D1002017

ARMIES
AND THE ART OF REVOLUTION

KATHARINE CHORLEY

ARMIES AND
THE ART OF REVOLUTION

BEACON PRESS *BOSTON*

Preface copyright © 1973 by Katharine Chorley

Armies and the Art of Revolution was first published in England in 1943 and is reprinted by arrangement with the author

Beacon Press books are published under the auspices of the Unitarian Universalist Association

Published simultaneously in Canada by Saunders of Toronto, Ltd.

All rights reserved

Printed in the United States of America

9   8   7   6   5   4   3   2   1

Library of Congress Cataloging in Publication Data

Chorley, Katharine Campbell (Hopkinson) Chorley, Baroness, 1897–
    Armies and the art of revolution.
    Reprint of the 1943 ed., published by Faber and Faber, London; with a new preface by the author.
    1. Revolutions.   2. Armies.   I. Title.
JC491.C5   1973   301.6'33   73–6250
ISBN 0–8070–4380–X
ISBN 0–8070–4381–8 (pbk.)

ACKNOWLEDGEMENTS

I would like to thank my friends, Mr. H. L. Beales and Professor Harold Laski, both of whom read a first draft of the manuscript and gave me generous help with their suggestions and support. And in particular I wish to thank Captain Liddell Hart for his Foreword and his valuable constructive criticism. Time is a precious gift, and I am in his debt for the time he has given in the service of this book.

Finally, I am especially grateful to R.S.T.C. He has been willing, in season and out of season, to discuss my problems, and has more than once made it easy for me to gain opportunities for work. Without his never-failing encouragement I should hardly have been able to carry the book through to completion.

K.C.C.

Ambleside
March 1943

CONTENTS

PREFACE

The genesis of this book was a chance conversation in the late 1920s about Lenin. It was asserted that the Bolsheviks had won the October Revolution of 1917 because the Officers' Corps of the Tsarist armed forces had been decimated by war and the rank and file was already disaffected; whereas the Revolution of 1905 had been lost despite disaffection in the rank and file—the *Potemkin* mutiny in the navy, for example—because the Officers' Corps was still virtually intact. Was this true? In other revolutions of the past, whether social or nationalist, successful or unsuccessful, what had been the part played by the armed forces of the existing regime which the revolution was designed to overthrow? It was suggested that here was an exciting and novel theme for a book. I was interested and began a few years later when opportunity arose to read myself into the subject in a desultory way but very soon became completely absorbed as one facet after another emerged and began to form discernible patterns. Moreover, the possible practical application to one's own time of many of these lessons of the past was at once exhilarating and highly disturbing; increasingly so as the 1930s advanced.

Mussolini and his Fascists had been in power in Italy for more than a decade. Hitler won power in 1933 and very soon the stream of refugees began, serious, established professional men and women on the run for their lives. At the beginning of 1934, the socialist workers of Vienna finally revolted against the growing nazification of Austria in an unsuccessful insurrection of special poignancy. The defence of the Karl Marx Hof, the great block of workers' flats built by the Socialist Municipality of Vienna, lit our imaginations. Friends of ours went over to Austria to help the defeated. In 1936 Hitler occupied the demilitarized Rhineland in defiance of the Treaty of Versailles. In the spring of 1938 he swallowed Austria, and in the autumn, on September 29th, Chamberlain sold out the Czechs at Munich. The Spanish Civil War broke out in 1936. At home in England, the queues of unemployed outside the labour exchanges, the ignominy of the means test, the great hunger march from Jarrow to London, Victor Gollancz's famous Left Book Club publications, plus the events abroad, bred a profound lack of trust in the Government's capacity to handle any situation, whether domestic or foreign.

PREFACE

Briefly then, those were the political circumstances in which this book was written. It is in the nature of an exploratory essay, and I explained my method of working and the limits I set myself in an introductory chapter. One of these limits was to confine the enquiry to Europe, with the exception of the American War of Independence and the American Civil War, both of which provided evidence for important conclusions. A generation has gone by since the book was first published, and the data now available have so increased both in quantity and complexity as almost to overwhelm the student. It may require another generation before historians can properly sift and analyse all the evidence supplied by events since the close of the Second World War.

Nonetheless, I do not think that analyses of post–1945 revolutions are likely to invalidate the main conclusions of this book, though they will probably modify some of them. Nor will it be possible to confine a meaningful discussion any longer to Europe, a reasonable restriction a generation ago. Indeed, the most interesting new material will now come from outside Europe: Mao Tse-tung's Communist Revolution in China, the fortunes of Vietnam since before the French withdrawal, Algeria, Cuba, Che Guevara perhaps on account of his astonishing emotional appeal for students.

I would, however, like to comment very shortly on a few of the post-war events and developments.

The Hungarian rising of 1956 was both social and nationalist, since it was at once a revolt against a Communist system of government and against the domination of Russia. Emotionally, therefore, it had two strong sources of power, and it was fought with immense courage and tenacity. Yet it was put down quickly and without real difficulty by Russian armed force used with all the necessary ruthlessness. It provides a particularly clear illustration of one of the main contentions of this book, that a rebellion cannot succeed in direct confrontation against the armed forces of the *status quo* government so long as these are not prevented by political or other reasons from realising their full potential. Similarly, with the Czechoslovaks' attempt to liberalise their regime in 1968. This never issued in armed revolt; it was given no opportunity to do so, since a sufficient show of armed strength by the Russians successfully cowed the opposition and then liquidated it.

The Hungarian rising is a classic example of the fate of rebellions when the operation of professional opposing forces is unrestricted. It now looks as if this lesson has been learnt and revolutionary strategists have evolved a possible method of countering the actual immense superiority of professional armed forces. This method is a form of sustained guerrilla warfare which avoids direct confrontation and greatly reduces the value of technical superiority. Moreover, the eroding effect of continual har-

PREFACE

assment is cumulative and finally affects the public opinion behind the troops. The French experience in Algeria is an important case in point. The French army was never beaten; at the same time de Gaulle conceded finally that it could not win.*

The present troubles in Ulster, though the outcome is still unknown, provide a somewhat similar example. Here, from the first, the British army has been prevented by extraneous considerations from putting forth its full strength, since it is obvious that public opinion in Britain would never stand for the ruthlessness necessary to flush out the I.R.A. from the minority enclaves of Belfast and Londonderry. Further, the psychology of the local situation in Ulster demands that the troops should alienate the minority civil population as little as possible. By contrast, the Provisionals operate from areas where a dense population is in sympathy with their aims if not necessarily with their methods. They can emerge and fall back almost at will. They can also disappear into the surrounding countryside and slip over the border into Eire where again sympathy awaits them.

The Ulster problem also exhibits with particular clarity the kind of circumstances in which a militant revolutionary group moves in and exploits a situation which first developed as a peaceful protest against specific political grievances, in this case the Civil Rights Movement.

A further point that may now need reassessment is in regard to the political commitment of an Officers' Corps. I showed, using the British Officers' Corps as an important example, that where officers are drawn almost exclusively from the propertied and governing classes of the community they cannot be relied upon to lead their men into action at the orders of a government whose policies they deeply mistrust and dislike. The example I gave was Ulster in 1914. I doubt whether this is any longer true of the British Officers' Corps, partly because it has been considerably democratised, and partly because a mechanised army develops a different ethos. Based on technical skills and a degree of education and individual initiative unknown to the old army, the gap between leaders and led is psychologically narrowed. It could be that this results in an Officers' Corps whose prime interest is professional and where a closer approximation to the concept of the army as an impersonal instrument

---

*. . . de Gaulle avait cessé de croire aux victoires stériles de la force. Une armée puissante, nombreuse, commandée par des chefs éprouvés s'enfonçait dans la guerrre sans jamais en déterminer le terme. Dès lors, aux yeux du pensionnaire de l'Elysée, donner au combat une ampleur sinistre, consommer un génocide. . . . c'était surtout dépasser des limites au delà desquelles, à en croire le philosophe romain "la force cesse d'être efficace et se suicide." (Alphonse Juin, Amar Naroun. *Histoire Parallèle, la France en Algérie 1830–1962.*)

is achieved. If troops had been sent to Rhodesia when U.D.I. (Unilateral Declaration of Independence) was declared in order to support the British flag—a situation like that of Ulster in 1914 insofar as acting against "kith and kin" was involved—we should have had one significant answer to this problem. In regard to the general problem of marked political orientation in an Officers' Corps, it would be interesting and much to the point to have a study of the comparative psychology of officers and men during the United States commitment to the war in Vietnam.

The problem of revolutionary strikes will also need a fresh examination in the light of post–world war developments. For instance, the experience of industrial strikes in Great Britain during the last few years has shown that picketing in the hands of strikers who are not overmuch concerned with a strict interpretation of "peaceful" can be a very potent weapon. It can successfully prevent outside labour being used and it can prevent army technicians being brought in to run essential services, that is, unless the *status quo* government is prepared for a confrontation which would almost certainly lead to bloodshed. The British Government has not been prepared for such a confrontation, not because it mistrusted the loyalty of the troops but because it dared not face the social and political consequences of using them. The same has been partially true of the use of the police. Moreover, it is not only a question of the political dangers of using troops to break picket lines. Even if this were successfully done, it is doubtful whether civilians or soldiers would have the necessary specialised skills to run several of the key services of a modern state with no prior training. It is too soon to make a judgment, but it certainly looks as if the recent French experience of civil air lines control by the military in order to keep services going during a strike might prove a case in point.

In the circumstances of planned revolutionary strikes, picketing might prove crucial in effecting the escalation to violent revolution. It could also be seized upon by revolutionary leaders awaiting their opportunity to exploit a suitable situation as in the case suggested above regarding the I.R.A. Provisionals and the Civil Rights Movement.

Finally, I want to thank Mr. Brian Bond of King's College, London, for his generous help in discussing this new Preface with me; and I am grateful to Lady Liddell Hart for her permission to reprint the Foreword which Sir Basil Liddell Hart wrote for the original edition. I should like also to record how deeply I regret that Sir Basil, who was always keen that this book should be re-issued, will not see the new edition and I should like to dedicate it to his memory.

ARMIES
AND THE ART OF REVOLUTION

FOREWORD

by Captain Liddell Hart

The experience of the past two generations, and of the last decade especially, has made it plain that force forms the foundation of society as we know it—of the social and national order in what is called the civilized world. It is a bad reflection on *Homo sapiens*, but a fact that cannot be burked. A consciousness of this hard fact, which was temporarily obscured by the trend of the nineteenth century, has been gradually reawakened in the twentieth-century mind. Yet its implications have received inadequate attention. Despite all the study that has been given to social problems and military problems respectively, there has been curiously little attempt to explore their common foundation.

It may here be argued that both were embraced in the problem of international order and collective security, to which much discussion and study were devoted in the interval between the First and Second World Wars. That is true up to a point, and in part. But deeper examination of this problem leads to a realization that the attempt to find a solution of it, in an international scheme of collective security, did not go deep enough. It is possible that a solution could be found which would effectively check aggression between nations. It is no less possible that the solution, in its very partial perfection, might smooth the way for a *coup d'état* by a military clique among the staff of the international force, and the establishment of a world military dictatorship. That risk needs to be foreseen, and guarded against—which means carrying the study of the problem deeper than is usually done in considering the question of checking aggression by an international scheme of security. In other words, this is only the upper layer of the matter, not the foundation.

So long as force forms the foundation of order between nations and within nations, we are nourishing a delusion when we draw the customary dividing line between war and peace. In the sense that those terms are commonly used, they are not the antitheses of each other. Force has no place in real peace. We might go some way towards avoiding dangerous disillusionment if we scrapped the use of the word 'peace' to describe the conditions, or intervals, when nations succeed in avoiding armed conflict, external or internal. For under existing conditions, that avoidance depends

9

FOREWORD

fundamentally on the deterrent threat inherent in armed force—in might, not in right. A volcano is still a volcano even when it is not in eruption; and the same conclusion applies to belligerent society when it is in a state of quiescence.

In consequence, any study of what are called 'peace' problems—i.e. political and social problems—is not only dependent on an understanding of war but should start from an understanding of the relation of armed forces to society. Yet the student of military theory will find little reference to the question in the literature of his subject, apart from Alfred Vagt's notable work, *A History of Militarism*. There has been more discussion of the question in books dealing with social and economic issues, but there the approach is apt to be political rather than scientific, and the military aspects are usually treated as secondary.

Armies and the Art of Revolution goes a long way towards filling this important gap. Awareness of the gap made me all the quicker to appreciate the value of the work when shown a draft, embodying the results of several years' research, and I urged its publication in book form. While not agreeing entirely with the author's conclusions, I realize, even where I differ, how deeply she has gone into the various questions both in study and thought. And I have no hesitation in saying that her book is a most significant contribution to military history and knowledge of war, in the wider sense. It should prove an incentive as well as an aid to further exploration of the fundamental problems with which it is concerned. Meanwhile, it is an addition to that very small number of military books that are really essential to knowledge.

INTRODUCTORY

When Karl Marx wrote *Das Kapital*, he tried to do for the study of revolution what Darwin a few years earlier had done for the science of biology in *The Origin of Species*. He related isolated historical instances in a basic theory which accounted in his view for the incidence of violent upheavals of one class against another at specific points in time. Since his day, not only the underlying causes of revolution but also theories of how to make revolutions have always been seriously discussed by the more militant socialist parties. But strangely enough, in spite of all this discussion, few attempts seem to have been made to assemble the historical facts of various revolutions in an endeavour to deduce from them whether there be any general laws which govern the practical conduct of a revolutionary outbreak and account for its success or failure. Practical revolutionary leaders, with the exception perhaps of the Russians, seem to have attacked their problems *ad hoc* with little reference either to theory or to the experience of the past. In particular, beyond occasional reflections of socialist thinkers or of long-headed politicians, generally of the Right, whose job has forced them up against dealing with revolution in action, little serious attention has been given to an effort to make an historical analysis of armed insurrection in its relation to the character and strengths of the defending forces of the *status quo* government which the insurrection is designed to overthrow. Yet armed insurrection in some form or other is the classic method of making a revolution and, in modern times at any rate, it is bound to imply a clash with professionally trained troops equipped with all the gear of scientific warfare. History shows that, in the last resort, success or failure hinges upon the attitude which those armed forces of the *status quo* government will take towards an insurrection.

This attitude will be mainly determined by the general political circumstances in which the insurrection takes place. It will also be influenced by the tradition of political function and the organization and character of the particular armed forces which are called into action.

A country's army is generally accepted as the guarantee and buttress of the political system on which the State is built. This conception is not always frankly expressed, but it is in fact implicit throughout the relation of the State to its armed forces. It is usually taken to mean a guarantee and

11

buttress against aggression from the militant Left. But experience has shown that at present aggression against democratic systems is more likely to take an authoritarian and reactionary form, and that this type of attack is more insidious and therefore more menacing than anything which may be expected from the revolutionary Left.

The relation of the State to its armed forces and the techniques of revolution are matters of vital concern. We should know where we stand. And we can only know this by studying the lessons of the past. This book is an attempt to discuss, in the light of history, the practical issues raised by these broad considerations and to deduce from them conclusions which may have a certain practical value.

The problems which will emerge are complicated and frequently overlap. The whole subject is after all sprung on human emotions, and human emotions even when taken in the mass make a tangled complex of feeling. It will be necessary to analyse various types of insurrection in order to find out the inherent reasons for their strength and weakness. And in doing this a distinction must be borne in mind between those insurrections which are the result of social or political upheaval and those which are nationalist in their aim. It will be necessary to establish the external conditions which favour success or failure. Here it will be found that the political position and consequent action of the armed forces opposed to the insurrection is pivotal. The main part of the book must therefore be devoted to a discussion of the causes which will determine this position. These causes will fall under various heads, but in practice they intermingle and react upon each other so that it may not be feasible to discuss each group separately.

The effective strength of armed forces which are opposed to a revolution and prepared to fight it can be crippled either by quite extraneous political circumstances such as the pressure of public opinion at home and in other countries, or by technical considerations such as the geographical layout of the insurrection.

The armed forces as an effective weapon may also be crippled or in practice paralysed by the disaffection of a set of key officers—this situation raises in acute form questions of the first importance. We must find out whether the attitude of the officers has in practice a determining influence out of all proportion to their numbers and in what circumstances the attitude of the rank and file depends on that of their officers. We must find out whether to seek the causes for a passive attitude on the part of the rank and file in connection with the internal structure and organization of armies. We must assess the political instability of an officers' corps when it is not in sympathy with the government which it serves. We must examine the so-called military pronunciamento.

The next important group of causes determining the attitude of the armed forces to revolution are those which may be expected to influence the rank and file so strongly that they will take the law into their own hands and refuse to oppose an insurrection even against the orders of their officers. We must find what solvents are capable of disintegrating the rank and file of a modern army.

Finally, an attempt must be made to analyse the structure and character of different types of army in order to find out in what way structure and organization determine the political outlook, on the one hand of the officers, and on the other of the rank and file.

These conditions, however, do not take the general subject to its possible limit. Revolution in relation to armed force does not stop short at a seizure of power. A revolution must not only be won; it must be held and consolidated after the initial victory. And in fact it always is held by some sort of armed force. The special character of the army created by a revolutionary government and the reasons for its success or failure in its task of defending the new system are also matters of vital practical concern. An attempt will be made to analyse the character of revolutionary armies and to account for their sufficient strength or inadequate weakness.

The various aspects of the whole subject are so entangled and bear upon each other so closely that it is almost impossible to discuss them without a certain confusion. It will therefore perhaps be as well to indicate here the points where a confusion of thought is likely to occur. The method I have used is illustrative and deductive, e.g. I have examined the more important revolutions of the past and tried to deduce from them the relevant lessons. In doing this, it appeared that the only feasible way to get any sort of clear grouping of cause and effect was to base the various groups on the technical issues involved. Revolutions are not, therefore, classed according to their political cause but rather according to the technical means employed to make them or to crush them. It is obvious that there is a fundamental difference separating a social upheaval such as the Russian Revolution, and a nationalist rebellion such as the Irish of 1918–21, and again separating either from an officers' pronunciamento such as the Curragh Mutiny or the Franco Rebellion. These differences, however, do not necessarily issue in an equally fundamental difference of revolutionary technique. Lessons from one may apply to the other. It has therefore seemed wiser to class them according to their technical characteristics and to refer to their political bases only when these have affected their technical conduct.

Since the material of history is men's emotions and aspirations in action, it is not perhaps humanly possible to write of these things with complete objectivity. I have, however, tried hard to look at my collection of facts as if they were the passionless data of the chemist or the biologist, and I do not think that I have twisted the deductions made from them much out of shape on the rack of my own feelings.

The facts themselves are representative, and by no means a full collection. The hundred and one revolutions of the South American Republics would no doubt provide a good deal of interesting material. These are omitted altogether. But the American War of Independence and the conflict between North and South provide so much significant evidence that I have not liked to pass them over. The discussion is, however, mainly confined to Europe.

1

ARMED FORCES AND THE BODY POLITIC

Theory of relation between the armed forces and the State—
contrast between theory and practice—technical superiority
of professional armed forces to any rebel force—insurrections bound to fail against professional armed forces operating at full strength—attitude of the armed forces therefore
pivotal.

To fit professional fighting forces into the body politic has always
been a dangerous and an anxious task. The difficulty confronted
the Roman Republic two thousand years ago:

'In the days before Marius, a Roman army was composed of
peasant proprietors enlisted from their farms for a summer campaign and
afterwards, when the fighting was over, well content to return to the plea-
sant livelihood which awaited them at home. Levies so composed and so
supported constituted no danger to the Republican state. . . . The military
reforms of Marius marked a revolution. The Roman army became in practice a long-service force of professional soldiers. . . . The Senate failed to
realize that, unless the Republic controlled the professional armies by
making itself responsible for their pay and pensions, the professional armies
would master the Republic.'[1]

During the Middle Ages, the problem was in abeyance, since those who
made war relied on feudal and militia levies raised *ad hoc* and on the mercenary companies who served the highest bidder and whose numbers and
activities were perforce kept in check by the poverty of princes. Moreover,
the lag between the amateur and professional soldier in technical equipment and skill was scarcely existent. The longbow-men who won Agincourt
for King Harry ranked among the finest troops in Europe, but they were
farmers from English shires who had learned their skill by Sunday practice
on the local greens, and who had been drawn to France through a spirit of
adventure, or half-unwillingly by the Commissions of Array. But as central
government re-emerged and monarchies grew strong and rich enough to

[1] H. A. L. Fisher, *A History of Europe*, vol. i, p. 71.

15

consider the raising and maintenance of a professional army, the difficulty rose again. It was now accentuated by an increasing complexity in the methods of and equipment for warfare, a complexity which has been steadily growing through the centuries and is now so intense that whatever government or party has the full allegiance of a country's armed forces is to all intents and purposes politically impregnable.

In this country, the political importance of the armed forces had become pressing as far back as the seventeenth century. The early Stuarts had no standing army; they raised troops as they required them, but sometimes they conveniently forgot to disband their levies. For them, the problem centred round control of the militia, a national levy which could be raised by counties for certain specific purposes and was organized by the Lord Lieutenant of each county and officered by the local gentry. In Charles I's time, power over the militia was one of the chief points of controversy between Crown and Parliament. Indeed, it was considered so important that the right of Parliament to control the militia had place among the nineteen fundamental propositions put up to Charles at York in 1642.[1] It became, therefore, one of the immediate causes of the Civil War. After the Restoration, the problem shifted to the King's efforts to form a standing army of professional character and personally bound to him by the terms of its service. Clarendon, for instance, was impeached 'for that he hath designed a standing army to be raised and to govern the country thereby.'[2] James II succeeded in maintaining such an army and showed up again the possible dangers of the system to a frightened and embittered country which still remembered the military dictatorship of Cromwell's major-generals. After the Revolution, however, the problem was to all appearance solved by a shrewd and typically English compromise. It was frankly recognized that a modern state of rising importance, with Continental commitments of one kind or another, did require a professional army; and the army was allowed to remain, nominally at any rate, in the personal province of the King. But its existence was only legalized and its discipline regulated by Parliament for one year at a time.[3] Every year supply must be voted, and the Annual Mutiny Act passed afresh; and though that Act has now been altered, the principle which governs the maintenance of the British Army is still almost exactly similar, and still the Army Act has to be renewed from year to year by a certain date in March or April. If this were omitted, the army would be automatically disbanded, since there would be no power to pay it, discipline it, or generally maintain it in existence. The supreme importance of this arrangement as a check on governments was demonstrated during the Ulster crisis of March 1914, when the Unionists in the House of Lords seriously contemplated throwing out or amending

[1] Maitland, *A Constitutional History of England* (Camb. Univ. Press), p. 326.
[2] Ibid., p. 327.   [3] Ibid., p. 448.

the Army Bill as a practical protest against the possibility of the army being used against Ulster.[1] They were probably prevented from taking this course only on the strength of representations from Asquith's government pointing out the extreme seriousness of such tactics in view of the international situation.

The solution of 1689 gave a firm basis for the theory, which has now been fully developed, that the fighting services must be set apart from political strife in order to prevent their arbitrary or partisan use and made merely a part of the legal machinery of a *status quo* government. Pitt, speaking in the House of Commons on the subject of the '45, said:

'The right of inquiring what measures may conduce to the advantage and security of the public belongs not to the army, but to this House. . . . Our armies have no better right to determine for themselves than any other body of men, nor are we to suffer them to prescribe laws to the Legislature or to govern those by whose authority they subsist.'[2]

Dicey, a very strong Unionist, took a similar line when the conduct of the army in regard to Ulster was under discussion. Drawn by Carson's remarks during a speech at Manchester in December 1913 he wrote to him in a private letter:

'I have always entertained the strongest conviction that, in a civilized country, obedience to lawful orders is the absolute duty of soldiers and that the British Army would, in circumstances however painful, fulfil this duty.'[3]

Unfortunately, the theory, like others which depend upon refractory human material, will not always stand the rough application of practical life. And when policies of vital importance are in question which arouse those ultimate political passions for which men are prepared to fight and die, the professional soldier may forget that he is by definition a passive instrument and remember only that he is a man with emotions like another. As Bonar Law exclaimed in the House of Commons during the Ulster Vote of Censure on the Liberal Government in March 1914: 'If it is a question only of disorder, the army I am sure will obey you, and I am sure it ought to obey you, but if it is really a question of civil war, *soldiers are citizens like the rest of us.*'[4]

The same point of view had been put forward more than once in Parliament nearly 150 years before during debates on the American War. There was a considerable feeling amongst army officers that they were being called on to suppress rebellion in a just cause. Lord Amherst, the Commander-in-Chief, refused to take command in the field in America, though

---

[1] *Vide* Callwell, *Field-Marshal Sir Henry Wilson*, vol. i, p. 138. Also Denis Gwynn, *Life of John Redmond*, p. 251.

[2] Quoted by Asquith, *Fifty Years of Parliament*, vol. ii, p. 152.

[3] Colvin, *Life of Lord Carson*, vol. ii, p. 238.   [4] Ibid., vol. ii, p. 311.

inconsistently enough he retained his office of Commander-in-Chief.[1] Lord Howe went half-heartedly, salving his conscience by promising himself that he would do everything in his power to bring about a peace. Other less important officers refused to go at all despite the probable damage to their careers. In the spring of 1775, the Earl of Effingham was ordered to America with his regiment and repudiated his orders. He made his explanation in the House of Lords, an explanation worth quoting since it shows up so clearly that perennial problem with which the soldier is faced, the problem of his dual personality as a citizen and as a unit in a military machine: 'When the duties of a soldier and a citizen become inconsistent,' Effingham told the House, 'I shall always think myself obliged to sink the character of the soldier in that of the citizen, till such time as those duties shall again, by the malice of our real enemies, become united.'[2] A similar point of view was put forward six months later by a soldier who had served under the Duke of Cumberland and in particular had fought with reckless gallantry at Lauffeld and Fontenoy. Conway argued that there was a great difference between a foreign war, where the whole community was involved, and a domestic war on points of civil contention, where the community was divided. In the first case no officer ought to call in question the justice of his country; but in the latter a military man, before he drew his sword against his fellow-subjects, ought to ask himself whether the cause was just or no.[3]

An ironical comment on the limitations in practical life of the theory of the passive military instrument may be found in the attitude of Pitt, now Earl of Chatham, whose speech laying down that very theory has just been quoted above. In 1773 Chatham bought his son a commission in General Carleton's regiment in Canada and arranged that the boy should receive his military education on Carleton's staff. In 1776 we find a letter to Carleton from Lady Chatham, written at her husband's request, in which she thanks the General for his attentions to young Pitt, but finishes: 'Feeling all this, sir, as Lord Chatham does, you will tell yourself with what concern he communicates to you a step that, from his fixed opinion with regard to the continuance of the unhappy war with our fellow subjects of America, he has found it necessary to take. It is that of withdrawing his son from such a service.'[4]

Chatham had no use for Jacobites and Highland chieftains, but he had every respect for American colonists who were fighting to maintain the fundamental Whig principle of no taxation without representation.

It will be observed that all the protests just quoted come from the mouths of officers or of highly placed civilians who were voicing the opinion of officers. This fact may be found of fundamental significance as the evidence

[1] G. O. Trevelyan, *The American Revolution* (rev. ed.), vol. iii, p. 202.
[2] Ibid., vol. iii, p. 208.   [3] Ibid., vol. iii, p. 203.   [4] Ibid., vol. iii, p. 207.

of succeeding chapters lays bare the points at which the theory of the impassive military instrument is in fact most vulnerable in practice. The British Army has, of course, always been, with the exception of the present war and the first World War period, a long-service force, based on voluntary enlistment and officered by men drawn from the propertied classes of the community. But the theory of its relation to the State holds good for the armed forces of all civilized nations. The calculation of successful rebellion will be based on a just assessment of the limitations of the theory in any given revolutionary situation.

It is the application of science to warfare that has weighted the scales so heavily in favour of the political side which controls a professional army as against the party which controls only volunteers, however brave and even fanatical. The technical resources and skills of modern troops make it in practice impossible for amateur soldiers, untrained and necessarily unequipped with the instruments of modern war, to stand up against them, if they are exploiting these resources to the full. Rebels, for instance, have to buy and collect their arms secretly; they are limited by relatively meagre financial backing, by awkward conditions of storage, by the impossibility, where preparations must be carried through underground, of training large groups to act together. In modern times, for instance, it is obvious that rebels can never command aeroplanes in any quantity, or tanks, or big guns, nor can they control any mass source for the supply of munitions. It is worth considering that even so long ago as 1642, when technical differences between amateurs and professionals were relatively slight, the Parliament could probably never have won the Great Rebellion in this country unless the King's Navy had come over to its side at the very start of hostilities. This made the great technical difference in strength between the two parties, since it gave Parliament the means of importing arms and ammunition from abroad and enabled the vitally important Port of London to be kept open exclusively for the use of the Roundhead city. Similarly, during the American Civil War, the naval superiority of the North, which made possible the successful blockade of Southern ports, cut the South off from the outside world and thereby prevented the Confederates from marketing their cotton crop on which depended exclusively their financial ability to get money and supplies to carry on the war for more than a limited term.

Here, while considering the technical disadvantages with which rebels have to cope by comparison with the forces employed against them, it is important to recall the distinction between an internal social revolt and the revolt of an oppressed nationality. It will generally be found that a nationalist revolt is better placed technically than an internal revolt. Where a subject province or country rises against its rulers, it can be safely premised that on the whole the active rebels will have a sympathetic and homogeneous population behind them. Moreover, the rebellion will be grounded on a clearly cut geographical as well as on a clearly cut political unit. This gives a great advantage in guerrilla warfare where the fighters must rely on a sympathetic population. But in an internal social revolt the dividing line between revolutionaries and counter-revolutionaries will probably be clear-cut neither geographically nor politically. Geographically, active insurrection will be based on focal points dotted over a country and, owing to difficulty of communication, linked together precariously or not at all. Time and again plans for concerted rebellion at various separate centres have come to grief. And even in cases where rebellion is based on a widespread peasant jacquerie the difficulty of bringing the towns into line with the rural areas may prove insuperable. Politically, internal insurrection suffers almost invariably from the absence of a homogeneous population behind the revolutionaries. The dividing line comes between various classes of the population and is therefore bound to entail confusion and uncertainty.

These technical distinctions between internal and nationalist revolt do not, however, always hold good. It may occasionally happen that a straight civil war produces an alinement both geographical and political which carries all the advantages for the rebels which may be expected in a nationalist revolt. The Spanish Civil War, for instance, after a time alined itself geographically into two or three well-defined areas controlled by each side. This is also true of the American Civil War. Indeed, no better example could be found of the particular advantages which are apt to go with a nationalist revolt. The rebellious Southern provinces formed a compact geographical unit with clear interior lines of communication. They were peopled by a population to all intents and purposes exclusively in sympathy with the rebel cause. The leaders could, therefore, concentrate their forces and move them with complete freedom behind the actual battle front. They could raise and train armies in the open. They could use at will the whole administrative machinery of government. In fact, only when Sherman's stupendous V-shaped march, south through Georgia to the sea and up north-west again to take the rebel capital of Richmond in the rear, broke up the unity of their territory did the military preponderance of the North become decisive. From the standpoint of a perfect rebel layout, the Southern position is probably unique. Yet the American Confederates with all their special advantages could not in the long run stand up against the weight of men and material and money mobilized by the Union.

The rule then emerges clearly that governments of the *status quo* which are in full control of their armed forces and are in a position to use them to full effect have a decisive superiority which no rebel force can hope to overcome. The outstanding apparent exceptions, which are discussed later in this book, the American War of Independence, and the Sinn Fein Revolution, had both of them special features which in effect neutralized to a considerable and probably decisive extent the striking power of the British Army. And in the case of the Americans, foreign intervention on their side can certainly not be discounted as a very important if not a decisive factor in their success.

An analysis of a sample batch of straight insurrections over the last 150 years, where the armed forces of the *status quo* have brought their full technical resources into play, puts the validity of this rule beyond reasonable doubt. During the nineteenth century, it was a question of the possession and use of artillery. In Paris, seed-bed of insurrections, the magnificent boulevards were driven through the city, not so much with an eye for the aesthetics of town-planning, but because guns operate awkwardly in city fighting and that kind of street is the only one that gives an adequate opportunity for their use. Napoleon's exclamation about the 'whiff of grape-shot' was no mere rhetorical flourish. It laid down the serious strategy for dealing with urban insurrection which has been in use ever since.

The phrase was first used in connection with the insurrection of Vendémiaire in 1795. Some thirty thousand men of the better-to-do 'Sections' of the Paris National Guard were in arms against the Convention. The Conventional troops numbered only four or five thousand soldiers of the line and a couple of thousand Guards from the working-class districts. Young Bonaparte was asked at the last minute to take charge of them. His method marked off for good the old haphazard way of combating a rising from the modern treatment which he inaugurated. The insurgents had no guns, but guns were available at the artillery park at Sablons for whoever could seize them first. Bonaparte at once sent Murat galloping off to Sablons to get the guns. They were brought into Paris and mounted in the Tuileries. Just too late, the revolting Sections themselves made an attempt to get hold of these cannon which they now found ranged against them and commanding the streets north of the Tuileries and the Pont Royal. When the rebel attack broke on the Tuileries, the guns were at once ordered into action and tore away the heads of the advancing columns. They swept the Pont Royal too, thus preventing the insurgent reinforcements, which were due to cross the river at that point, from making a junction with the troops on the Tuileries side. The artillery was used quite ruthlessly and with conclusive effect. During the night, the Conventional soldiers, outnumbered though they were by about five to one, were able to take the offensive and clear the streets neighbouring the Palais Royal. Next morning, the Sectional troops had melted away.[1]

Yet insurgent fighters, even where they are not led by men of marked capacity, can generally win the initial rounds in street fighting. The element of surprise is on their side and the terrain is in their favour. They can raise their barricades like mushrooms, they can use every house to shelter a

[1] This account follows J. H. Rose, *Life of Napoleon* (3rd ed.), pp. 71 sq.

sniper and, within the revolting area, they have complete freedom and great speed of movement. Armed with modern rifles and machine-guns, they can fight on superior terms against professional soldiers who are using only equivalent weapons. Even where, weapon for weapon, the balance of efficiency is on the side of the trained troops, insurgents can win by sheer heroism. It is, for instance, clear that the Franco Rebellion in Spain would have established itself successfully at the outset both in Madrid and Barcelona had it not been for the valour and the brilliant capacity in street fighting of the workers who had risen against the revolting army in defence of the Government of the Republic. The workers were not, of course, politically insurgents since they had the legal government behind them, but they were the same fighting type as insurgents. Their rifles were second-rate and insufficient in numbers, for the Government hesitated to arm such explosive elements of the population. Yet in Madrid they succeeded in storming the Montana barracks which formed Franco's key to the military domination of the city, and in Barcelona the fury of their attack against the forces of the rebel generals broke all organized resistance within forty-eight hours. It is, of course, true that the workers had important support on their side from loyal groups in the army and the Civil Guard. A couple of aeroplanes, two guns, and two police tanks were in action against the barracks in Madrid, but these seem to have been relatively ineffective, and there is no doubt that the final and conclusive reduction of the building was entirely due to the energy of the workers' mass assault. Again, in Barcelona, a measure of support for the workers came from loyal Civil Guards and Shock Police and the weight of the rebellion was considerably eased by the fact that numbers of soldiers fraternized with the people and brought over their arms. None the less, the saving of Barcelona for the Republic cannot be ascribed either to the Civil Guard or to the fraternizing soldiers. It was due to the gallantry and determination of the workers' militias.[1] But it must also be remembered that superior weapons such as tanks and artillery were not used against the workers during this opening round of the Civil War.

The Moscow Insurrection of 1905 provides another excellent example of the possibilities of city warfare against trained troops—until the latter bring technically superior weapons into serious action. The revolutionaries held a large block of Moscow for ten days. Yet it is reckoned that there were not more than three thousand actively engaged combatants. Numberless barricades were erected, and the insurgents slipped from one barricade to another with astonishing mobility as the tactics of the fighting demanded. Against these barricades and in the tortuous streets, the Tsarist infantry and cavalry were almost powerless. It was only when long-range artillery was established in positions outside the town and a two-days' bombard-

[1] For a vivid account of the street fighting in Madrid and Barcelona, *vide* Frank Jellinek, *The Civil War in Spain*, parts ii, iii, iv.

ment carried out that revolutionary Moscow finally fell. The whole industrial quarter of the city was shelled indiscriminately.[1]

Somewhat similar conditions killed Mazzini's Roman Republic of 1848, when France came to the rescue of the expelled Papal Government. Battling on equal terms, the Roman rebels and the young Italians who had come in from other parts of Italy to help them might well have sustained a fight against the seasoned soldiers of Louis Napoleon. They had already repulsed Oudinot's troops in an engagement outside the city. The Republic fell only when the investment of the city was undertaken in form, and Oudinot's guns at last ordered into action to blast in pieces the defence of the Janiculum heights which was the key to the town's integrity.[2]

Thiers's investment of Paris in 1871 and his ruthless use of artillery against the Commune, an enterprise which will be discussed in more detail later, provides another example. But there is no point in trying to multiply instances. Nineteenth- and also twentieth-century evidence on this score is conclusive. Insurrections cannot be permanently won against a professional army operating its technical resources at full strength. They can be won only when the introduction of some extraneous factor cripples the striking power of the professional fighting forces for one reason or another. The part to be played by the army is, therefore, decisive in any revolution, whether social or nationalist.

[1] *Vide* Mavor, *Economic History of Russia*, chap. xi.
[2] *Vide* G. M. Trevelyan, *Garibaldi's Defence of the Roman Republic* (Nelson, 1920), chaps. vii, ix, x.

2

INSURRECTIONS AND THEIR CONDITIONS

Various types of insurrection—the spontaneous mass uprising—the planned insurrection—the revolutionary situation—seizing its opportunity—artificial creation of the revolutionary situation—problems of timing—unsuccessful war the prime producer of revolutionary conditions.

Before making an insurrection it would appear that the first business of the leaders is to calculate the probable attitude and strength of the armed forces which are opposed to them. In practice, however, insurrections are frequently the result of uncontrolled and half-instinctive movements—this is particularly true of deep social revolts—which do not admit of a nice calculation of opposing forces before the actual outbreak. Such explosions appear to happen spontaneously and without any prearranged direction or dating, when some outside event touches off the latent combustible material of a discontented and restive class. In these cases all that serious revolutionary leaders can do is to try to gain control of the spontaneous movement and organize its violence for a deliberate seizure of power. They will have no alternative between standing aside altogether and gambling on the attitude of the armed forces, influencing this as best they can in the circumstances of the moment. In other conditions, insurrection can be deliberately timed as the final move in a carefully prepared and matured plan of revolutionary action. In such cases, the resources of the *status quo* and the resources of the revolutionaries will have been balanced against each other so far as is humanly possible before the outbreak. Again, insurrection may come as the result of some unexpected shift in a dangerous set of political circumstances which suddenly presents waiting leaders with a ripe revolutionary situation, a fruit that must be plucked with decision and without delay. These categories hold good either for nationalist or for social revolutions.

The spontaneous insurrection in its nature is an almost automatic mass reaction against a set of political conditions which have suddenly, perhaps owing to the added weight of some new and relatively unimportant griev-

24

ance, become too galling to bear. Like every popular insurrect
pends fundamentally upon a general revolutionary situation, bi
plosion is almost invariably caused by some specific event or circun
the dropped match which may light up a moorland fire when the l
dry for burning. Thus the insurrection of 1848 in Paris depended t
general revolutionary situation worked up by the anti-government
banquets which had been held throughout France and were due
minate in a great banquet arranged for Paris. Owing to the repres
more direct methods of expressing discontent, these banquets were tl
means of agitation open to the reformers. The Paris banquet was car
by the Government, and its proscription unloosed all the battened-
discontent of the people. Angry crowds demonstrated through the st
But the actual rising occurred as the direct and immediate and spontar
result of a musket shot fired by an untraced hand while crowds were den
strating in front of a force of soldiers posted outside the Ministry for For
Affairs. The troops, believing that they were to be attacked, loosed a vo
on the crowd.[1] That night the barricades were up all over Paris and
spatter of musketry fire announced that the people had passed the Rubic
between demonstration and armed revolt. Again, the insurrection of t
Paris Commune in 1871 depended upon the revolutionary situation set t
by the emotional reaction in Paris after the Prussian siege and the deteste
attitude of Thiers's government and the Bordeaux Assembly. But the out
break occurred as the immediate outcome of Thiers's attempt to get possession of artillery which had been subscribed for by the National Guard
and was considered to be their property.[2] In both these cases feeling was so
tense that almost any additional exasperation would probably have provoked the outbreak. The tinder was so well dried and laid that the merest
friction only was necessary to make a spark and ignite it.

These insurrections were spontaneous manifestations of crowd emotion.
The outbreaks had not been clearly envisaged beforehand. There was no
preconceived plan of action and indeed their salient feature is absence of
any sort of competent revolutionary leadership. In regard to 1848, Lamartine says that when it was seen that an outbreak was inevitable, Committees
of Insurrection sat around in the rooms of the Secret Societies and in the
offices of Republican newspapers discussing the situation. But they do not
seem to have made any plan of action and Lamartine comments with unconscious sarcasm that 'they were probably rather engaged in observation
than in action'.[3] Louis Blanc relates that a few minutes before the fusillade
outside the Ministry for Foreign Affairs, he was engaged on drafting a

[1] Lamartine, *The Revolution of 1848* (Eng. trans. of 1849), pp. 56 sq.
[2] For a more detailed account of this situation, and for the actual outbreak
of the insurrection *vide infra*, p. 156.
[3] *The Revolution of 1848* (Eng. trans. of 1849), p. 38.

manifesto issued by the members of the Electoral Democratic Committee. Louis Blanc was scarcely a socialist in the modern sense, but he was a leader of the people as distinct from the discontented bourgeoisie. The tone of his manifesto is therefore significant. It laid down that the capacity to distinguish between a revolution and a riot belonged exclusively to the National Guard, whose ranks should be thrown open to every citizen, and it demanded that the use of the army to put down civil disturbances should be expressly forbidden by legislation.[1] The idea that the army could be paralysed 'by legislation' when a revolt was actually breaking out seems particularly naïve. No attempt was made to call the people to arms in this manifesto or to define for them the political aims of the insurrection or to appeal to any popular spirit in the army with a view to winning over its support. Yet the army, as was proved a few hours later, had considerable sympathy with the revolting populace. It is probable that Louis Blanc and his colleagues would have preferred a change of Ministry and a radical alteration of policy within the framework of the monarchy to full-dress revolution. They failed to see that this had passed beyond the realm of practical politics in a Paris where the barricades were up and the people already ranged against the troops. The obvious task under these circumstances was to gain the leadership and manage the revolt, in particular leaving no effort unmade to find out the feeling among the troops and win them over so far as possible. As it was, the successful result of the insurrection was a gift. The National Guard sympathized from the outset, the temper of the troops was hesitating, and any action they might have taken was in fact paralysed for reasons which will be described in detail in a later discussion on fraternization. So the revolution, launched by the angry populace and their anonymous leaders, was won without any calculation of opposing forces and with no consideration or provision for the regime which was to embody it.

In the case of the Paris Commune it may be well perhaps to sketch in more detail the events which led up to the explosion since they show with particular vividness that there was every indication for weeks beforehand that discontent was bound to issue in revolt sooner or later.[2]

The armistice with Bismarck was signed and the Prussian siege lifted on January the 29th. Political passions in the city were already violent and daily rising nearer to a temperature of open revolt. There was an undercurrent of generalized revolutionary feeling made up out of the secret revolutionary tactics of Blanquism, the spread of Proudhon's notions among the workers concerning an elementary sort of syndicalism, and the ill-understood Socialist theory of the First International. There was an enthu-

---

[1] Louis Blanc, *Histoire de la Révolution de 1848* (Paris, 1880), vol. i, p. 45.

[2] This discussion is based on Jellinek, *The Paris Commune of 1871*. *Vide* also Lissagaray, *La Commune de 1871*, for an admirable contemporary account.

siastic revival of the Jacobin ideas of 1793 with their emphasis on radicalism and the necessary leadership of the capital for French life and politics. This undertow was deepened and strengthened by various specific grievances. For instance, the Parisians felt that in some sense Paris had been let down by the remainder of France during her long siege and was now to be jettisoned and in addition humiliated by the formal entry of the victorious Prussians, an entry which Thiers had agreed upon in exchange for the retention by France of Belfort.[1] Then, when the new Assembly met at Bordeaux, it was found that the French provinces had elected a predominantly Royalist chamber, whereas the forty-three deputies from Paris were all enthusiastically Republican.[2] Further, the new government wasted no time in showing its fear and dislike of radical Paris by various administrative measures such as the appointment of an unpopular and reactionary Governor and the suppression of left-wing newspapers. Finally, the Assembly, from its meeting-place at Bordeaux, saw fit to pass three decrees which aroused the most bitter resentment. The Assembly elected to meet and sit for the future at Versailles, thereby in effect decapitalizing Paris and wounding her people in the tenderest spot of their pride.[3] The second and third decrees hit them economically, workers and bourgeoisie alike. During the siege, exchange had been carried on to a large extent by means of promissory notes. A moratorium had been declared on these, but they had now become concentrated in the hands of a few financiers who wanted to call in their moneys. The Assembly decreed that all such bills should be payable with interest within seven months after they were originally due. The first lot were due for payment on the very day on which this decree came into force. 'It meant utter ruin for thousands of small traders.'[4] The second measure related to rents on land and buildings which had been held up by consent during the war. It was decreed that all such rents could be collected immediately. 'The poor were faced with eviction and even the largest tenants could not find the money to pay so suddenly.'[5]

The explosion took place as we have seen when Thiers attempted to capture the guns belonging to the National Guard. Thiers was only too well aware of the ripening revolutionary situation; hence his correct counter-revolutionary scheme to get hold of the guns. The men on the other side must have been equally well aware of it. There was no excuse for vacillation or failure to have a plan of action ready for taking control of the revolt when it broke out. Yet they failed to prepare a plan for the inevitable insurrection, and after it had broken out they failed entirely to understand the development of the military situation.

The only possible insurrectionary authority was the Central Committee of the Federation of the National Guard. It had made no effort to control

---

[1] Jellinek, *The Paris Commune of 1871*, p. 92.   [2] Ibid., pp. 85, 87.
[3] Ibid., p. 100.   [4] Ibid., p. 97.   [5] Ibid., p. 98.

the course of events, but a few hours after Thiers's failure to capture the guns at Montmartre and his consequent decision to withdraw every regular soldier from Paris, it found itself master of the city. Its situation has been well described:

'The Committee sat in the Hôtel de Ville in the utmost perplexity. They had never had the slightest idea that they might be called upon to act as a Government. . . . Their political claims had been purely local; their activities hardly more than those of supervision. None had any political experience. A few were members of the International, notably Varlin, an efficient co-operative and union organizer. Brunel and Duval were good soldiers, but not actually Committee members. The rest were a collection of mere delegates, personally vague. The only man who had some realization of their task was a young commercial traveller, Edouard Moreau, who quite suddenly emerged from complete obscurity to lead their deliberations.'[1]

The Government of revolutionary Paris sat on in the Hôtel de Ville while the demoralized army retreated gloomily along the road to Versailles. The National Guard had presented it with an insurrection whose opening phase had been completely and decisively won. But in its first session the members wasted precious time discussing arrangements for immediate elections for a new municipal council—such was their passion for legality. They could not see themselves as custodians of a revolution or realize that the political situation had now clarified to a direct issue of civil war. It does not seem to have occurred to them that Thiers's retreat to Versailles was simply the strategical prelude to an attempt to recapture Paris by a fresh and increased concentration of armed force The more realistically minded leaders such as Eudes and Duval strove in vain to make the majority understand the insurrectionary logic of the situation, the correct application to the circumstances of the rule that the defensive attitude brings failure to an armed uprising. Eudes and Duval wanted an immediate attack on Versailles.[2] If this had been undertaken at once, it might very well have been successful. The demoralization of Thiers's army at that stage was considerable. It might have been caught before there was any opportunity to reform it and retune it to the necessary counter-revolutionary pitch. Moreover, Fort Valerian, the key to the Versailles road, was held only by a detachment. It could quite easily have been captured and in the hands of the National Guard would have made a redoubtable obstacle to any advance from Versailles. Eudes and Duval were overborne and the Committee continued with its preoccupation about the elections, and for the rest devoted its attention to civil measures, excellent no doubt in themselves, but largely irrelevant to the pressing facts of the situation. It was no doubt important from the point of view of conserving revolutionary energy and enthusiasm that Paris should be administered with the minimum of friction. But to concen-

[1] Jellinek, *The Paris Commune of 1871*, p. 124.   [2] Ibid., p. 132.

trate on this sort of thing and avoid the military implications of the situation was no more than childish playing at revolutionary government. In the event it was Thiers who opened the civil war on Palm Sunday, April the 2nd, after he had been given six peaceable weeks in which to reorganize his army. The crucial days in which the revolution might have been won had been frittered away.

Even had Versailles been captured and the Bordeaux Assembly sitting there dispersed, it is still not possible to say that a government based on the ideals of Communard Paris could have captured and held France. There were outbreaks sympathetic to the Commune in several of the great industrial towns, but it is doubtful whether sympathy in the provinces was sufficiently widespread or serious to make the necessary foundations for a permanent revolution on Communard lines. Moreover, Bismarck, who had permitted Thiers to increase his army beyond the numbers laid down in the preliminary treaty terms in order to reduce Paris,[1] would almost certainly have thrown all the weight of German influence against a national Communard government. He was glad for France to become a bourgeois republic because he thought that form of government would keep her weak, but it is hardly to be supposed that he would have tolerated anything so extreme and explosive as the Commune.

This, however, does not invalidate the general principles of insurrectionary strategy which we have been discussing and which emerge so clearly from a study of the Commune.

Perhaps the greatest example of spontaneous insurrection comes from our own time. It is the March Revolution of 1917 in Petrograd. Here the general revolutionary situation was set up by the sufferings of war, coupled with the realization that the Tsarist Government, owing to its incompetence, and its lack of sympathy with every popular need and aspiration, was directly responsible for most of the economic privation and also to a large extent for the disastrous conduct of military operations. Weeks, and indeed months, however, might have dragged on without an armed outbreak but for a purely fortuitous coincidence of events.

On March the 8th, which was observed by the Socialist parties as Women's Day, crowds of women marched through the streets of Petrograd shouting for bread and bearing banners inscribed with anti-Tsarist slogans.[2] Now, on the previous day, the management of the great Putilov works had ordered a general lock-out. Some 20,000 Putilov workers, the most revolutionary section of the Petrograd populace, were therefore free to join in the demonstrations. On the 9th, the lock-out became a strike of alarming dimensions. Nearly 200,000 demonstrators were on the streets and there were fairly frequent clashes with the police. It was, however, noticeable that

[1] Jellinek, *The Paris Commune of 1871*, p. 207.
[2] Chamberlin, *The History of the Russian Revolution*, vol. i, pp. 75 sq.

the demonstrators avoided provoking the troops, and that the soldiers, for their part, were already showing unmistakable signs of sympathy with the workers. The spontaneous movement, thanks to the coincidence of the women's march with the Putilov lock-out, had gathered an impetus which nothing could arrest. This impetus in itself clarified the political situation and posed it in simple terms. The demonstration could no longer stop itself; it must go forward to the final overthrow of the Tsarist regime or be violently broken against the resistance of the troops. The analysis of the relation between the troops and the people and the final swing-over of the soldiers belongs to a subsequent chapter. Here it is only necessary to emphasize the spontaneity and the almost fortuitous character of the outbreak. 'The idea of going into the streets', wrote the Bolshevik Kayurov, a member of the Viborg Committee, 'had long been ripening among the workers; only at that moment nobody imagined where it would lead.'[1]

In all these cases of spontaneous insurrection the salient feature is the absence of planned revolutionary leadership either before the outbreak of revolt or during its initial stages. In no case was there a revolutionary organization competent and ready to take over the immediate control and direction of the insurrection. Trotsky devoted a chapter of his *History* to the question of who led the March insurrection in Petrograd. His answer is the rather vague generalization: conscious and tempered workers educated for the most part by the party of Lenin.[2] Shorn of the glamour of Lenin's name, this can really mean little more than that once on the streets and committed to an ultimate course, the more politically educated workers were able to give a certain aim and purpose to the almost blind thrusts of the demonstrating masses. They worked consciously, for instance, to avoid clashes with the soldiers so that the troops might not be alienated but rather persuaded over to the side of the uprising by sympathetic methods. The Bolshevik Shyapnihov says, for instance: 'I decisively refused to search for arms at all and demanded that the soldiers should be drawn into the uprising so as to get arms for all the workers.'[3] They realized no doubt that the attitude of the troops was the pivot on which the insurrection would swing and, once on the streets, they had the insight to see that the troops were vacillating and might be won. Thus, these anonymous leaders did to some extent take hold of a situation which they had not sought but which was rather presented to them as a *fait accompli*. It is obvious, however, that the insurrection had received its impetus before any attempt had been made to assess the probable attitude of the armed forces; and in this sense its success must be regarded as a gift of perilous chance rather than as the expected outcome of a judgement. The lack of any organization or group

[1] Trotsky, *History of the Russian Revolution* (one-vol. ed.), p. 121.

[2] *History of the Russian Revolution*, p. 171.

[3] Chamberlin, *The History of the Russian Revolution*, vol. i, p. 76.

able to take control of the revolt at the outset may be largely explained no doubt by the fact that most of the best-known and ablest revolutionary leaders were in exile or prison. Lenin, for instance, did not get back to Russia till April. Trotsky did not return till May.

The subsequent Bolshevik insurrection of November 1917 is an example of that kind of rising which is the direct result of a planned political campaign and a planned overthrow of the existing government. The plan is made as watertight as possible both as regards a calculation of the opposing forces and the choice of a suitable date for the uprising in view of the various factors involved. For example, in dealing with a conscript army, a revolutionary leader may time the insurrection for the period when a fresh class of recruits has just been called to the colours and a trained class dismissed. Young recruits are more amenable to revolutionary influence than old soldiers. This kind of factor may well influence ultimate success.

In Russia, the political campaign was developed by Lenin throughout the late summer and autumn. It was based on the assumption that, in order to carry the nation forward to the revolutionary goal which he had set, all power must be transferred from Kerensky's Provisional Government to the Soviets.[1] Throughout the late summer and early autumn months, the ground was prepared by a series of simple and masterly slogans. The Bolsheviks dinned into the country's ears the idea of 'All power to the Soviets', which by this time meant the Bolshevik Soviets, and linked this conception indissolubly with the two most popular cries that they could have chosen: 'Peace with Germany and an end to the disastrous war', and 'The land for the peasants'. This last slogan really belonged to the Social Revolutionaries who were the traditional party of the peasants and at that time numerically the strongest party in Russia, but they had made no attempt to implement their own programme during the summer and their supporters began to lose faith and to look to the more resolute Bolsheviks for action.[2] The cunning theft of this slogan probably did more than anything else to ensure mass support for the Bolsheviks when the hour for insurrection had arrived. By September, Lenin had decided that power could only be

[1] This statement needs a certain qualification. After the Bolshevik setback in July, Lenin himself temporarily abandoned the slogan of 'All power to the Soviets' since, if it meant all power to the then existing Soviets, it was useless and deceptive (*vide* Chamberlin, *The History of the Russian Revolution*, vol. i, p. 84). The slogan was abroad, however, and was hotly used at meetings and conferences. Later, when he saw how events were shaping for a Bolshevik policy, Lenin based his plans on obtaining a Bolshevik majority in the Soviets (ibid., vol. i, pp. 286, 288).

[2] *Vide* Rosenberg, *A History of Bolshevism*, pp. 96 sq., for an analysis of the position of the Social Revolutionaries; *vide* also Trotsky, *History of the Russian Revolution*, "The Peasantry before October", pp. 85 sq., and Chamberlin, *The History of the Russian Revolution*, vol. i., "The Peasant Upsurge", pp. 242 sq.

attained through an armed insurrection.[1] The rising was dated to coincide with the meeting of the All-Russian Congress of Soviets in Petrograd. The timing was the result of careful deliberation and balancing up of the various factors involved. It was assumed that the rank and file of the Petrograd garrison would not offer serious resistance and that a good proportion of them would in fact go over to the insurrection. The fighting was to be entrusted to Kronstadt sailors and to the battalions of the Red Guard who had been drilling and arming throughout the summer and who had come into the open at the time of the Korniloff push in August, when the Provisional Government had been forced into using their services as a part of the city's defence against the counter-revolutionary movement. The immediate tactics of the insurrection have no universal application. It is not, therefore, necessary to discuss in detail, for instance, what points in the city the Bolsheviks decided ought first to be seized or how they allotted their forces. Matters of this kind obviously depend upon the special circumstances of a given situation, upon the resistance offered, and upon the particular seats of administrative machinery and symbols of power of the *status quo* government. It is, however, worth remarking that the Bolsheviks paid most attention to the capture of two particular buildings: the fortress of Peter and Paul, which contained a valuable arsenal and whose guns commanded the Winter Palace, and the Winter Palace itself which was the seat of the Government. The fort fell without the firing of a shot, thanks to Trotsky's oratory which effectively brought over the wavering garrison to the side of the insurrection. The Winter Palace, inadequately defended by junker (cadet) forces and exposed to artillery fire from the fortress, was stormed by the most casual methods, but quite successfully.

Both the fortress and the Winter Palace represented not only objectives of great practical value, but also symbols of power of an old regime. The capture of such symbols of power may have an importance out of all proportion to its practical effect by reason of the psychological repercussion. The capture of the Bastille, for instance, in July 1789, relatively unimportant in itself, symbolized the release of France from a reactionary system. The emotional effect can hardly be exaggerated. The instinct of the Paris populace in choosing the Bastille for their attack was therefore perfectly correct. During the nineteenth century, almost every Parisian insurrection has concentrated first upon occupying the Hôtel de Ville, largely perhaps because during the Great Revolution the Hôtel de Ville was the seat of the radical Commune of Paris and the rallying-place for any fight against threatened counter-revolution, and so became not only the centre from which Paris could be administered, but also a significant symbol of revo-

[1] For an account of the development of Lenin's mind in regard to immediate insurrection, *vide* Chamberlin, *The History of the Russian Revolution*, vol. i, pp. 287 sq., and for the insurrection itself, vol. i, pp. 306 sq.

lutionary power. Again, during the 1916 Easter Week Rebellion in Ireland, plans were laid for the capture of Dublin Castle, the centre of government which symbolized more sharply than any other place in Ireland the bitterness of English rule. These plans completely miscarried; but there can be little doubt that, had the Castle been captured, the effect throughout the length and breadth of Ireland, in raising the people to an open support of the Republican cause, would have been tremendous. It might conceivably have turned a hopeless insurrection into a widespread rebellion which the English, with almost all their resources engaged in a European war, would have found almost beyond their available strength to put down. 'No other achievement would have had such an effect upon the imagination of the Irish people' is the comment of the ablest historian of the Irish Revolution.[1]

These references to tactics should perhaps be read as it were in parenthesis. It is of more general importance to observe that the success of the Bolshevik insurrection was really due to the correct reading of the general situation. In the first place there was the broad assumption that the people as a whole were ripe for the turnover from a bourgeois democratic revolution to a proletarian. This assumption was fiercely combated by several of the Bolshevik leaders. On October the 23rd, the Central Committee of the Bolshevik party met to thrash out finally the question of immediate insurrection. A long resolution was passed at this meeting setting forth in detail the reasons for assuming that the correct hour for a rising had arrived. Both Zinoviev and Kamenev voted against this resolution and next day issued an appeal to various party organizations to use their influence against a rising.[2] They held the view that an immediate insurrection was a dangerous gamble on which not only the fate of the Bolshevik party, but the fate of the whole revolution would be staked. They believed that the soldiers were too warweary, that the Bolsheviks could not rely on the railway and telegraph workers, that the sentiment in the factories was not what it had been three months back. They also greatly overestimated the quality and the amount of military resistance that might be expected. In addition to these objections on grounds of opportunity there seems to have been a trend of opinion in certain quarters against insurrection on the score that the proletariat would not be capable of holding and administering state power under Bolshevik leadership even if it could successfully seize it. This latter line of thought had been bitterly castigated by Lenin during the summer.[3] It does not seem to have been shared by Kamenev and Zinoviev; and the interest and importance of their objections lie in the light they throw upon the type

[1] McCardle, *The Irish Republic*, p. 177.

[2] Chamberlin, *The History of the Russian Revolution*, vol. i, pp. 292, 293; *vide* also Trotsky, *History of the Russian Revolution*, p. 999.

[3] Chamberlin, *The History of the Russian Revolution*, vol. i, pp. 289 sq.

of practical problem which revolutionary leaders have to judge before embarking on a planned uprising. The event proved the objectors wrong and Lenin right.

In regard to the amount of armed resistance that might be expected in Petrograd, the assessment of Lenin was even an overestimate. Not only was no resistance offered by the rank and file of the garrison, who in most cases threw in their lot actively with the insurrectionaries, but the officers and junker cadets, whose strenuous resistance it was certainly correct to allow for, put up no serious fight at all.[1] It is, however, interesting to note that Lenin underestimated the probable resistance in Moscow. He believed that Moscow would fall more readily than Petrograd,[2] whereas in the event ten days of bloody fighting was required to seize the city. The military preparations for revolt had been less complete in Moscow and the officers and junkers offered a gallant fight. And once they were fighting in earnest, their superior training told in their favour. Finally, they were overborne by the weight of numbers on the Bolshevik side—the Bolsheviks had a numerical superiority of something like five to one and expected further reinforcements—and by their own hopeless feeling that they were isolated from the rest of Russia.[3]

Every revolution which must depend for its ultimate success upon popular support demands an active revolutionary situation before insurrection can be safely undertaken. The general revolutionary situation as a prelude to the actual outbreak of violence has emerged clearly in all the uprisings which have been under discussion in the foregoing pages. In these cases the revolutionary situation has ripened as it were naturally in the particular political climate preceding the violent explosion. It has derived from a given set of political conditions. But it may sometimes happen that some new and to all intents quite extraneous event occurs and suddenly transforms a merely dangerous set of political conditions into an active revolutionary situation on the strength of which insurrection may be safely launched.

A clear example of this type of insurrection may be found in the English Revolution of 1688. Here, the birth of a son to James II, followed a few weeks later by the trial of the Seven Bishops, produced the immediate revolutionary situation which made it justifiable for the leaders to stake everything on sending the famous invitation to William of Orange to land forces in England. The birth of a Prince of Wales drove home to the country at large as no other event could have done that the Protestant succession was finally imperilled and with it the freedom of the Protestant faith in England. The majority of the English would probably have been prepared passively to put up with James's tyrannies—he was himself never personally unpopular—so long as they believed that he would be succeeded by his Protestant

[1] Chamberlin, *The History of the Russian Revolution*, vol. i, p. 306.
[2] Ibid., vol. i, p. 287.   [3] Ibid., vol. i, pp. 335 sq.

daughter Anne. When this was ruled out, the smoulder of discontent throughout the country became a flame and it was clear that the people were prepared to act, or rather to support those who would plan and take action. The trial of the Seven Bishops served as a further valuable inflammation to public feeling. It caught the popular imagination :

> And have they fixed the where and when?
> And shall Trelawny die?
> Here's twenty thousand Cornish men
> Will know the reason why!

The scenes of rejoicing in London when the verdict of acquittal was made known seemed a conclusive indication that the time for revolutionary action was ripe. That day seven of the Opposition leaders, Shrewsbury, Devonshire, Danby, Lumley, Bishop Compton, Edward Russell, and Henry Sydney met to make a final decision, and while the joy bells swung in the towers and steeples of London, and the night sky flushed tawny from numberless bonfires, they sat and drafted the definite invitation to William.[1]

Although the 1688 Revolution was only made possible for a given date by a coincidence of extraneous events, yet it was in every sense a directed and not a spontaneous revolution. The leaders had been awaiting their opportunity for months. Envoys had been constantly passing between them and William of Orange and they had calculated at least to some extent their chances of success. They had gauged the feeling in the country. They had taken soundings in the army and had secured the support of men like Churchill. They had also approached naval officers. These overtures to the army and the navy had convinced them that when the decisive moment came they would not be opposed by a united army or a united fleet. The details of the attempt to win over military and naval officers make fascinating reading in Burnet's *History* and Byng's *Memoirs*. Some of them will be quoted in a subsequent chapter where the final and complete paralysis of the Royal Army is discussed in full.

The scheme of insurrection in 1688 has no particular general interest. The promoters appear to have made no plan beyond arranging to send leaders into the provinces to rouse the country as soon as William's landing was an accomplished fact. For the rest, they seem to have decided to wait and see how events would shape themselves when William had actually set foot on English soil. They wanted at all costs to avoid a full-dress civil war and probably believed that the presence of William's army coupled with the obvious feeling in the country would be sufficient to overawe the king into granting adequate guarantees for future freedom. The revolution would thus be in fact accomplished by a shift of power within the system of the

[1] Lodge, *Political History of England*, vol. viii, p. 278.

Stuart monarchy. The actual outcome they do not seem to have concerted beforehand.

The revolutionary situation in 1688 was a gift of fortune. Attempts have also been made to create such a situation artificially as the necessary prelude to insurrection, or to use the introduction of some new political circumstance as a mechanism whereby popular feeling can be deliberately worked up to the insurrectionary level. The desire to create artificially a revolutionary situation which can issue in armed revolt is almost certainly the correct explanation, for instance, of the Gunpowder Plot. The organizers of the plot were not primarily engaged on a gratuitous act of terrorism. There is evidence to show that the plot was designed to throw the country into a general state of consternation and confusion. The active revolutionary—in this case the active Catholic—elements in the country would then be able to take advantage of this to rouse their supporters to an armed revolt. Plans had actually been drawn up for a rising on this basis. They included the storing of arms in country houses throughout the shires, but they also necessarily involved the drawing of influential Catholic outsiders into the gunpowder secret so that when the moment for action came the chaos in London consequent on the successful outcome of the plot could be linked correctly and swiftly to the general discontent in the Catholic country houses. It was obviously of the first importance that the revolt should be launched on as wide a base as possible before the opposing forces could have time to recover and organize. The necessity for enlarging the original group of promoters was of course the wreck of the whole scheme. The story of Tresham's smitten conscience and warning letter to Monteagle is part of the historical equipment of every English child. The serious revolutionary strategy of the Gunpowder Plot is perhaps less generally understood.[1] Given the strength of Catholic feeling in the country and the possibility that an insurrection successful in its initial stages might draw support from Spain, given the fact that there was no standing army to oppose rebellion, such a rising might have had a genuine prospect of success. It seems clear, however, that no rising could have been engineered as it were in cold blood. Some dramatic and terrible stroke was necessary at the outset, on the one hand to disorganize initial resistance and cash in on the general confusion, and on the other hand to shake up the Catholic elements to a sense that the last and crucial hour for action had come.

It is not here necessary to discuss the moral aspect of terrorist tactics. The moral aspect has, however, a practical repercussion. Tresham's con-

[1] Gardiner, *What the Gunpowder Plot Was*. *Vide* in particular p. 36, part of Guy Fawkes' confession after his arrest, and pp. 57 sq. Winter's confession. *Vide* also p. 45 a letter from the Sheriff of Worcestershire *re* his suppression of the 'rebellious assembly' in his county; also G. M. Trevelyan, *England Under the Stuarts*, pp. 92 sq.

science, when it came to the point, could not stomach a major act of terrorism and he preferred to betray his cause. And it is possible that Catholic feeling in the country would have been so shocked by the outcome of the gunpowder explosion that many supporters would have refused to rise.

A further possible example of the artificial creation of a revolutionary situation might be the use of the weapon of the general strike. The revolutionary strike has been used on more than one occasion as a prelude to violent uprising; but history so far provides no instance of a revolutionary strike issuing in a successful insurrection. It is, therefore, only feasible to discuss the chance of such a strike developing conditions which would admit a revolutionary seizure of power in theory. This chance will be referred to in a later chapter in an attempt to analyse the inherent strength and weakness of the general strike as a revolutionary weapon, particularly in regard to the opportunity it may give to cripple the power of opposing armed forces.

The proposed application of conscription to Ireland in 1918 produced that kind of revolutionary situation which leaders can exploit in order to inflame smouldering popular discontent to the heat necessary for open insurgence. The Irish insurrection was of course a long-term insurrection in the sense that it was not launched by a single spectacular outbreak but was rather conducted through numberless apparently isolated acts of terrorism and small guerrilla engagements over a period of years. The conscription issue dominated the opening period and enabled the Sinn Fein leaders to rouse the country to an active support of militant tactics. The Irish Volunteers pledged themselves to resist by force the imposition of conscription. By this means they induced thousands of men who wanted to avoid military service to join their ranks. In Galway at the beginning of 1918 only 25 per cent of the population were said to be Sinn Feiners. Towards the end of the year, the proportion had risen to 80 per cent. In County Mayo an official report reads that Sinn Fein derived its first great impetus from the proposal to extend the Military Service Act to Ireland. The people credited the movement with successfully staving off the introduction of conscription. In the West Riding of Cork, when it was announced that conscription would be applied, there was a serious outbreak of raiding private houses for arms.[1] Practically the whole of Nationalist Ireland signed the anticonscription pledge,[2] and for the first time in the history of the Sinn Fein movement, the issue drove the constitutional Nationalist leaders on to a common front with the militant Sinn Feiners.[3] A twenty-four hours' general strike was staged as a protest. With the exception of Belfast the stoppage of all branches of work throughout Ireland seems to have been singularly complete.[4] In capitalizing the conscription issue the Sinn Fein

[1] I.O., *Administration of Ireland 1920*, pp. 13, 50, 60.
[2] McCardle, *The Irish Republic*, p. 263.   [3] Ibid., pp. 260 sq.   [4] Ibid., p. 263.

leaders showed considerable revolutionary acumen. It is an example which exhibits clearly how a specific grievance may be used in order to create a necessary psychology of revolt. The insurrectionary organization and method of Sinn Fein in relation to the armed forces opposed to the insurrection will be discussed in a future chapter.

It may sometimes happen that some sudden event over which revolutionary leaders have no control may upset entirely calculations of time in a planned insurrection. Thus, the Franco Rebellion in Spain was planned for the middle of August 1936, but the murder of the Right leader Calvo Sotelo on July the 5th produced such tense emotion, both in the Right and Left political camps, that the rising could not be held back. In spite of the fact that their preparations were by no means matured, the leaders were forced to strike at once.[1] Preparation for insurrection naturally presupposes a generally explosive situation, and an uncontrollable interference of this kind must always be allowed for. It shows up sharply that the supreme characteristics needed for a revolutionary leader are adaptability to a kaleidoscopic alteration in conditions, the capacity to take quick decisions, and the power to steer his party without confusion on some necessarily altered course.

It is clear from the foregoing discussion that the problem of correctly timing a revolutionary outbreak is of the utmost importance to its success. This problem has a long-term as well as a short-term aspect. Examples of the short-term aspect of timing for a particular set of favourable conditions have already been given, and it has also been shown how correct timing may depend upon taking swift advantage of some sudden change in a potentially revolutionary group of political circumstances. Long-distance timing belongs rather to the ebb and flow of large historical sequences than to the handling of an immediate practical policy. It is concerned with such questions as whether a revolutionary policy is more likely to gain support and grow to the necessary strength for a violent outbreak during periods of economic depression or whether, on the other hand, seasons of relative prosperity do not make better breeding grounds for revolutionary energy. Long-distance timing in this sense falls outside our purpose here. But there is one salient situation in which long- and short-term timing appear to meet. This is the situation created by war.

There can be little doubt that under modern conditions the last stages of an unsuccessful war provide the surest combination of circumstances for a successful revolutionary outbreak. It is indeed probable that in a strong modern state, where the efficient machinery of government is backed by military force and controls almost every aspect of community life, unsuccessful war is alone capable of disintegrating the structure of government

[1] *Vide* Borkenau, *The Spanish Cockpit*, p. 62, and Duchess of Atholl, *Searchlight on Spain*, p. 71.

sufficiently to make revolution practicable. It is not only a question of disintegrating the structure of the government, but also of rousing a closely governed population to a sufficiently acute and widespread sense of grievance to take violent revolutionary action. It will be shown in a subsequent chapter that failure in war produces solvents which are potent enough to crumble the rank and file of the army; in a modern army no other set of conditions seems likely to be able to produce these solvents. But failure in war also provides conditions of administration so difficult that the civil machinery of the state creaks and breaks down, at least partially. Thus the civil machine and the military machine are no longer powerful to withstand the rising revolutionary pressure from a disillusioned and suffering populace.

The difficulties and dangers of carrying a revolution past its initial stages towards the close of a losing war are, however, obviously enormous. For, once the initial stage of revolution is successfully past, the leaders will be faced with the task either of continuing the war as best they can with a necessarily disorganized and war-weary country behind them or of making an almost certainly humiliating peace. In practice there can be no real alternative to making peace. From the standpoint of the prestige of the revolutionary government and the successful consolidation of the revolutionary gains, the consequences of such a peace may well be disastrous. The Bolsheviks, it is true, lived down the Treaty of Brest-Litovsk, but the German Social Democrats never freed themselves from the stigma of having accepted and signed the preliminary peace terms in November 1918 or the final terms of the Treaty of Versailles. This point will be referred to again in more detail when the German Revolution of 1918 comes under review. It is perhaps only indirectly relevant to a discussion on the technique of seizing the most suitable conditions for revolutionary action.

Where a revolutionary party is sufficiently sure of itself and sufficiently ruthless to work for a social upheaval in the midst of war, or to endeavour to seize control and direct an outbreak which has taken place as a spontaneous protest against intolerable conditions, the general plan of action is clear. The party will concentrate upon propaganda among the troops and the civilian populace and, when the smouldering fires of discontent finally burst into flame, it will concern itself not so much with inventing the most advantageous organization and technique for opposing regular troops as with the task of winning over the wavering soldiers by persuasion. At every stage it will work to break down any feeling of military isolation and in its stead build up a sense of the essential solidarity and identity of interest between the army and the people. This technique is, of course, true only for social revolution. An oppressed nationality which takes advantage of a war situation to revolt does not aim at winning over the opposing troops but rather at fighting them with the best organization possible. It has been shown above, and will be described in more detail later, how from the very outset of the March Revolution in Russia, the Bolsheviks realized the importance of distinguishing those general conditions of revolution which make this technique of insurrection the correct one, and concentrated upon undermining the already discontented army and persuading it to the revolutionary cause rather than perfecting a strong insurrectionary fighting organization to oppose it. In a case such as the German Revolution of 1918, where an outbreak among the armed forces precedes the explosion among the civil population, revolutionary technique must vary again. In these conditions, it will become the leaders' business to gain immediate control of the tremendous revolutionary force which has been released. This force will tend to have a negative rather than a positive character. It will derive from a blind reaction against unbearable conditions rather than from a conscious urge to reach some positive political goal. And its revolutionary power will rapidly be lost unless it can be controlled and directed to a clearly seen and constructive political aim. The failure of the Social Democratic leaders to take control and lead the armed forces, using them both as the spearhead and the buttress of the revolution which they had themselves made, is one of the major calamities of the months after November 1918.

It is clear that a general technique for insurrection must depend to a very large extent upon quick adaptability to factors over which the revolutionary leaders have no control. The two main classes into which insurrections fall, the spontaneous mass uprising and the planned revolt, stand at either end of a scale of varying possibilities for control. Before leaving this subject, it may therefore be as well to try to assess in some degree the comparative strength and weakness of these two types. The contrast between them which emerges most vividly is in their difference of impact against the regime of the *status quo*. The spontaneous mass uprising throws itself blindly against the regime which it holds responsible for its sufferings. It commands a volume of violent support which a planned revolt can probably seldom obtain and it goes forward by the sheer impetus of its own tremendous weight. From this standpoint it has revolutionary qualities superior to those of the planned revolt. It has the qualities of the rising flood-tide or the mountain avalanche. At the same time it has the defects of these qualities. The tide turns from flow to ebb and the avalanche expends itself perhaps before any objective of real importance has been swept out of its track. Unless the spontaneous mass uprising can be captured and directed by competent leadership it will end in failure. It may topple over a weak *ancien régime* but it will be unable to hold its gains. The direction of its drive is without purposeful and positive political aim and unless its energy can be harnessed to a constructive political purpose it will dissipate itself in confusion and bewilderment. This is the underlying explanation of the confused and essentially weak layout of politics in Russia during the spring and summer of 1917. And it is clear that the basic task which the Bolsheviks shouldered during that period was to get control over the surging currents of revolutionary energy released during the March outbreak and direct them to a constructive end. Their success can be measured by the success of their own planned revolution in November.

The planned revolution does not bear this characteristic of a natural force released into overwhelming motion. In this sense it is artificial and may lack mass drive; it may show weakness where the spontaneous uprising is strong. It depends for its success partly upon a correct timing in relation to popular feeling and a shifting set of political conditions, partly upon a correct timing in regard to purely technical considerations and partly upon a sound judgement regarding the strength of the forces which can be marshalled against the revolt. The strength of the planned revolution by comparison with the spontaneous uprising lies in the greater ease and efficiency with which it can be handled, in the fact that the leaders can, at any rate to some extent, choose suitable political weather before embarking, and finally in the fact that a planned revolution will have almost certainly a deliberate political aim towards which the varying and veering currents of revolutionary energy can be directed by able and determined leadership.

3

THE UNSUCCESSFUL INSURRECTION

Value of unsuccessful insurrection as a factor in long-term revolutionary strategy.

The object of an insurrection is to effect a seizure of power; and it has been shown in the opening chapter that straight insurrections have never been won and probably never can be won against the full strength of a professional army. But insurrections have frequently broken out spontaneously in conditions where any chance of permanent success was impossible and have even occasionally been launched deliberately in the accepted knowledge that they could achieve no positive and direct success. Regarding revolutionary strategy by and large it does not necessarily follow that such insurrections are always unjustifiable. Indirectly, they can sometimes alter the whole political situation so deeply that from a revolutionary standpoint they may be a valuable factor in long-term strategy, even though foredoomed to military failure.

The Moscow insurrection of 1905, already described, was perhaps almost successful from this point of view. In fact, the Moscow rising did not hold out quite long enough to modify fundamentally the general revolutionary situation in 1905. Also it came too late. It did, however, prove that a quite small number of determined and self-regardless men may be able to hold a government at bay over a short period of time and that, if only this period can be made to last long enough, the mere fact of sustained defiance can force alterations in the whole trend of events. In order to assess their value, such insurrections must be placed in their general revolutionary setting. The general character of the 1905 revolution is a curious series of ebb and flow of revolutionary activity lasting for many months. There were several sporadic mutinies in the army and a rash of agrarian disturbances, but the peak periods were marked by general strikes.[1] The temper of the people, surging up, made action essential, but this action was never planned and thought out in terms of a rising curve of revolutionary pressure and enthu-

[1] The Russian general strikes of 1905 will be referred to in more detail in the following chapter.

siasm in the sense that Lenin tried to control the pressure of the flooding tide of political feeling during the summer of 1917. The Moscow rising broke out towards the end of this period as the culmination of the last of these strikes. The strike was transformed into a rebellion, the best of the striking workers being used as the rebel force.[1] The leaders knew well enough that the rising could win no permanent revolutionary objective unless the army should refuse to act against the rebels, but they realized that the temper of the people at that moment was such that a rising was an essential and inevitable outlet for their emotion. The abscess of discontent had come to a head and could only burst. It burst too late to affect the course of events in any fundamental way because the tide of general revolutionary feeling was already on the ebb and the psychology of the Tsar's government was swinging back from the state of nervousness into which it had been thrown by the tremendous pressure of the first General Strike. Had the Moscow rising come as the culmination of the first General Strike when revolutionary feeling was most active, united, and general, it is possible that it would have forced basic concessions even though it was not able permanently to seize power.

Again, from a long-term point of view, the Dublin Insurrection of 1916 was extraordinarily useful to Sinn Fein. The rebels held the centre of Dublin for six days in the name of an Irish Republic, thereby giving a concentration and a kind of actuality to national sentiment such as perhaps it had not known since the great days of the '98. The Irish lost 56 volunteers killed in action and the English 130 combatants. Considering the circumstances, the rebellion was liquidated by the English with surprising leniency. There were 3,500 arrests, including 79 women. Of these, 1,000 men and all but five women were subsequently released; 90 were sentenced to death by court-martial, but the actual number of executions was only 15.[2] It is worth comparing these figures with similar ones for the Paris Commune of 1871. It is, of course, true that the Communards held Thiers at bay for more than six weeks instead of six days, but this can perhaps be offset by the special danger and exasperation of the Irish Rising at a time when England was straining every resource in a European war. At any rate, taking into account those who were killed in the street fighting as the Versaillese Army closed on the centre of Paris and in the massacres after the army's entry, those who died in prison, on the convict transports, or in New Caledonia, those who were gaoled on long sentences or deported, it has been reckoned that Paris lost more than 50,000 workers—an unpleasant but not unimpressive comment on the capacity of the French for vengeance and class terror. The mass shootings of prisoners were peculiarly ruthless and undiscrimin-

[1] *Vide* note 1 on p. 84.
[2] McCardle, *The Irish Republic*, pp. 188, 195, 196.

ating. It is reckoned that 1,900 were shot at La Roquette in two days and 400 at Marzas.[1]

Judged by such standards, the English behaved in Dublin with extraordinary forbearance; yet out of their handful of killed and wounded and executed, the Irish were able to construct a brand-new martyrology, in all seriousness an essential feature of Irish revolutionary method. They were able to fan opinion to burning pitch with their tales of 'British brutality' and to give the country a renewed sense of national manhood through the memory of those few days when the Republican flag had floated over Dublin.

The promoters of the rising[2] had originally planned it in terms of serious help from Germany, not only as regards the landing of arms, but also in the rather optimistic hope that the Germans might follow up the outbreak by an attack on the east coast of England and an offensive in France. Casement was in Germany acting as liaison. When it became clear to him that the Germans intended no more serious help than the landing of a cargo of arms, he did everything in his power to get the rising stopped, but his messages failed to get through. It was only when the news of his own landing and arrest became known that the insurrectionary leaders realized that they were embarking on a forlorn hope, a hope made even more forlorn by the confusion which had resulted from the efforts of Eoin MacNeill, who had never believed in the strategy of the rising and who had been kept out of the promoters' councils, to countermand all movements of volunteers when he heard what was being prepared. The insurrectionary leaders and many of the rank and file, with a truer instinct for psychology, determined to go on. 'Anything, they felt would be better than to disperse now without one blow struck—reduce all their great purpose and brave preparation to an empty boast. No army would ever recover from such a humiliation; the leaders would never be forgiven or trusted again; for a generation, Irish freedom would be a lost cause.'[3]

Arthur Griffith had been among those who were strongly against the rising beforehand, since he realized that so far as the permanent seizure of power was concerned, it was almost bound to be a failure. Griffith, indeed, had been excluded from the confidence of the planners. The indirect results, however, made him change his opinion. In 1917, commenting on the shooting of the rebel leaders by General Maxwell, Griffith said: 'I knew the English were brutal enough to do it; I did not think they would be stupid enough. Had I foreseen that, perhaps my views on the whole matter

[1] Jellinek, *The Paris Commune of 1871*, pp. 381, 365.

[2] The most important account of the preparations for the rising and the course of the fighting is in McCardle, *The Irish Republic*, chaps. xiii, xiv, xv, xvi. Cf. the account in I.O., *The Administration of Ireland 1920*, pp. 16 sq.

[3] McCardle, *The Irish Republic*, p. 170.

might have been different.'[1] MacNeill said afterwards that the English should have suppressed the insurrection by using the Royal Irish Constabulary. The whole thing would then have been regarded merely as a farce. But the troops and the artillery made it dignified and tragic and enlisted a great mass of otherwise neutral or even hostile opinion on the side of the rebels.[2] This view may be psychologically correct, but it is difficult to believe that the rising could in fact have been suppressed by the unaided R.I.C. The rebels only surrendered when the searing artillery fire had made their positions untenable—another instance of the decisive advantage in the hands of those who control the big guns. In this connection it is interesting to note that certain of the leaders had reckoned that the artillery might not be employed by a capitalist government which would fight shy of wrecking the capitalist centre of Dublin. Dillon, a leader of the old moderate Home Rule party, took a view similar to that of Griffith about the effect of the executions. Speaking in the House of Commons in May, he said that thousands of Irish people who ten days before had been bitterly opposed to the whole Sinn Fein movement and to rebellion were now becoming infuriated against the Government and that this feeling was spreading right through the country.[3]

The official British reports bear out the same theory. From the British point of view, recruiting for the war was then the most pressing problem in Ireland. Conscription had just been applied to the rest of the United Kingdom, but Ireland had been excluded from the Act. A report from Westmeath in 1917 emphasized the large number of Sinn Fein sympathizers and asserted that the chief reason for this was the belief that the rebellion had saved the country from conscription. Other reports from various parts of the country complained of its disastrous effect on voluntary recruiting. In Kilkenny, prior to the rising, recruiting had been satisfactory; after the rising, the number of recruits dwindled to eight or ten a month. In County Kilkenny there were only 158 recruits taken during the year. In the East Riding of Galway, the majority of people had gone over to Sinn Fein.[4]

Piaras Béaslai, Collins's biographer, describing the return to Dublin of those leaders of the rebellion who had been imprisoned in England and were released when an amnesty was granted for the meeting of the Irish Convention, wrote: 'Little over a year ago they had been marched prisoners through these streets to the boats amid silence or hostile demonstrations. To-day, they were received as heroes and leaders.'[5]

[1] Quoted by Piaras Béaslai, *Life of Michael Collins*, vol. i, p. 124.

[2] Report of an interview with MacNeill in *Michael Collins' Own Story Told to Hayden Talbot*, p. 33.

[3] Piaras Béaslai, *Life of Michael Collins*, vol. i, p. 127.

[4] I.O., *The Administration of Ireland 1920*, pp. 44, 45, 47.

[5] Piaras Béaslai, *Life of Michael Collins*, vol. i, p. 157.

THE UNSUCCESSFUL INSURRECTION

A further interesting example of the indirect importance of an unsuccessful revolt may be found in the Asturias Rising of 1934. The Asturias Rising was a desperate protest against the failure of the 1931 Revolution to hold its gains and effect any deep alteration in the social system of Spain. During the three years before 1934, the parties of the Right had improved and consolidated their position and by 1934 they were strong enough to control the government and make the running throughout Spain. The Left realized that the revolution was at a cross-roads and risings broke out also both in Madrid and Barcelona. These were dismal failures owing to the inability of the Left parties to combine. In the Asturias, where the U.G.T. was supreme, the working classes rose in a revolt as determined and heroic as any in all European working-class history. They held out for a fortnight, and were finally subdued by Moorish troops, foreign legionaries, and air-bombing. The liquidation of the revolt was particularly cruel—some 30,000 prisoners were kept in gaol for eighteen months apart from bloodier and more spectacular acts of vengeance—and the fact that Moors and foreigners were used in the work of repression added a nationalist element to the social anger of the working classes throughout Spain. The working classes now had a tradition and a heroic myth. Asturias combined for them 'the pride of an army in its previous feats of military glory and the pride of a Church in its religious martyrs.'[1] It was a welding iron to fuse the differences of the Left parties into a common aim. The Republicans, for instance, who had refused to take part in the insurrection agreed to an electoral alliance with the Socialists. The Communists joined in too. The Anarchists, whose refusal to go into the Barcelona revolt had ruined its chances from the start, now agreed to persuade their followers to support the Popular Front at the polls.[2] It is not, therefore, going too far to say that a direct result of the splendid failure in Asturias was the triumph of the Left in the elections of Feburary 1936, the decisive turning-point in the path of the revolution.

Two more examples can be taken from the history of the Italian Risorgimento.

On the 17th of March 1848, the people of Milan, already excited and encouraged by the success of the February Revolution in Paris and hopeful of Piedmontese help against Austria, heard the news that Vienna had risen in insurrection against the oppressions of Metternich's Government and that Metternich himself had been compelled to resign. Feeling had been boiling up in Milan for some while past, demonstrations were continuous, and Radetsky, the Austrian commander, fearing both insurrection in the city and war with Piedmont, had sent for reinforcements for his garrison. The news of the Viennese rising fired the explosive material. Barricades were thrown up all over the city and the soldiers of Austria, attacked with every weapon which came to a citizen's hand, failed to clear the streets. Radetsky

[1] Borkenau, *The Spanish Cockpit*, p. 57.   [2] Ibid., p. 58.

THE UNSUCCESSFUL INSURRECTION

held the castle, the cathedral, the walls, and numerous outposts in the town. But his men could make no headway when they tried to assault the barricades. These were held with heroic determination. It is said that at one barricade two lads fought back an Austrian company for a whole day. Demoralization set in, and Radetsky began to fear also for his food supply. He proposed an armistice. The Milanese refused. On the fifth day of the fighting, the Austrians had lost all but the walls and the castle. That day volunteers from neighbouring towns attacked the gates from outside and the Milanese joined the attack from within. By evening they had captured the Porta Tortosa and the volunteers could enter to reinforce them. Radetsky spent the night in a futile bombardment of the city from the castle. Then he evacuated his beaten army and retired slowly behind the forts of the Quadrilateral.

By their action alone, the Milanese could never have beaten the Austrians permanently out of northern Italy. It was clear that Radetsky had retreated behind the Quadrilateral in order to come back in his own time. His return could only be barred by the professional army of Piedmont. The story of that war, the splendid fighting quality of the Piedmontese troops thrown away by the indecisions of Charles Albert and the blunders of generals, the final disaster at Custozza, does not belong here. On August the 4th, the Piedmontese were taking refuge behind the walls of Milan. The generals decided that further resistance was useless and the king agreed to capitulate. During the night the Piedmontese army moved out of the city, and more than half the population is said to have gone with the army rather than experience once more the humiliations of Austrian rule.[1]

The 'five days of Milan' had won the Milanese but five short months of freedom. The positive gain must have seemed fleeting and bitter enough. But they had done something which no returning Austrian army could undo. They had created a legend and 'they had registered a claim upon the future and Austrian rule was henceforth too odious ever again to seem a settled and legal government'.[2]

The defence of the Roman Republic against the French in the following year had an even greater effect on the emotional strength of the fight for Italian unity. For Rome held a unique place in the annals of Italy and men's thoughts must be turned back from her dismal present to the days when she had been not only the centre of the peninsula, but the heart of the civilized world. The knowledge that not only Romans but the finest elements among all Italian youth had fought and died upon the walls of Rome reawakened the old tradition and gave it a contemporary significance. Mazzini realized this special position of Rome when he determined to carry on the struggle even though he knew that the result could only be defeat.

[1] *Vide* Bolton King, *History of Italian Unity*, vol. i, pp. 216 sq., 256 sq.
[2] G. M. Trevelyan, *Garibaldi's Defence of the Roman Republic*, p. 57.

THE UNSUCCESSFUL INSURRECTION

With his words we may finish this chapter:

'To the many other causes which decided us to resist, there was in my mind added one intimately bound up with the aim of my whole life—the foundation of our national unity. Rome was the natural centre of that unity, and it was important to attract the eyes and the reverence of my countrymen towards her. The Italian people had almost lost their *Religion* of Rome; they too had begun to look upon her as a sepulchre and such she seemed. . . .

'A few individual exceptions apart, the Romans had never shared that ferment, that desire for liberty, which had constantly agitated Romagna and the Marches. It was therefore essential to redeem Rome; to place her once again at the summit, so that the Italians might again learn to regard her as the temple of their common country. . . .

'I remember that when the question as to whether we should resist or not first arose, the chief officers of the National Guard, when I assembled and interrogated them, told me sadly that the main body of the Guard would not in any case co-operate in the defence. It seemed to me that I understood the Roman people far better than they, and I therefore gave orders that all the battalions should defile in front of the Palace of the Assembly on the following morning, in order that the question might be put to the troops. The universal shout of 'Guerra!' which arose from the ranks drowned in an instant the timid doubts of their leaders.

'The defence of the city was therefore decided upon; by the Assembly and people of Rome from a noble impulse and from reverence for the honour of Italy; by me as the logical consequence of a long-matured design. Strategically, I was aware that the struggle ought to have been carried on out of Rome, by operating on the flank of the enemy's line. But victory, unless we were to receive assistance from the other provinces of Italy, was equally impossible within and without the walls; and since we were destined to fall, it was our duty, in view of the future, to proffer our *morituri te salutant* to Italy from Rome.'[1]

[1] G. M. Trevelyan, *Garibaldi's Defence of the Roman Republic*, p. 117.

4

FIGHTING PROFESSIONAL ARMED FORCES

Can armed insurrection succeed in any circumstances against a professional army?—the Irish Revolution, 1916–21—the American War of Independence—Garibaldi's Sicilian campaign—general strikes as a revolutionary weapon.

Armed insurrection can be carried out in various ways; and it would appear that there are certain conditions in which a particular type of insurrectionary technique has a chance of succeeding even against the professional armed forces of a *status quo* government, because for one reason or another these forces cannot put out their full strength.

A technique of insurrection suited to a given set of conditions was tried out in Ireland between 1916 and 1921. The Irish Treaty of 1921 is a proof of its success. It is not suggested that the Irish Republican Army had in fact beaten, or indeed could beat, the British Army in a 'straight' war. The Irish leaders themselves knew that; at any rate the more realistic among them knew and admitted it. Otherwise, they would not have accepted the treaty terms which represented a considerable whittling down of their original demands. Michael Collins, for instance, agreed to put his signature to the treaty only when refusal faced him with the prospect of an immediate renewal of hostilities on the scale of a full-dress war. It has been described how Mr. Lloyd George came to the conference table when the delegates were tired out after hours of haggling and said: 'I have to communicate with Sir James Craig to-night. Here are the alternative letters I have prepared, one enclosing the Articles of Agreement reached by H.M. Government and yourselves, the other saying that the Sinn Fein representatives refuse the Oath of Allegiance and refuse to come within the Empire. If I send this letter it is war, and war within three days; which letter am I to send?'[1] Collins put his signature to the treaty because he believed that if hostilities were renewed on a fresh and much extended scale the Sinn Fein military campaign could be carried no further to meet them. Defending his

---

[1] Quoted by McCardle, *The Irish Republic*, p. 608.

action later in the Dail, he said : 'We as negotiators were not in the position of conquerors dictating terms of peace to a vanquished foe. We had not beaten the enemy out of the country by force of arms.'[1]

Indisputably, however, the Sinn Fein revolutionary strategy had produced a condition of affairs where the Irish could wrest from an unwilling England the major part of what they wanted. Moreover, it had knocked completely out of the sphere of practical politics any notion that the English could hold and govern Ireland by civilized methods. If they were to try again, they would first have to reconquer the country by force of arms from cabin to cabin and then hold it as a foreign army holds a conquered province. Theoretically, the country could no doubt be reconquered by methods similar to those used in South Africa, but in practice, to embark on such a war would have involved a number of extremely difficult political considerations. In order to reconquer Ireland the experts reckoned that 100,000 new special troops and police would have to be raised ; thousands of motor-cars would need to be armoured and equipped ; the three southern provinces would have to be laced with cordons of blockhouses and barbed wire ; a systematic rummaging and questioning of every individual must be put in force.[2] But England was still convalescent after the most gruelling Continental war of her history. Her people were sick of soldiering and military adventus reheld no glamour for them. Moreover, a section of English opinion, indeed perhaps the best of English opinion, was sympathetic to the Irish cause, and a much larger section was quite unable to face up to the necessary reign of frightfulness and terror which must ensue in Ireland if the country were to be reconquered. This had been proved to the British Government by the outcry which had arisen in England against the policy of official reprisals in the late winter and spring of 1921 and the relatively mild and spasmodic excesses of the 'Black and Tans'. Moreover, in those years immediately succeeding the war, there was in England an uncertain current of political feeling more revolutionary perhaps in character than anything the country had known since the days of the Chartists. In addition, England had imperial and foreign reactions to consider. Mr. Winston Churchill, speaking in the House of Commons on the treaty terms, admitted the Government's nervousness : 'Our whole army was tethered to Ireland. Our great interests . . . in India, in Egypt were sensibly affected by that weakness. So were our interests all over the world, especially in our Dominions and in the U.S.A.'[3]

[1] McCardle, *The Irish Republic*, p. 635.

[2] McCardle, *The Irish Republic*, p. 475, quoting Winston Churchill. Other experts rated the difficulties still higher. General Macready, Commander-in-Chief in Ireland, for instance, asserted that if the truce had broken down in December 1921, 150,000 men would have been needed to reconquer Ireland. Before the truce he could have succeeded with 80,000 men. (Macready, *Annals of an Active Life*, p. 562.)   [3] Quoted by McCardle, *The Irish Republic*, p. 627.

FIGHTING PROFESSIONAL ARMED FORCES

Given these considerations, the Sinn Fein leaders were justified in planning a strategy of revolution which would bring them up against the professional armed forces of England because they could count that these forces would in practice be hamstrung to a considerable extent. It is possible, indeed, that they might with success have risked rejecting the treaty terms. Mr. Lloyd George's ultimatum to the Irish delegates might not have been without an element of bluff and, had the bluff been called, the Government might have retreated. In any case, had Mr. Lloyd George stood by his threat and forced England into a full-dress war, the outcome, granted the background conditions, might well have been unpredictable. This, however, can only be a matter for historical speculation and, in discussing it from the point of view of revolutionary strategy, the position of the Irish Republican Army has also to be considered. There appears to have been a considerable conflict of opinion on both sides as to the real strength of the I.R.A. when the truce was declared in July 1921. Both Sinn Fein and British observers seem to have believed that it had passed the possible zenith of its activities. And some at any rate of the Sinn Fein leaders were uncertain as to whether it would be possible to renew insurrectionary tactics adequately even after the breathing space of the truce. Piaras Béaslai quotes a British report on the military situation in September 1921 :

'Three months ago the rebel organization throughout the country was in a precarious condition and the future from the Sinn Fein point of view may be said to have been well-nigh desperate. The Flying Columns and Active Service units . . . were being constantly defeated and broken up by the Crown forces ; the internment camps were rapidly filling up, the H.Q. of the I.R.A. was functioning under the greatest difficulties, many of its officers having been captured. . . . Reinforcements were pouring into Ireland. Martial Law was about to be proclaimed throughout the twenty-six counties and three months of suitable weather was still before us. . . . Such were the conditions on the 11th of July, and it is small wonder that the rebel leaders grasped at the straw that was offered and agreed to negotiations.'[1]

Béaslai himself seems to have thought that from a military point of view this summing up was fairly correct. And it seems clear that after the inevitable slackening of organization and discipline during the truce it would have been extremely difficult to reorganize and launch hostilities afresh if the negotiations had broken down.[2] He points out, however, that from a political point of view the English administration of Ireland had been completely broken up. Morally, the English had been beaten out of the country. 'Where all the science and all the massed battalions of the Central Powers failed, the methods of Sinn Fein succeeded. They did so because they reduced, not the British Army, but the British Government

[1] Piaras Béaslai, *Life of Michael Collins*, vol. ii, p. 249.
[2] *Life of Michael Collins*, vol. ii, p. 271.

and the British people to that mood of surrender which is the essence of defeat.'[1] And the treaty terms, even though they embodied a compromise, were in reality little less than a capitulation.

'They were passed with a revolver pointed at your head,' exclaimed Lord Carson in the House of Lords. 'You know it and you know you passed them because you were beaten, because you had failed, that the Sinn Fein army in Ireland had beaten you.'[2]

When there is a point to be made derogatory to England, Irishmen who normally display the bitterest animosity against each other, can develop for a moment an engaging exhibition of mutual admiration.

The insurrectionary technique of Sinn Fein combined terrorist tactics with guerrilla warfare. It was part and parcel of a largely conceived revolutionary strategy designed to make the English administration of Ireland impossible. In order to understand it properly, it is therefore necessary to set it in its place as part of the larger design. The basis of this design was to boycott English government by setting up an alternative Irish administration and whenever possible inducing the Irish people to refer to this Sinn Fein organization. Thus, in the realm of justice, Sinn Fein set up courts alternative to the English courts. Piaras Béaslai asserts that the practice of refusing to plead before an English tribunal or provide jurors had become general by the beginning of 1920.[3] This is corroborated by Alison Phillips, whose bias is Unionist, and who says that by the summer of 1919 Sinn Fein justice was alone available throughout two-thirds of Ireland and the King's Writ had ceased to run. The Royal judges still went on circuit, but their courts were guarded by police and soldiers and empty of litigants.[4] Lord Justice Ronan, addressing the grand jury of north Tipperary at the March Assizes in 1920, pointed out that only three trivial cases had come up to him, all arising out of a trade dispute. Yet there should have been forty-nine cases, including two murders, two attempted murders, three woundings, three arsons, four raids for arms, etc. No-one had been made amenable for these crimes. It was obvious that there could be but two causes for this—either sympathy or terrorism.[5] In course of time people of all political parties found it advisable to apply to the improvised courts of the Republic if they were to have any redress. Solicitors, deprived of practice in the ordinary courts, made no bones about appearing before the Sinn Fein judges, and even Loyalists, compelled to sell their property, occasionally applied to the Sinn Fein courts, when they found that these imposed a higher price for land compulsorily purchased than was allowed by the Land Commission.

[1] Alison Phillips, *The Revolution in Ireland*, p. 245.

[2] Ibid., p. 244.

[3] *Life of Michael Collins*, vol. 1, p. 427, and vol. ii, p. 34.

[4] *The Revolution in Ireland*, p. 181.

[5] I.O., *Administration of Ireland 1920*, p. 77.

Moreover, at its zenith, the authority of these courts was absolute, the ultimate penalty for disobedience being death.[1]

Sinn Fein also turned its attention to gaining control of local government. The municipal elections of January 1920 gave the party a majority in most of the Councils of the south and west. In May, the Dublin Corporation resolved formally to acknowledge the authority of Dáil Eireann and to give effect to its decrees. Other Corporations followed suit and also County and District Councils. With this advantage, Sinn Fein proceeded to rig the Councils. Old councillors were to stand aside and let young men take their places who would refuse to recognize the competence of the English Local Government Board. These young councillors, being without property, could not be made liable for damages. The elected bodies would then proceed with a refusal to submit their accounts to the Local Government inspectors or to pay in their rates to English offices—an ingenious scheme.[2]

Sinn Fein election tactics were also thought out in terms of providing the country with an entire system of government alternative to the English. In the 1918 election, the more obvious revolutionary policy might have seemed to boycott the polls, thereby showing that the party took no interest in the electoral activities of the United Kingdom. Instead, Sinn Fein went into the election wholeheartedly. Candidates were put up in every constituency but two, and out of the hundred and five members returned for Ireland, seventy-three were Republicans. The remainder consisted of twenty-six Unionists, and six Nationalists.[3] The Irish Parliamentary Party had been wiped out. The strength of Sinn Fein and the justice of its claim to represent the feeling of the Irish people was patent to the world. A blow far heavier than a boycott of polling booths had been successfully struck at the English administration. For, with consummate political insight, the Sinn Fein leaders proceeded at once to organize this legally elected majority into Dáil Eireann, the National Assembly of Ireland.[4] Throughout the years of the rebellion, Dáil Eireann continued to function, in whatever chequered cirsumstances, as a freely elected parliament. Its debates helped to shape the party policy and to give it a national basis, and its decrees helped to establish a conviction among the Irish people that they had in fact, and not only in theory, an alternative government of their own on which they could rely for guidance.

As a basis for insurrectionary tactics, the alternative administration, both as a conception and a fact, was enormously important. It gave the insurrection a national standing which it could not otherwise have won. The Irish Volunteers became the Irish Republican Army, the accredited military

---

[1] Alison Phillips, *The Revolution in Ireland*, p. 181.

[2] Alison Phillips, *The Revolution in Ireland*, p. 180; *vide* also McCardle, *The Irish Republic*, pp. 340–2.

[3] McCardle, *The Irish Republic*, pp. 274 sq.   [4] Ibid., pp. 283 sq.

force of a republic which was fighting for its life. The leaders were thus able to apply the conception of a nation at war, a conception which enabled them to justify and make sense of those unpleasant tactics of murder and boycott which were in fact an essential part of the campaign for undermining the English hold on the country, but which otherwise might have been taken as purely pointless and gratuitous acts of terrorism. The point of view is well shown in the following extract from *An t-Oglach*, the paper of the Irish Volunteers, for the 31st of January 1918:

'The state of war which is thus declared to exist, renders the national army the most important national service of the moment. It justifies Irish volunteers in treating the armed forces of the enemy, whether soldiers or policemen, exactly as a national army would treat the members of an invading army. . . . Every volunteer is entitled morally and legally, when in the execution of his duty, to use all legitimate methods of warfare.'[1]

If we join to this two further extracts, one from an article by Michael Collins in the *New York American*, written in 1922, and the other from a pamphlet issued by the Headquarters of the Irish Volunteers, we get a fairly complete picture of the militant strategy Sinn Fein intended to adopt. Michael Collins wrote:

'To paralyse the British machine, it was necessary to strike at individuals. Without her spies England was helpless. It was only by means of their accumulated and accumulating knowledge that the British machine could operate. Without their police throughout the country, how could they find the man they "wanted". . . .

'We struck at individuals, and by so doing we cut their lines of communication and we shook their morale. . . . Only the armed forces and the spies and criminal agents of the British Government were attacked. Prisoners of war were treated honourably and considerately and were released after they had been disarmed.'[2]

In this regard, Collins paid particular attention to dislocating the British Intelligence Service by introducing his own agents into its ranks and also into the Post Office. His view was that England could replace her soldiers but not so easily her intelligence officers. This drive against the Intelligence Service explains a particularly cold-blooded assassination such as that of the magistrate Alan Bell, who was dragged in broad daylight from a tramcar in Dublin and shot out of hand. Bell had done a great deal of work on the Intelligence and was at that time engaged in ferreting out the financial relations between Sinn Fein and various Irish banks.[3]

The instructions to the Irish Volunteers run as follows:

'To attack troops or police would be a mistaken policy. The method

---

[1] Piaras Béaslai, *Life of Michael Collins*, vol. i, p. 275.
[2] McCardle, *The Irish Republic*, p. 319.
[3] McCardle, *The Irish Republic*, p. 347.

adopted should be to act in small numbers in suitable localities, thus compelling the authorities to disperse in search of them. . . .

'Destruction of communications should be carried out as systematically as possible.'

The instructions then go on to give detailed suggestions for destroying telegraph and telephone communications, railways and roads, transport and stores of petrol. They suggest that whenever possible fighting should be done by night, since in a locality familiar to the Volunteers this would offer them obvious advantages.[1]

The extent to which this strategy was successfully put into action may be shown from the following statistics of successful Sinn Fein insurrectionary and terrorist activities for the eighteen months between January 1919 and June 1920 and during the latter half of 1920:

	January 1919 to June 1920	*2nd half of 1920*
Courthouses destroyed	33	39
Vacated R.I.C. barracks destroyed	351	167
Vacated R.I.C. barracks damaged	105	15
Occupied R.I.C. barracks destroyed	15	11
Occupied R.I.C. barracks damaged	25	30
Raids on mails	98	894
Coastguard stations and lighthouses raided	19	26
Police killed	66	127
Police wounded	79	192
Soldiers killed	5	47
Soldiers wounded	2	118
Civilians killed	15	30
Civilians wounded	41	69
Raids for arms	*no figures given*	2,229[2]

These methods of direct attack were supplemented in two further important ways. In the spring of 1920, Sinn Fein set going a serious campaign to disorganize the entire transport system of the country so far as the carrying of troops and military stores was concerned. Dublin dockers were instructed to refuse to handle suspect cargoes and railwaymen throughout the country were ordered to refuse to work trains carrying men or material for the British Government. Attempts were also made to derail trains. This campaign so far succeeded that an official report for October 1920 visualizes the almost complete dislocation of transport throughout great areas of the country:

'Whenever the necessity arises, soldiers and police present themselves as passengers by train. If they are carried, well and good; if not, the defaulting

[1] I.O., *Administration of Ireland 1920*, p. 60.　　　[2] Ibid., pp. 93, 97.

railwaymen are suspended, and a shortage of staff ensues, resulting eventually in a curtailment of services. It is obvious that sooner or later complete paralysis must overtake the Irish railway system. When this occurs, it will be impossible to institute an alternative road transport service. . . . In the first place, the necessary lorries and drivers are not available; and in the second, it is unlikely that the Republicans would allow such a service to operate without interruption.'[1]

General Macready refers to these transport strikes as setting back the work of the military seriously during the best six months of 1920.[2] They were called off in December of that year. No doubt the strain on the financial resources of Sinn Fein in providing for the dismissed men coupled with the general discomfort caused to the civilian population was too great to allow of their becoming a permanent feature of strategy.

A similar weapon, which the Sinn Fein leaders do not appear to have used, is industrial sabotage. Ireland is primarily an agricultural country, and sabotage could only have been made important in one or two areas such as Cork or Dublin. In the north, owing to the Unionist strength, it would probably have been impossible to practise it on any seriously influential scale. In any event, its effect on the Irish situation would have been through the pressure on England and would, therefore, have depended principally upon the proportion of English to Irish capital invested in Irish undertakings.

It is, however, important to refer here to the possibilities of industrial sabotage, since it is obviously a weapon of very great potential power. And the more heavily a country is industrialized, the more powerful this weapon will be. Again, it is probable that it would prove more valuable in a revolution whose political basis was social rather than nationalist.

The second supplementary method of attack was the boycott of the Royal Irish Constabulary. This boycott was ordered by the Dáil. It was laid down that Volunteers should have no intercourse with members of the R.I.C. Persons associating with them should be subjected to the same boycott, and lists of such persons should be prepared by local area commanders of the I.R.A.[3] Phillips alleges that any young man who was known to be about to join the force was promptly shot. It is unlikely that the social ostracism of the R.I.C. by itself could have broken their morale, but combined with the policy of direct attack and the conditions under which the constables had to do their work it was sufficiently disastrous. In August 1920, Sir Hamar Greenwood said in the House of Commons that there had been 556 resignations from the force during the previous two months, and

---

[1] Macready, *Annals of an Active Life*, p. 472.

[2] I.O., *Administration of Ireland 1920*, p. 260; *vide* also p. 87, 244 sq.

[3] I.O., *Administration of Ireland 1920*, p. 130.

313 magistrates had also resigned.[1] The position in which the R.I.C. found themselves was vividly summed up in the report of a Divisional Commissioner:

'. . . Shut up in their barracks, watching nightly for attacks, murdered if they go out singly, ambushed if they go in parties, liable to be shot in the back at any time by an innocent civilian, unable to get exercise or recreation except at the risk of their lives.'

The same report points out the advantageous conditions under which the enemy worked compared to the police:

'He is conducting warlike operations against us and we are not permitted to do so against him. He also enjoys the usual advantages of guerrilla warfare without suffering any of the penalties attached to it. We have to act largely on the defensive, for we have no-one to take the offensive against. As far as we possibly can we take the offensive but our blows fall on empty air, as the enemy forces at once take up the role of innocent peasants whom we must not touch.'[2]

Gradually, the British were forced to evacuate the smaller and more isolated barracks and to concentrate in larger centres which were properly fortified. This meant that great areas of the country came under the exclusive sway of the Sinn Fein organizations. The operations of the I.R.A. increased in scope and daring, and more and more the campaign took on the aspect of a regular guerrilla war.

In judging the success of the Sinn Fein methods, the enormous advantage and impetus that was given to them by the initial slackness of the English cannot be discounted. In contrast to English indulgence and inertia, the Sinn Feiners pursued their course with energy and utter ruthlessness. From the very start they had made it clear that they considered their country to be at war with England and that hence every English agent deserved to be treated without any sentimentalism as the agent of an enemy nation. Whereas the English, with their touching belief that unpleasant spades may be conjured into polite implements if only you call them by a prettier name, refused to admit this state of war, and directed the policy of their troops and police accordingly until quite late in the campaign. English colonels drove out unarmed and unescorted to tennis parties along country roads and were

[1] Piaras Béaslai, *Life of Michael Collins*, vol. ii, p. 48. It was on account of this depletion that the Government decided to increase the force by recruiting for it in England. Hence the 'Black and Tans', so called because owing to a shortage of R.I.C. uniforms, they were fitted out partly in dark green and partly in khaki. The original 'Black and Tans' were a famous Limerick pack of hounds. In every other respect the 'Black and Tans' were full members of the force. They should not be confused with the Auxiliary Division of the R.I.C., which the British raised about the same time. These men were all ex-officers, a sort of *corps d'élite* of rebellion breakers. *Vide* I.O., *Administration of Ireland 1920*, pp. 277 sq.

[2] Quoted by Alison Phillips, *The Revolution in Ireland*, p. 185.

naturally shot or kidnapped. The English preferred thus to sacrifice their servants rather than face up to the obvious facts. A 'state of insurrection' was finally declared in the south and west in December 1920 and various measures were taken to strengthen the English position.[1] The Crown Forces were declared to be on active service; the death penalty was introduced for anyone who harboured arms or ammunition, for anyone who took part in insurrectionary activity or who gave asylum to an insurgent. The disheartened and disintegrating R.I.C. were stiffened by new troops, the Black and Tans and the Auxiliaries, highly paid, and largely recruited from that driftwood set of tough adventurers who are left in any country by the receding tide of a war—the same set, in fact, who helped to ruin the Weimar Republic for Germany by their activities in the ranks of the Free Corps. Finally, the Government introduced an official policy of reprisals. This seems to have been unquestionably effective, but was called off owing to the revolt of public opinion. General Macready believed, as we have seen, that given some 80,000 troops, he could reconquer Ireland on these lines. He was not given the chance to prove it. The British people and the British Government could not stay the course. Moreover, the effect of this kind of warfare, even on regular troops, was so deleterious that a British general could write:

'Law and order have given place to a bloody and brutal anarchy in which the armed agents of the Crown violate every law in aimless and vindictive and insolent savagery. England has departed further from her own standards, and further from the standards even of any nation in the world . . . than has ever been known in history before.'[2]

General Gough had presumably forgotten the suppression of the Paris Commune.

The Irish Republican Army was small; it has been asserted that the number of volunteers in action over the greater part of the campaign was only about 10,000.[3] The number engaged in any one action was usually a mere handful. Béaslai states that there were never as many as 200 acting together in any single operation, not even in the burning of the Dublin Custom House.[4] This gave two great advantages. Thanks to the smallness of the numbers engaged, when a specific operation was completed, it was possible for the unit which had conducted it to break up easily. The members wore no uniform and could at once make themselves indistinguishable from peaceful peasants, or they could 'run' to the wild hills of the south and west. The second advantage is the general one that it is always easier to work to a detailed plan with small picked forces which can be implicitly

---

[1] Alison Phillips, *The Revolution in Ireland*, pp. 191 sq., 186.

[2] Quoted by McCardle, *The Irish Republic*, p. 448.

[3] McCardle, *The Irish Republic*, p. 358.

[4] Piaras Béaslai, *Life of Michael Collins*, vol. ii, p. 48.

trusted and controlled rather than with the spontaneously moving masses of a revolutionary populace. Given the conditions of the Irish Revolution, it was undoubtedly wise tactics to entrust militant operations to a picked body of men and to give the civilians only the revolutionary job of succouring the fighters and obstructing British administration by civil methods.

The actual organization of the I.R.A. seems to have combined a high and successful degree of centralization with elasticity and freedom of action in the localities. Broadly speaking, it was built up on a normal army model, but the tactical force was the company consisting of 76 to 100 men. This unit was presumably chosen so that it could be based locally. Company officers were elected by their men and higher regimental officers by a meeting of company commanders. These elections had to be ratified by headquarters in Dublin. Ultimately, the whole organization was responsible to the Dail when the latter was constituted as the National Assembly of Sinn Fein Ireland at the beginning of 1919. The Volunteers' oath then became an oath of allegiance to the Dail. This point is interesting, since previous to the setting up of the Dail the Irish Volunteers had been a part of the Irish Republican Brotherhood and bound by their oath. Now the Irish Republican Brotherhood was in effect a secret society whose object was to secure the independence of Ireland by force of arms and whose members were bound to obey all orders and to preserve the secrets of the organization. Thus the Irish Volunteers were bred in the traditions of the secret society with all its emphasis on implicit obedience no matter what the cost and on absolute reticence.[1]

The I.R.A., both as regards its organization and its methods, bears a much closer analogy to such a force as the Fascist militia before Mussolini's seizure of power than it does to the classic libertarian type of insurrectionary army. The Fascist squad, which was the smallest unit of the militia organization, was linked in an ascending hierarchy of direction to the party headquarters. In bigger operations, squads seem to have acted together as a group. How far local action was autonomous and how far it was directly ordered from headquarters, it is difficult to be certain; but there seems little doubt that all terrorist actions on a major scale were the result of a general headquarters plan and were specifically ordered.[2] The Red Guard, on the other hand, which fought for the Bolsheviks, was in its essence a spontaneous organization of workers without any real provision for the transmission of authority from a central military headquarters. The

[1] For the organization of the Irish Volunteers and their relation to the Irish Republican Brotherhood, vide I.O., *Administration of Ireland 1920*, pp. 162 sq.; vide also McCardle, *The Irish Republic*, pp. 317, 318; and Piaras Béaslai, *Life of Michael Collins*, vol. i, pp. 204 sq.

[2] There is a good picture of the organization of the Fascist Militia for carrying out terrorist tactics and the type of objective aimed at in Rossi, *The Rise of Italian Fascism*, chap. 9.

Bolsheviks relied on a straight seizure of power after one decisive action. For this purpose the loose organization of the Red Guard was adequate. It is obvious that such a type of organization would have been useless either to the Irish or to the Italians, whose campaign was not based on a single large-scale insurrection, but rather on a series of guerrilla and terrorist operations spread over years, and designed, not for a straight seizure of power, but rather in order to make any alternative administration to their own finally impossible.

In this campaign both the Irish and the Fascists were successful, but in comparing their success it must be remembered that the Italian authorities held the army inactive on almost every occasion of Fascist violence, whereas the Sinn Feiners had the much harder task of opposing trained troops, or rather perhaps of carrying out their plans so as to avoid any pitched clash with the troops. Against this disadvantage to the Irish, however, must be offset the fact that the Sinn Feiners had the mass of the people behind them, either through genuine sympathy or because they were terrorized, whereas the Fascists were bitterly hated by the majority of the Italian working class. The Sinn Feiners were working against a hostile garrison, the Fascists with the connivance of a garrison against a hostile working class. The basic difference perhaps is that the Fascist movement was an internal movement and therefore necessarily diffused, and sectionalized both regionally and politically; whereas the Sinn Fein movement was nationalistic and had, therefore, all the advantages of regional homogeneity and popular unity. These underlying conditions are so different that it is unwise to press the analogy between the Sinn Fein and Fascist revolutions. The strategy was roughly similar, but the conditions in which that strategy was applied were widely different.

It is, however, worth emphasizing the enormous advantage of a tightly knit military insurrectionary organization where this can be obtained without a loss of spontaneous enthusiasm and drive. During the Paris Commune, for instance, there can be no doubt that the loose federal organization which linked the battalions of the National Guard to the Central Committee was the worst possible foundation on which to build a military organization suitable to oppose the Versaillese Army. The federalist Central Committee jibbed at the notion of a properly centralized military command endowed with adequate executive authority, with the result that the defence of Paris was undertaken in utter confusion, haphazard and piecemeal:

'There was no general plan. There was never a general council for defence. The men were frequently abandoned to themselves, without care or supervision. . . . Some battalions remained twenty or thirty days in the trenches, denuded of necessities. Others were continually held in reserve. . . . This negligence quickly killed discipline. The brave men were ready to

rely only on themselves, the others shirked their service. The officers behaved likewise—some quitted their posts to fight with their neighbours,
others abandoned them. . . .

'Before the end of April . . . the offensive promised by Cluseret was impossible. Internally, the active devoted men wore themselves out in ener-
vating conflicts with officials, committees, sub-committees, the thousand
pretentious functionings of rival administrations—and wasted a day in trying to get delivery of a cannon. . . . It was like a steam engine whence the
steam escapes by a hundred vents.'[1]

To sum up the analysis of the Sinn Fein Revolution, it would appear
that given certain favourable conditions, it is practicable for a relatively
small party of fighting revolutionaries to embark on war against a professional army and that such a war has a fair chance of success. The most
important of these conditions are:

(1) That the opposing army is for one reason or another prevented from
exerting its full strength.

(2) That the general population is sympathetic to the revolutionary forces
and prepared to give secret support.

(3) That the insurrectionary organization is closely controlled and can be
directed to a strategical plan.

(4) That operations can be carried on over a long term and on a rising
scale so as to wear down both the civilian and military morale of the opposition; and that they can be carried on in a countryside whose social make-
up and topography will give quick cover to insurgents while at the same
time they tend to disperse the opposing forces into isolated groups.

In this last regard, Ireland is an ideal country. There are no real industrial
areas with the exception of Cork and Dublin. A thin population is spread
over peasant holdings, little villages, and market towns. Great stretches of
bog and mountain land, where modern communications are almost non-
existent, march with the lush pasture country. Topographically, everything
favours guerrilla fighters working in their own countryside against stranger
garrison troops.

Here the distinction between a social and nationalist revolt becomes important since it involves technical considerations of strategy. The Sinn Fein
rising was nationalist; and certain of the favourable conditions just enu-
merated are much more likely to obtain in a nationalist rather than in a
social rising. The advantage of operating among a population which is
unitedly sympathetic, either actively or tacitly, is almost always denied to
social insurgents. In Ireland the Southern Unionist minority was small in
numbers and was still branded to a considerable extent as representative of

[1] Lissagaray, *La Commune de 1871* (edition E. Dentu), pp. 223, 224; *vide* also
Jellinek, *The Paris Commune of 1871*, pp. 199 sq.

a conquering race, so that this advantage of a sympathetic population was very marked. Coupled with it, there goes the further advantage of a homogeneous geographical background. Such a background permits a smooth spread of revolutionary infection and movement to the natural limits of a given geographical area. It may not always be combined with effective revolutionary control over the area in question so that the rebels can work openly from their bases. In Ireland, the British garrison, except for a short period when they were to a large extent driven back on the large towns, held isolated points dotted over the whole area. But they held these points almost as a garrison holds a besieged place from which it can make sorties. Such a geographical layout is far stronger from a revolutionary point of view than the type of geographical conditions which usually make the background of social revolt—separated storm centres which can only be linked together by tenuous and uncertain communications. To comprehend this advantage fully, it is only necessary to recall the position of Paris in regard to the remainder of France during the Commune, and also during the Revolution of 1848. In both cases, one serious cause for the weakness of the revolutionary position was the isolation of Paris from the provinces. Paris made the running, but the provinces failed to keep in step. There was no real equation between revolutionary activity and a political-geographical area. During the Great Revolution, except for definite pockets of counter-revolutionary activity, the pace set by Paris was more uniformly kept.

From the two advantages of a sympathetic population and a homogeneous geographical layout, there springs another which has considerable psychological value. In a nationalist revolt, the military forces opposed to the rebels are not part and parcel of the same community. They can be regarded as aliens and treated by the whole community—as they were in Ireland—as a foreign foe. They must therefore do their work under all the disadvantages of operations conducted in hostile territory where every hedgerow may shelter a civilian enemy with a gun and every cottage may be the headquarters of a guerrilla group. In a national revolt, the troops may be branded as the instruments of a foreign oppressor, a conception which always has a wide and flaming appeal and which may reach the heart of an entire community.

It can also be borne in mind that the English were defeated in Ireland before they had learned their North-West Frontier technique for using aeroplanes to subdue isolated and remote outbreaks. It is doubtful though how far this technique could have been successfully applied to Ireland. English public opinion would probably have forbidden it, and in any case the Irish forces were so mobile and so adept at disappearing into the normal population that it would have been difficult to find an objective unless bombing had been used simply as a method of reprisal.

The Sinn Fein Revolution has been chosen as an example of a successful revolt against the opposing force of a professional army because it provides a modern and particularly concise instance. The factors which crippled the effective striking power of the British Army were partly technical and partly psychological; but all could be reproduced again in some other analogous situation.

To most people's minds, however, the American War of Independence will come as the supreme example of revolutionary success against professional troops. But this war was fought a hundred and fifty years ago and many of its characteristics and some of the causes which contributed to the Colonists' ultimate success, though fascinating in themselves, have little bearing on any events that could take place in our own time. It is, for instance, clear that in many cases the firearms of the Colonials were considerably superior to those of the British regulars. The poor quality of the flints in the British Army was a byword and to pick up an American flint on a battlefield was regarded by the British private as an enormous piece of luck. In wet weather English muskets could frequently not be fired at all. Moreover, the British private was not taught to shoot either at individuals or individually, and his volleys fired almost at random frequently did practically no damage. But the American volunteer or militiaman was often a first-class sniper. He needed marksmanship in the course of his ordinary day's work at home and he learned to hold his fire and pick individuals with deadly effect. At Bunker's Hill, Lieutenant Clarke of the Marines related how he observed an American rifleman standing high above his fellows and discharging musket after musket while loaders below handed the weapons up to him. The proportion of British officers to men, 92 to 948, lost at Bunker's Hill is a sufficient proof of American marksmanship.[1] In modern times any such technical superiority on the part of rebels is almost inconceivable.

It is, therefore, only proposed here to pick out certain salient conditions of the war which had a major influence in preventing the British Army from putting out anything like its maximum strength. In this way it can be shown that the War of Independence conforms to the general rule that only the introduction of special circumstances which militate against a professional army employing its full resources can enable a rebel force to achieve victory.

The fundamental technical cause of trouble and weakness on the English side, a cause which operated in favour of the Colonists with increasing strength as the war years dragged on, was the difficulty of communication between England and America. The Atlantic Ocean was worth a trained army to Washington. Transports took anything from two to four months to make American ports and conditions on board were so bad that reinforce-

[1] Curtis, *The British Army in the American Revolution* (Yale Historical Publications), pp. 16–21. G. O. Trevelyan, *The American Revolution* (rev. ed.), vol. i, pp. 307, 315.

ments arrived, not in fighting fettle, but already decimated by death and disease. In 1781, for example, 2,400 German reinforcements were embarked for New York; 66 men died at sea from scurvy and on landing it was found that 410 others could only be reported as 'sick'.[1] This was not an isolated case. The British commanders were constantly complaining of the ill-health of the reinforcing troops when they reached American shores. The same conditions interfered with the transport of horses. Even along the American coast conditions were too difficult for the resources of the time. General Clinton, for example, asserted that in his South Carolina campaign he lost every horse on the voyage between New York and Charleston.[2]

The natural difficulties of transport were further complicated by a shortage of tonnage due partly to the reluctance of merchants to lease ships to the Government owing to the empty return journey, partly to the difficulty in finding men to man the ships—a whole fleet was delayed at Cork for a month owing to lack of seamen; and again to the slackness at the American ports in returning the transports immediately they had unloaded. Finally, not only transport, but the whole administration of the war suffered from the familiar malady of jealous and badly co-ordinated government departments, whose mutual suspicion and lack of co-operation damaged the efficiency of almost any administrative measure. The Admiralty, the Treasury, and the Colonial Office bickered perpetually. And the army itself was administered by a series of 'Boards', each dealing with some more or less separate aspect of army affairs, and the whole characterized by a muddle of overlapping, duplication, and decentralization of authority, which was painfully apparent in peace-time, but became in a war of the American order a serious obstacle to the success of British arms.[3]

As a result of the transport shortage, supplies and necessary military equipment from England arrived months overdue or perhaps not at all, and operations were consequently held up. Lord Howe, for instance, gave as one of his reasons—or excuses—for not taking the field earlier in the spring of 1777 that he had to wait for the arrival of camp equipment from England.[4]

The transport problem also very seriously affected the food supply of the British troops. In modern times, it is feasible adequately to feed an army separated from its base by some three thousand miles of ocean. Canning has solved the worst of the problem of long-distance transport of provisions; moreover, the ingredients necessary for health have now been properly worked out and, if they cannot be prepared fresh and direct from the land, they can be supplied in other forms that will keep wholesome for

[1] Curtis, *The British Army in the American Revolution*, p. 126.   [2] Ibid., p. 127.
[3] *Vide* Curtis, *The British Army in the American Revolution*, pp. 127 sq.; also his chapter 'The Administrative Machinery of the Army'.
[4] Curtis, *The British Army in the American Revolution*, p. 102.

months. But in the 1770's neither the type of food essential for fitness nor the technique of keeping foods over long periods was really understood. An attempt was certainly made to supply antiscorbutics in the form of sauerkraut, spruce beer, and vinegar, but how regularly the soldiers got their rations of these is quite another story.[1]

It was therefore imperative, if the British Army were to keep physically and psychologically fit, that it should be fed mainly from American soil. This was originally the intention of its organizers. In practice, however, it proved impossible to feed the troops adequately off the countryside. The organizers in Whitehall forgot, or failed to envisage the fact, that America was a pioneer country with huge spreads of untamed land over which troops must move from one operation to another, and that the populated areas, where the soil was yielding, were relatively mere pockets of cultivation which could scarcely support an army in addition to their normal needs. Moreover, Whitehall had assumed a population friendly at least in considerable areas. As the war developed this assumption proved increasingly illusory. The high-handed methods of the troops, and in particular of the German auxiliaries, regarding other people's possessions rapidly alienated sympathetic elements. It is, however, only fair to say that the English army in America probably compared well with the current practice of the times and that pillaging was severely censured by commanding officers such as Howe. Foraging parties found, therefore, that they frequently had to work in hostile territory where they were liable to be cut off from their bases and were exposed to the crack marksmanship of the American rifleman-farmer; or at best hampered by his indifference or refusals to meet their needs.

In spite of consignments of rice from the south and periodic hauls of grain, cattle, and forage, it became obvious that the army would have to depend for its staple source of supply on provisions from England, In the circumstances of the day, provisioning from England with any sort of adequacy presented administrators with a superhuman task and the results were lamentable. The records are full of complaints about the quality of the food unloaded; maggoty bread and biscuit and beef, rancid butter, worm-eaten pease. When General Howe evacuated Boston in March 1776, he left behind as 'unfit for his Majesty's troops to eat', 61 barrels of pork, 32 firkins of butter, 1,000 lb. of cheese, 12 casks of raisins, 393 bags of bread, and a quantity of mutton; this not including 4,000 barrels of flour which had been condemned the previous October.[2]

These difficulties affected strategy. For example, the impossibility of maintaining a steady food supply on any large scale meant that it was not feasible in practice to keep big concentrations of troops together over a long period. During the winter of 1776–7, for instance, Howe reckoned that provisions at New York would be far too limited for him to keep his whole

[1] Curtis, *The British Army in the American Revolution*, p. 89.   [2] Ibid., p. 96.

army concentrated there throughout the season. He therefore arranged to place most of the troops in scattered cantonments throughout New Jersey, where small groups would be able to get provisions locally. But the dissipation of the army into these small groups made possible Washington's daring and dramatic midwinter passage of the Delaware and his capture of Princeton and Trenton; a campaign which is generally regarded as one of the turning points of the war in favour of the Colonists. And this was no isolated instance of the damaging influence of the difficulties of the commissariat on fighting efficiency. Howe's campaign in the middle colonies in 1776 was delayed at Halifax while he waited for provisions from England. Cornwallis's pursuit of Washington across New Jersey in November 1776 was hampered and held up because his troops had to get flour from the countryside and then stop to bake their bread. Howe's dilatoriness in starting for the spring campaign of 1777, already mentioned, was not only due to the non-arrival of his equipment from England. He had to rely on American forage for his horses and thus had to wait until the grass was on the ground.[1]

These are all instances in which active military operations were interfered with through lack of supplies. They were offset, no doubt, to a considerable extent by the parallel difficulties which frequently troubled Washington. The continental soldier was often as short of food as his opposite number in the English army; in his case largely owing to the inefficiency of Congress in management and distribution rather than to actual shortage of possible supplies. His sufferings at the winter camp at Valley Forge during the first months of 1778 both from cold and hunger were pitiful. Immediately after their arrival at the end of December, Washington had to inform Congress that he had 2,898 men in camp 'unfit for duty, because they are barefoot and otherwise naked'. For want of blankets many had 'to sit up all night by fires, instead of taking comfortable rest in a natural and common way'. And Valley Forge was no isolated instance of the endurance of desperate privations both in regard to food and clothing. At the end of the campaigning season Washington had had to abandon the execution of a promising movement against Howe because the troops were mutinying from starvation. They had had no bread for three days and no meat for two days.[2] Moreover, in the province of Pennsylvania it would seem that the conditions of supply off the country as between the English and the continentals were reversed. Howe, after his occupation of Philadelphia, apparently found no difficulty in getting fresh provisions, whereas Washington was reluctantly forced to class Pennsylvania as enemy country where he could obtain supplies and transport only by force.[3]

[1] Curtis, *The British Army in the American Revolution*, pp. 101, 102.

[2] Fiske, *The American Revolution*, vol. ii, p. 29.

[3] Lecky, *History of England*, vol. iv, p. 425.

FIGHTING PROFESSIONAL ARMED FORCES

The framing of the major strategy of the war produced a final problem of communication. Much of this difficulty might have been obviated if a single war chief had been appointed in America with supreme powers and a free hand to choose his own strategy as conditions on the spot might best dictate. But this was never done, and plans were discussed between New York and Whitehall in dispatches which took many weeks to travel from one destination to the other. Alternatively, some general would go home for the winter season, gain the ear of Lord George Germaine, the Secretary for War, and concoct a strategy with him in accordance with his private ideas. This happened in the case of Burgoyne prior to the disastrous campaign of 1777 which ended in Burgoyne's capitulation at Saratoga. Indeed, the story of the laying down of strategy for the 1777 summer campaign, which was designed to finish the war, is so instructive of practical inefficiency and almost incredible carelessness that it is worth sketching even at a little length.

The general plan was to gain firm possession of the Hudson and Mohawk valleys from bases at New York and in Canada. With the British power thus thrust like a wedge through the centre of the Confederate States, it would become impossible for New England to co-operate with the Southern States. It was hoped that by splitting the geographical areas of resistance into two separate halves the union between the thirteen states would be broken and the war brought to an end. This plan undoubtedly had attractive features and would probably have attained its object had the military strategy adopted to compass it been successful. But here the scheme broke down hopelessly. It was decided that three distinct armies should operate on converging lines. Burgoyne was to take a strong force down from Canada, capture Ticonderoga and proceed down the Hudson valley to Albany. St. Leger was to take a smaller force up the St. Lawrence to Lake Ontario, land at Oswego, and then turn east and reduce Fort Stanwix, after which he was to come down the Mohawk valley and join up at Albany with Burgoyne. At the same time, Howe with the main New York army was to ascend the Hudson and meet the other two. The junction of the three armies would complete the driving in of the wedge. This plan undoubtedly looked very well on paper and from a distance of three thousand miles. But unfortunately for the English, its many practical disadvantages were entirely overlooked, disadvantages which Burgoyne who did know the country ought to have realized and pointed out.

Granted the difficulty of intercommunication in America and the immense distances to be covered, the division of the army into three separate —and separated—forces was rash to a degree. It left the Americans with the great advantage of interior lines of communication, whereas the English could scarcely communicate with each other at all. Moreover, in Whitehall the risks and difficulties of the long marches which must be incurred were grossly under-estimated. It was supposed that these would lie through relatively friendly country; but the event proved that both St. Leger and Burgoyne must operate through what was in effect almost exclusively enemy territory. Burgoyne in particular, as he marched south, was formidably harassed by movements of New England militia on his flank. This was an interesting lesson in rebel psychology. Washington had the greatest difficulty in recruiting his continental army for the general campaign; but in the face of immediate enemy invasion the farmer militiamen would rise with enthusiasm. So much for the lack of practical judgement on the issues involved which made a too clever paper plan so rickety when translated into deeds on the spot.

The key to the whole campaign was, of course, the effective junction at Albany between the three forces and in particular between Howe and Burgoyne. Since neither could communicate with the other except by slow and devious methods, it was essential that both should have clear and binding instructions, binding both as to time and to the routes to be followed. Burgoyne had express orders to make his way down the Hudson whatever should happen until he could link up with Howe's army. But Howe received no unconditional orders. He understood the plan of campaign and knew that he was expected to ascend the Hudson, but he was left with discretionary powers to proceed as he thought best. The upshot was that he took up with the idea that before going to Burgoyne's assistance he might have time to make a movement southward and take Philadelphia, the rebel capital. This enterprise was foiled by Washington after Howe had spent three weeks on it. He then went back to New York and spent further precious time in hesitating whether he should go up the Hudson to meet Burgoyne or attack Philadelphia from the sea. After hearing of Burgoyne's success at Ticonderoga he decided to leave him to look after himself, at any rate until after he had had another drive at Philadelphia. Burgoyne advanced south through thickening difficulties with no prospect of immediate aid while Howe was pleasing himself in Pennsylvania. On October the 17th he was forced to surrender his whole army at Saratoga, a blow to British prestige that can hardly be exaggerated.

The explanation of the differing orders given to Howe and Burgoyne belongs to one of those errors which creep in, owing to the vagaries of a single individual, and alter fantastically the probable course of history. A dispatch giving positive orders to Howe to ascend the Hudson was duly drafted at the War Office and placed with other papers for Lord George Germaine's signature. He called in at his office on his way down to the country for a short holiday, signed his dispatches, but found that the one to Howe had not been 'fair copied'. He put it aside so that this might be done. But when he returned to town the dispatch had inexplicably slipped from his mind. It was never signed and never sent, and was only discovered after the catastrophe at Saratoga had already become history.[1]

[1] Fiske, *The American Revolution*, vol. i, p. 267.

FIGHTING PROFESSIONAL ARMED FORCES

It is too much to say that the English lost the war on account of the physical difficulties of carrying on campaigns at a distance of three thousand miles from the army's base, coupled with their incapacity to fashion their strategy in accordance with conditions on the spot. But it can be safely said that they lost more than one opportunity of winning the war, and presented to Washington balancing advantages which, given the essential weakness of his army, he ought never to have had.

Washington had his own troubles, chief among them the difficulty of keeping his regiments recruited, equipping them satisfactorily, and turning his raw farmer lads into professional soldiers. More than once his army was on the verge of complete disintegration owing to the short-service engagements in the earlier periods of the war and the continuous difficulty of getting a sufficient number of men to respond to calls to the colours. When Washington made his brilliant crossing of the Delaware on Christmas Night, 1776, he could rely on his troops for only six days longer. Their terms of engagement expired with the old year and on Christmas Eve he had written to the President of Congress: 'I have not the most distant prospect of retaining them a moment longer than the last of this month, notwithstanding the most pressing solicitations and the obvious necessity for it.' His success rallied the soldiers' spirits and induced many to stay on.[1] Except for rare and fleeting periods, then, Washington was chronically shorthanded; and on his side had to forgo opportunities of attack which might conceivably have ended the war months or even years earlier in the Colonists' favour.

Saratoga had certainly disposed of the idea that the Hudson and Mohawk valleys could be conquered and the states thus split, and the news of Burgoyne's surrender was a severe blow to bear when it came through to England. But given the internal resources effectively at his disposal, it is unlikely that Washington could ever have forcibly shifted the English from their holding points on the American coast. The position then must have had the elements of a stalemate but for the introduction of a new strategy on the British and a new factor on the American side. Lord George Germaine's new strategy had two aspects. Realizing that it was now unlikely that America could be conquered outright, he decided to try to wear down the Colonists' resistance by continual harassments. For this purpose he launched that barbarous frontier warfare with the help of the Indians which perhaps did more than any other British action to ruin what remnants there might be of affection and loyalty to Britain in American hearts. At the same time he decided that if it became necessary to make peace with the American States and acknowledge their independence, it might at least be possible to hold the Southern states for Britain. He therefore planned invasions of Georgia and the Carolinas.

These invasions were successful, and by the summer of 1780 Cornwallis

[1] Lecky, *History of England*, vol. iv, p. 386.

was boasting that in a very short time he would have the whole country south of the Susquehanna at his feet. American fortunes seemed at their lowest ebb; General Gates's army had been cut to bits at Camden and Washington was too weak to send further reinforcements to the South. Owing to the depreciation of the continental currency he could scarcely find means to feed and clothe his troops except by requisitions from the countryside. The soldiers' pay became in practice valueless. Desertions to the British lines were said at this period to average more than a hundred a month;[1] a very serious figure when the small size of the army is taken into account. Washington himself was almost at the end of his tether. In August, even before he had heard of Gates's egregious disaster at Camden, he had written to the President reminding him that the term of service of half the army would expire at the end of the year and that the shadow of an army which would remain would have every motive except patriotism to abandon the service. 'This is almost extinguished now and certainly will not outlive the campaign unless it finds something more substantial to rest upon.'[2] It looked, therefore, as if Lord George Germaine for once would be proved right; and in both aspects of his strategy. The American people were almost wearied out and the South was in British hands.

The new factor which had been introduced on the American side had, however, yet to make itself decisively felt. After Saratoga, the French had realized that American resistance to England was a serious element in the pull and counterpull of European politics and had agreed to a military alliance with the Colonists in February 1778. A declaration of war by England against France naturally followed. This war was maritime and, though it involved England in very grave dangers, so grave that the British situation must sometimes have seemed to contemporaries wellnigh desperate, it did not immediately give that decisive help and encouragement to the Americans which they so sorely needed. Indeed, during the first two to three years of the alliance, French co-operation must have seemed to them half-hearted and without direct effect. But in the early spring of 1781 the American sky began to brighten. The Southern States had not taken their beating lying down, and Cornwallis and his commanders had for some time been considerably harassed by partisan armies whose daring raids and attacks kept them perpetually ill at ease. This type of action was developed to an amazing degree of brilliance after General Greene took command of the Southern forces, including a nucleus of Washington's regulars. Cornwallis decided to shift his ground altogether and marched off into Virginia. But here he was harassed on his western flank by Lafayette. He could not break through to the north and deemed it advisable to get nearer the seaboard for safety. At this point the French alliance made possible the final stroke of the war.

[1] Fiske, *The American Revolution*, vol. ii, p. 200.   [2] Ibid., p. 200.

FIGHTING PROFESSIONAL ARMED FORCES

Washington had information that Admiral Grasse would be available in the summer off the American coast and would co-operate with any land movements. He also had available a small French army under Rochambeau. He therefore decided to try one of two strategies according to the dictate of immediate circumstance. He gave Grasse the choice of going for New York or for Chesapeake Bay. According to where the French fleet should make the coast, he arranged either to attack New York from the land with his own continental army plus the French troops or throw his forces with all speed south to cut off Cornwallis. The capture of New York, or alternatively the capture of Cornwallis's army, lying in the peninsula of Yorktown and barred landwards by Lafayette while relying on a seaward retreat if necessity should arise, would almost certainly prove a knockout blow for British arms and issue in the evacuation of the continent. Either scheme was, of course, dependent on French co-operation from the sea. In the middle of August Washington had news that Grasse was making for Chesapeake Bay. With 2,000 continentals and 4,000 Frenchmen he marched south and by September the 18th he had reached the scene of action at Yorktown. Meanwhile, on August the 31st, the French had made the Chesapeake, only six days after Hood with the British fleet had himself looked in at the river and then, finding no enemy, sailed north for instructions from Admiral Graves at New York. It was only when Hood reached New York that the British got the bearing of Washington's strategy. Graves raced the fleet back to the Chesapeake and on September the 5th fought the French. But the engagement was indecisive and Graves withdrew, leaving Grasse in undisputed possession of Virginian waters. The trap had now closed on Cornwallis. His seaward retreat was cut off and Lafayette, reinforced by 3,000 Frenchmen from the fleet, lay across the neck of the Yorktown peninsula. Washington's men were arriving by detachments and by September the 26th were concentrated 16,000 strong at Williamsburg. Three weeks later the British Army marched out of Yorktown to lay down their arms to the ironically chosen tune of 'The world turned upside down'. The war was in effect at an end.

Washington's plan was daring but by no means foolproof. Cornwallis, for instance, could have legitimately risked everything on a break-through of Lafayette's lines before the northern troops arrived in overwhelming force. Such a break-through was discussed but turned down as being too costly. Cornwallis at the time did not realize that Washington was close upon him in addition to Grasse and Lafayette, and believed that Graves would return and make another effort to destroy the French fleet. In fact, Graves did return, considerably reinforced, but five days after Cornwallis's surrender. A fortnight sooner and this force might well have been sufficient to foil Washington's entire plan.

Yorktown has been discussed in more detail than other phases of the war because it exhibits decisively the value of French intervention as a contributing cause for the failure of British arms, a cause which at a critical moment temporarily raised the Americans to a level of complete technical equality with their opponents. Whether the Americans might ultimately have won without this intervention in much the same manner that Sinn Fein won in 1921 must be a matter of historical conjecture.

This brings us to the last cause of British weakness that need be discussed here. The trends of public opinion in England and their influence on the course of the war cannot be ignored. There can be no doubt that public opinion at home was to a very considerable extent half-hearted, or even warmly sympathetic to the American cause. This was particularly the case in the earlier phases before the country united in face of the French intervention in hostilities. And it affected the British Army adversely in quite specific ways. Both the army and the navy had to be enormously increased at once to meet the emergency, but voluntary recruitment broke down completely owing to the indifference or active dislike of the war amongst the classes from which recruits could be drawn. Recourse was therefore taken to the press gang. G. O. Trevelyan has drawn a savage picture of the activities of the press gang in providing recruits for His Majesty's forces particularly by sea.[1] It functioned without regard to the individual as a human being, but equally without regard to his niche in the community. As a result, seagoing commerce was frequently dislocated owing to the capture of crews by the pressmen. Such methods were not likely to popularize the war in the coastal towns. And in the City of London, where the Lord Mayor and the City Fathers and the four Members of Parliament consistently opposed the war from start to finish, irritation ran so high that the Lord Mayor actually issued an order to arrest all naval officers who should carry on the work of the press gang within the area under his jurisdiction.

As regards the army, efforts were made to fill the ranks partly by voluntary enlistment with the promise of a bounty, partly through the press gang, and partly by the raising of regiments of Scottish Highlanders who alone in the United Kingdom seem to have joined the colours in this cause with enthusiasm. But no combination of these methods could produce the necessary men, and the Government therefore was forced to fall back on the system of hiring foreign mercenaries.[2] The innocent German peasants who were torn from their homes by needy princes, anxious only to lay hands on English gold, and then drafted off to fight English battles on the other side of the Atlantic did more to ruin sympathy for English arms both at home and in America than any other military cause, except perhaps the later use of the Indian tribes. The decent English were made ashamed and the Americans made angry, bitter, and disillusioned. Moreover, the argument was

[1] *History of the American Revolution*, vol. iii, pp. 192 sq.
[2] Curtis, *The British Army in the American Revolution*, pp. 51 sq.

forced upon them, that if the English were willing to fight them with ⟨
man mercenaries, there was no moral reason why they should not use
their side French assistance if they could enlist it.

A definite example such as this recruiting difficulty shows clearly h
the lack of popular response to the appeal to force against the Colon,
affected adversely the power of British arms. It is much harder to es\
mate in general terms how far the unpopularity of the war affected i\
efficient conduct. Trevelyan has devoted a large section of his *History* t(
describing the various trends of public opinion in England. It is hard to
combine these trends in anything like a consistent picture. They include the
loathing of the Whigs for the personal rule of George III and of his Ministry, the genuine political disgust at the coercion of the Colonies, the annoyance felt by many among the merchant classes at the interference with
trade, the indifference of the common people, the reaction because all the
old Jacobite elements in the country suddenly found themselves with a
cause suited to their mentality and showed their true political feelings by a
volte-face which brought them into active sympathy with the Hanoverian
monarchy. It is, however, probably safe to conclude that at no time until
French intervention menaced the basic security of Britain itself did the
nation put its back into the conflict and then only in regard to the European
issues involved. The American War, as has been shown, was perhaps technically beyond the competence of England to win, granted the resources of
the times. But the fact that half the country had no desire to see it won can
scarcely be discounted as a vital element in the causes of Britain's defeat.

We cannot turn away from this subject without a reference to Garibaldi's
Sicilian and Neapolitan campaigns in 1860. The story of these as told by
Mr. G. M. Trevelyan in the second and third volumes of his Garibaldian
trilogy makes perhaps the most exciting and romantic reading in revolutionary history. I do not propose to recapitulate it here, but merely to
notice some of the factors which contributed to Garibaldi's success.

There was the tacit understanding with Cavour which alone made the expedition possible and enabled it to maintain itself with men and munitions;
the fact that England in a sense held the European ring so that Italy could
fight out her quarrels without foreign intervention; the final march of the
Piedmontese to free Romagna and the Marches and then link up with Garibaldi so that the Neapolitan army could be defeated in form by regular
troops; the almost miraculous luck which again and again seemed to attend
on Garibaldi personally, or which enabled him to snatch some advantage
out of the very teeth of disaster. Coupled with his valour, determination,
and daring conception of how to fight the war, this luck made him seem
possessed of an invincible force both to his friends and his foes.

There is, however, another and more prosaic reason which contributed in
considerable measure to Garibaldi's successes up to the time when the regu-

lar army of Piedmont took over the task of dealing the *coup de grâce* to the Neapolitans, an operation which would have been beyond the strength of the volunteers. This reason bears out the main contention of this chapter. Garibaldi was fighting a professional army which could muster 90,000 effectives. When the Neapolitan soldiers evacuated Palermo, there were 20,000 of them. But the army was not in practice putting out anything like the strength which might be expected from such a force. The incompetence, or the indolence, or the indecisions, or the nervousness, or all four combined of the Neapolitan generals, in the short Sicilian campaign and later on the mainland, lost them chance after chance of annihilating the little band of volunteers, at first hardly more numerous than a single modern battalion. The lower ranks of the officers were equally distinguished for inefficiency. The average age was far too high. It was said that a non-grey-headed captain was an exception. The quality was bad, since decent Neapolitans refused to serve in an army whose main duty was internal suppression and whose methods were as much the methods of spies as soldiers. Consequently the officers' corps was miserably manned. Some were illiterate. Some had been common thieves. The N.C.O.'s were no better. Or, if they were better, they were men of liberal sympathies. Trevelyan says that three-quarters at least of those who came over to Garibaldi after the capture of Palermo were corporals and sergeants. The men seem to have been recruited from the peasantry, which was 'among the most grossly ignorant in Europe'. And, though they were naturally brave enough, they were given few chances to show their mettle, thanks to their fantastically bad leadership. It is clear then that the real strength of such an army would bear no relation to its numbers. 'Against it a thousand picked men, moving with a common impulse under a chief for whom each would gladly die, might achieve astonishing results.'[1]

We have discussed three examples of rebellion carried to a successful issue against the armed forces of the *status quo*. The first was nationalist; the third, as part of a larger long-term strategy, was nationalist in the interests of a united Italy and social in its limited aspect of revolt against the oppression of the Royal Government of Naples. The second is politically more difficult to define. When the Americans embarked on their rebellion, they certainly regarded themselves as British subjects whose loyalty had been called in question only as a protest against what seemed to them an intolerable injustice. The stream of their emotion had its source in the

[1] This account is taken from G. M. Trevelyan, *Garibaldi and the Thousand* and *Garibaldi and the Making of Italy*. It is possible that Trevelyan, in his admiration for his heroes of 'the Thousand' may underrate the part played by the Sicilians themselves in the fighting. Their erratic quality is, however, emphasized by Bolton King in his *History of Italian Unity*. It seems fairly clear, however, that *fear* of what the squadri might achieve played a not insignificant part in weakening the effective striking power of the Neapolitan army.

English Civil War of 1642 and the Revolution of 1688. Their argument was that the rights of government which the home country had won for itself in those conflicts belonged equally to her colonists across the ocean. From this point of view, it is fair to claim the American Revolution as an internal revolt. But when the Americans emerged from the war, they were no longer British in feeling. They had welded themselves into a separate nation. Moreover, technically, the layout of the war had given them most of the advantages which usually go with nationalist as opposed to internal revolt.

There now remains the question whether any set of conditions may obtain in a true internal social revolt which will enable an insurrection launched against the armed opposition of the *status quo* to be carried to success. In countries which are highly industrialized, this raises the problem of the General Strike as a prelude to insurrection.

This is a sterile and difficult problem which it is a temptation to pass over altogether. It has such an obvious bearing, however, on the strategy of insurrection that it cannot be omitted. The discussion is difficult for various reasons. In the first place, the term 'general strike' has never been employed with any accurate definition. It has been used to describe a nation-wide stoppage such as that of 1926 in this country when industries, selected by the Executive of the Trades' Union Congress for their key position in economic life, were brought on progressive days to a standstill. It has been used to describe the great German strike of January 1918 in favour of peace by negotiation which began in Berlin and extended to most of the big industrial towns. Since, however, this strike at its peak covered only a million workers, it is clear that it was neither nation-wide nor industrially inclusive. It has been used in Spain to cover the revolutionary strike of August 1917 when the industrial districts of Catalonia, Aragon, Valencia, and Andalusia were virtually paralysed, but in which the peasants were not involved. Roughly speaking, then, the common use of the term is to define a series of linked strikes, sufficiently widespread geographically and sufficiently inclusive industrially to cause effective economic dislocation at least over a given region. In that sense it will be used here.

A further difficulty of discussion is the diversity of aims to which an identical mechanism, the mechanism of the strike, can be applied. General strikes have been called for purely economic reasons, for example, the British general strike of 1926 or the Swedish general strike of 1909. They have been called to win a limited political objective. The Belgian general strike of 1893 aimed at forcing an unwilling government to grant universal suffrage, and the German strike of January 1918 aimed at forcing the government to undertake peace by negotiation. They have also been called as part of a revolutionary campaign, or in order by their own pressure to force the overthrow of an existing system of government. The main goal of the Spanish strike of August 1917 was the creation of a republic, socialist for preference. The three great Russian strikes of 1905 were direct expressions of the revolutionary urge of the Russian people, and the last of them—in Moscow—was a more or less organized prelude to armed insurrection. Finally, general strikes can be called for a negative end. The Italian general strike of the 31st of July 1922 was expressly called in order to coerce a weak government into taking active measures for the suppression of fascist violence. Since its ultimate design was to strengthen the hands of the government and since the effect of a general strike is so to dislocate the community that normal administration is impossible, it was a contradiction in terms. And in spite of a loyal and courageous response by the workers it turned out an ignominious failure.[1] The only factor common to the examples given above is the aim to coerce a government rather than to win the desired result through channels of constitutional persuasion.

The issues are further involved by the fact that though general strikes have rarely, if ever, been seriously planned as the opening move of an insurrection, yet they have sometimes ended in armed clashes which are indistinguishable from insurrection.

Finally, there is the added complication of the syndicalist theory of the revolutionary general strike,[2] as a sort of ultimate battle between the workers and their masters for which actual strikes are but introductory skirmishes or rehearsals; a battle which is always staged for the future, so that a great working-class myth is created in terms of which real victories and defeats can be suitably explained. It is a conception analogous to the Christian theory of the Church Militant which shall one day, in some unspecified future, issue for the faithful in the Church Triumphant.

The discussion of general strikes as a prelude to insurrection is also difficult because, though there are instances of political strikes for a limited objective succeeding, there appears to be no instance of a revolutionary strike which issues in armed insurrection succeeding in an overthrow of the existing system of government. All such have failed. Arguments as to the possibility of success must therefore be carried on in a somewhat rarefied theoretical atmosphere, an unsatisfactory atmosphere which I would wish to avoid as far as possible.

For the purposes of this discussion, general strikes may be divided into three categories: (1) the economic general strike, (2) the general strike for a limited political objective, and (3) the thoroughgoing revolutionary general strike. The first two concern us partly because they throw light on the general possibilities of the strike as a revolutionary weapon and partly because unintentionally they have sometimes issued in a definite revolutionary situation. This is true of the Italian 'Red Week' of June 1914.[3] Riots

---

[1] Rossi, *The Rise of Italian Fascism*, pp. 214 sq.

[2] *Vide* Sorel, *Reflections on Violence*.

[3] Finer, *Mussolini's Italy*, p. 57.

broke out at Ancona in protest against the prohibition of an anti-militarist meeting. The movement was transformed into a general strike which spread throughout Romagna and the Marches and then to all the great cities. There was a good deal of violence; for days the towns were held by the people, soldiers were besieged in their barracks, and it was expected that the Republic would be declared in Rome. Then, after a week, the Reformist wing of the workers' parties deserted and engineered a truce. The desertion of the moderate Socialists and the sympathetic lower-middle class elements left the Syndicalists isolated. The revolutionary situation had been thrown away. Whether or not the movement could have been transformed into insurrection had the Reformists stood by it and could have received a sufficiently clear and united direction to make a successful seizure of power is another matter. The mass impetus seems to have been there though not to the extent that it was in Russia in 1917, but the attitude of the troops was never put to an ultimate test. Finally, the movement was suppressed by the Nationalist party led by Corradini, Federzoni, and Rocco, Mussolini's future friends.

The classic example of a successful general strike for a limited political objective is the Belgian strike of 1893.[1] This strike is worth examining on account of the reasons which contributed to its success. It was called during a bitter fight in the Chamber on the question of universal suffrage. A motion for universal suffrage was brought forward by the Radicals and heavily defeated by the Right. The working classes then struck in support of the Radicals. The Government held off the troops and there seem to have been no serious outbreaks of violence. But the situation grew daily more dangerous and explosive. The working-class leaders realized that they were losing control of their followers and, fearing that they would lose Radical support if the movement developed a violent character, they went to Janson, the leader of the Radicals, and proposed to him that they should call off the strike if he could make the Chamber agree to a compromise on the suffrage question, a compromise which combined universal suffrage with the plural vote. This was clever tactics. The working classes would win the right to vote while the propertied classes would be pacified by the principle of plural voting. At the same time the onus of refusing a peace offer would be thrown exclusively on the Right, so that the sympathy of the Radicals would be assured. Janson accepted this compromise and put it to the Chamber. It was carried a week after the declaration of the strike. In view of the compromise, it is perhaps not correct to say that the Belgian strike was a hundred per cent successful. There can be no doubt, however, that it was a considerable victory for the working classes, and a victory won exclusively by the coercive method of the strike. The most interesting point that emerges is the reliance which the working classes were forced to place on middle-

[1] Terlinden, *Histoire de la Belgique contemporaine*, tome ii, pp. 195 sq.

class support. They dared not alienate the Radicals in the Chamber or the mass of sympathy outside; and there can be little doubt that the success of the strike was due to the successful holding of the alliance between the working-classes and the Radicals which brought with it at least the benevolent neutrality of masses of the middle class. Against this middle-class and working-class combination, the Government dared take no action. It is a significant comment on the importance of the middle-class support that a second effort, in 1902, to force the grant of universal suffrage by strike action failed entirely.[1] This time the Liberal bourgeoisie took fright because they considered that the movement was revolutionary and refused to support it. The Government was heartened to take firm repressive measures and the strike ended in disaster. The Belgian working-class movement was set back for years just as the British working-class movement was set back after the general strike of 1926.

Middle-class support, or at any rate middle-class neutrality, is important and perhaps essential from two points of view. In the first place a government which cannot rely upon its middle classes will, almost certainly, be unable to rely upon the unbroken loyalty of its army, or will, at any rate, be sufficiently intimidated to shirk putting the loyalty of the army to a severe test. History has proved this again and again. The general attitude of the army in Russia in 1905 is perhaps the one notable exception. Conversely, where a government has the support of its middle classes it will almost certainly be in a position to rely upon its army. The factors which govern the attitude of armies will be discussed in subsequent chapters. Here it is only necessary to say that there appears to be no instance of regular troops refusing their duty on any considerable scale in the suppression of a purely working-class demonstration unless, owing to the influence of other external circumstances, they are already ripe for disintegration. This point is well illustrated by comparing the attitude of the German Army to the great strike of January 1918[2] and its attitude nine months later when the sailors and soldiers themselves made the November revolution. The strike was backed by all the German working-class organizations, though the Spartacists were not represented on the strike committee because they desired to give the movement a definite revolutionary character. The majority, on the other hand, realized that the time was not ripe for an ultimate struggle, since the authority of the Supreme Command and the strength of military discipline was still far too secure to give any hope that the troops would support the strikers. The strike was, therefore, in its nature simply a great demonstration designed to force the Government to agree to the principle of peace by negotiation and to grant a democratic government to replace the virtual military dictatorship of Ludendorff. Ludendorff, feeling certain

---

[1] Terlinden, *Histoire de la Belgique contemporaine*, tome ii, p. 216.
[2] Rosenberg, *The Birth of the German Republic*, pp. 211 sq.

of the army, shouldered aside the civil administration and himself fought the strikers. Berlin was proclaimed to be in a state of siege and courts-martial were established. Hundreds of strikers, including Dittmann, a leading Majority Socialist member of the Reichstag, were arrested. Thousands of workmen were ordered to join the army reserve and then told to resume work immediately as soldiers. Various great factories were placed under military control. Against Ludendorff's arrangements, the strikers could do nothing. The strike was called off after less than a week. The victory rested with Ludendorff and the supporters of the view that the war must be fought on to a victorious finish. The strike failed to achieve any of its objectives because it could not make headway against the military opposition of Ludendorff, even though that opposition never took the form of an open armed clash. But after nine further months of war, which included the failure of the great March offensive and the results of the gathering strength of the United States contingents in France, the situation had altered fundamentally. The troops themselves were now deeply discontented and it only required the impetus of the sailors' revolt in Kiel to start a general mutiny.

The principles of peace by negotiation and democratization of the government had a good deal of bourgeois support throughout Germany. The strategy of using the strike weapon in time of war to fight for these principles had none.

Middle-class opposition can also be disastrous to a general strike from the point of view of the immediate technique of strike-breaking. The purpose of a general strike is to effect a dislocation of the economic life of a community so complete that a government is forced to accept the strikers' demands in order to restore that life to its normal pattern and rhythm. Now, if an alternative personnel can be found to run essential services, this dislocation will not be complete. This happened during the Swedish general strike of 1909.[1] The strike was purely economic in character, the main demands being for higher wages and the dismissal of non-trade-unionists. It was in fact a defence against a lock-out on the part of the masters, who had countered the men's demands by locking them out. It was planned that all trades should strike with the exception of health, sanitary, water, and light services. But when soldiers were sent to guard gas and electricity works, these services also joined the movement. It is important to note that neither the railwaymen nor the agricultural labourers came out, a very serious omission. At its height, the strike called out 285,000 out of 460,000 wage-earners. It is, however, generally agreed that the strike broke down because the upper classes and the professional classes took over those services which had been brought to a standstill and successfully ran them. This is also true

[1] Hiller, *The Strike*, p. 257; *vide* also A. D. Lewis, *Syndicalism and the General Strike*, p. 237.

of the British general strike of 1926[1] when emergency services were successfully organized by the middle classes. Troops were only necessary as a background to prevent violent clashes. With modern motor methods of transport for food distribution, it is obvious that it is not technically difficult to organize amateur services which will function adequately enough for a stopgap. And with the modern spread of engineering knowledge, it is possible to organize rapidly enough a set of skeleton services to run the more technical undertakings such as light, water, etc.

It is now necessary to take a look at the fate of general strikes which have been called for a frankly revolutionary purpose. In August 1917 such a strike was called in Spain in order to force the overthrow of the monarchist government and establish a republic.[2] Throughout 1917, feeling against the monarchy had been setting in a revolutionary tide. The insolence of the officers' Juntas de Defensa was one of the leading causes of disgust. Throughout the spring and summer, the slogans were: subordination of the army to the civil administration, parliamentary government, a constituent assembly. The Government refused to call a constituent assembly since this would have meant signing its own death-warrant. Then seventy members of the Cortes, most of them representatives of the Catalan bourgeoisie, repaired to Barcelona and formed themselves into a rump Constituent. They were enthusiastically greeted by most of the larger towns in Spain. A month later the masses rose in a general strike led by the Socialists and the Anarchists. The purpose of effecting a democratic revolution had, however, by now been deepened so as to include social revolution; and the bourgeoisie took alarm. They sat tight and did not co-operate. Since the Spanish Army was mainly officered by aristocrats, it is possible that it would not have been paralysed even had the bourgeoisie adhered to the strike movement. As things were, however, the Government indubitably had a clear field for the employment of the troops. A state of war was declared, machine-guns and artillery swept the streets of Barcelona and Madrid. The movement was put down in three days. The strikers paid with two thousand prisoners, several hundred wounded, and the smashing of their hopes. The stranglehold of the army was fixed more firmly than ever. But, unlike the results of the Belgian strike of 1904 and the British of 1926, the failure of the Spanish struggle did not set back the working-class movement in Spain. On the contrary, it gave it a new strength and a new definition. Perhaps the reason for this is to be found in the violent character of the outbreak. The impact of long years of trial would be needed before the diverse Left parties could be hammered into real unity, but at least they had shown themselves capable of giving to their aims a common signature of blood.

[1] The best account of the 1926 General Strike is Postgate's *The Great Workers' Strike*.

[2] Madariaga, *Spain*, p. 402; *vide* also Borkenau, *The Spanish Cockpit*, pp. 31 sq.

FIGHTING PROFESSIONAL ARMED FORCES

During the Russian Revolution of 1905 there were three general strikes. In order to understand the place of these in the revolutionary movement, it will perhaps be as well to sketch in its general character. The essential background which a revolution needs was provided in 1905 by the disastrous course of the war with Japan. The Tsarist regime was shaken by military defeat. The middle classes were restive and disgusted. And the people were being swept forward on a rising tide of economic and political discontent to formulate new and definitely revolutionary demands. The revolution may be said to have opened with the events of 'Bloody Sunday', January 1905.[1] A throng of workers assembled in the streets of St. Petersburg with the object of peaceably marching on the Winter Palace and presenting a petition to the Tsar. It is significant that the terms of this petition visualized a redress of grievances within the framework of the Tsarist regime. There were detailed suggestions for the betterment of working conditions, demands for the separation of Church and State, for the equality of all subjects before the law. Perhaps the most revolutionary demand was for ministerial responsibility.[2] Instead of allowing the procession to proceed and present its petition, orders were given to the troops to disperse it. When the workers refused to disperse, the troops were ordered to fire. The workers estimated their losses on 'Bloody Sunday' at 500 dead and 3,000 wounded. 'Bloody Sunday' killed once and for all the last lingering idea in the mind of the Russian worker that the Tsar was the father of his people and that if only you could get at him and explain your grievances to him direct, he would take pains to redress them. On 'Bloody Sunday' the Russian worker grew up politically. Twelve years were to elapse before he learned to organize adequately for revolution, or where and how to push in order to exert the maximum pressure, before he learned to formulate the basic demand for a workers' state. But in one day he had learned the lesson that only a complete overthrow of the Tsarist administration could open the road to reform. After January, the workers' slogan was for a constituent assembly and the peasants' for 'land and freedom'. The revolutionary movement showed itself in the country in the seizure of large estates and the destruction of landlords' property and in the towns in a series of strikes culminating in the great general strike of October.[3] The strike began as a countermove against the suspected arrest of a committee of railwaymen who were due to treat on pensions with one of the Ministers. The committee had formulated wide demands including that for a constituent assembly. The railway strike spread throughout Russia and other bodies of workers rapidly joined in. Trade and industry came practically to a standstill. The telegraph and postal systems of the country were paralysed, the telephone

[1] Mavor, *Economic History of Russia*, pp. 459–63.   [2] Ibid., pp. 472.

[3] Mavor, *Economic History of Russia*, chap. iv, 'The General Strike of October 1905.'

service partially so. Provisions were everywhere held up through lack of transport. Moreover, the movement was not confined to the working classes alone. The unions of professional men were also demanding a genuine representative assembly, and a meeting was held in the St. Petersburg University which was attended by eight hundred civil servants. This meeting also passed a resolution demanding a constituent assembly. Even manufacturers and financiers, whose businesses had been paralysed by the strike, joined in attacking the Government and protested against the use of troops to break the strike. The strike reached its peak on October the 17th, when the Tsar signed a manifesto promising the grant of a constitution. On the following day the Government made nonsense of the spirit of this manifesto by allowing several armed attacks by police and Cossacks on separate crowds which had gathered in the streets of St. Petersburg. The more far-sighted working-class leaders drew the correct conclusion that the manifesto was but a manœuvre and that they had been sold. They would fain have continued the pressure of the strike. But in Moscow it petered out on the 19th, and on various sides it was already disintegrating. It was obviously futile for St. Petersburg to continue alone. The whole strike was, therefore, called off for the 21st.

There are various points of interest which emerge in regard to this strike. In the first place, it was the result of internal combustion. It had not been organized or timed beforehand by any central group of revolutionaries. Actually, the timing was good, since it coincided with the peak period for the movement of grain for export from the great wheat areas to the sea.[1] The lack of previous organization was a severe handicap, since an *ad hoc* directorate had to be evolved while the strike was in full career. On the 12th a council of working men's deputies was formed in St. Petersburg to which almost all the revolutionary parties sent their delegates. Khrustalov was appointed President and Trotsky[2] Vice-President. This first Soviet had nothing like the moral authority of its successors in 1917. It was a beginners' Soviet, but it knew where its job lay. The original members at once issued a manifesto inviting every factory and trade to send delegates, one for each five hundred men. They then defined the purpose of the Soviet as being to organize and unite the working-class movement, to give it direction during the strike so that it should be ready to meet any eventuality and to act as its representative before the rest of society.[3]

Granted the volume of middle-class support and the solidarity of the workers, granted the fact the Tsarist government was evidently too shaken when the strike was at its height to employ troops for the active suppression of the movement, it seems difficult to explain why 1917 was not forestalled

[1] Mavor, *Economic History of Russia*, pp. 482, 485.

[2] Pares, *A History of Russia*, p. 434.

[3] Mavor, *Economic History of Russia*, pp. 487, 488.

by the development of the 1905 struggle into full-dress revolution. Why was the final push which should topple over the old regime never given? It is possible that the masses lacked that ultimate momentum which drove them forward in 1917. The crowds who demonstrated in St. Petersburg for an amnesty of political prisoners after the issue of the Tsar's manifesto are said to have seemed nervous, and Khrustalov is alleged to have remarked that such crowds would never have stormed the Bastille. But a more adequate explanation seems to lie in the slogan which had been chosen, the demand for a 'constituent assembly'. This slogan in effect sidetracked the bourgeoisie and also large sections of the workers from the straightforward goal of an overthrow of the entire regime. The Tsar's manifesto cut the ground from under the feet of the more politically awake working-class leaders and members of the intelligentsia. Since the promise of a constitution appeared to grant the main demand on which the movement had united, it was obviously impossible to develop further pressure or even to maintain the existing pressure once the promise had been made. The bourgeoisie and many of the workers accepted the promise in good faith.

If this promise had been withheld for a few days longer it is possible that the strike would have developed into a violent revolt just as the third general strike developed two months later in Moscow. Of its nature, a general strike cannot maintain a *status quo* position for more than a few days. You cannot freeze up every channel through which urban communities conduct their communal life indefinitely. Either the strike will disintegrate owing to the impossibility of the community living for more than a very temporary period under such conditions, or it will issue in definite insurrection. The frozen channels will thaw themselves in armed revolt. It is at least arguable that had there been no concessions to stay the driving force of the movement, this would have happened in 1905.

Events after the finish of the strike proved that those who had questioned the sincerity of the manifesto were right. The country was given over to the operations of 'Black Hundred' bands whose object was to break the workers, and the Government did little to suppress their terrorist activities.[1] A mutiny among the Kronstadt sailors was ruthlessly suppressed and the Government appointed a special tribunal to try the mutineers. Knowing the character of Tsarist tribunals, the workers decided that its findings would result in a massacre of the sailors who had been implicated. The second general strike of November was a direct attempt to stand by the sailors. The shrewder leaders believed that here was a chance to establish an *entente cordiale* between the workers and the armed forces, an alliance which might even result in drawing the army over to the side of the revolution. There was considerable evidence of unrest among the armed forces to support this belief.[2] And had the second general strike been as powerfully

[1] Mavor, *Economic History of Russia*, pp. 499 sq.   [2] Ibid., pp. 504, 510 sq.

supported as the first, it is possible that events might have reached a climax where the troops would have had to make an ultimate choice of allegiance and would have made it in favour of the revolution just as they did in 1917. The second strike, however, was a failure. The factory hands of St. Petersburg stopped work almost to a man, but the postal and telegraph employees did not come in because they were at that moment negotiating with the Government about betterment of their conditions and they did not want to prejudice their chances. The tramways continued to run; attempts to stop their operation were met by volleys from Cossack rifles. The professional groups who had made such an important backing for the first general strike held off altogether. After three days it was clear that the strike must collapse. Moreover, the Government again outmanœuvred the workers by conceding their immediate demands. The special tribunal was withdrawn and it was agreed to try the sailors in a normal military court.[1]

By the end of the month the Government felt that it had regained sufficient strength to proceed against the St. Petersburg Council of Working Men's Deputies. Khrustalov was arrested.[2] The removal of Khrustalov seems to have taken the heart out of the St. Petersburg leadership. The workmen themselves were still defiant, but the remaining leaders were uncertain what line to take.

The centre of resistance shifted to Moscow, where feeling worked itself up until the declaration of the third general strike became inevitable. From the point of view of this study, the Moscow strike is perhaps the most interesting of the three since it issued in large-scale insurrection.[3] The insurrection itself has already been discussed, both on its technical side and from the point of view of its effect on the general situation. Here it is only necessary to show the process of transition between strike and armed revolt. It appears that there was no definite plan on the part of the leaders to transform a strike into a rebellion, but there was a widespread realization that feeling was by now so explosive that a general strike would so transform itself. The leaders accepted this probability, all the more readily perhaps because there was good ground for believing that a part at any rate of the Moscow troops were sufficiently disaffected not to shoot. When it came to the point, this belief was proved to be unduly optimistic. The strike began on the railways. Three days later the Moscow Soviet issued orders for transforming this strike into a general strike. The response among the workers was adequate and thousands of government and municipal employees ceased work. But skeleton postal and telegraphic communication was still maintained. At this point, the Soviet seems to have been uncertain as to the correct lead to give. The workers were beginning to collect arms where they could, but no attempt was made by the leaders to precipitate an

[1] Mavor, *Economic History of Russia*, pp. 512, 513.
[2] Ibid., p. 530.   [3] Ibid., chap. xi.

insurrection, and no extreme provocation was given by the Government. This state of suspense was ended two days after the call of the general strike. On that evening dragoons fired into a building where some fifty people who had been present at a street meeting had afterwards assembled. A boy was killed and several people wounded. The people could hold back no longer. Without orders from the Soviet, the first barricades were there and then erected. Next day barricades were up all over the city and fighting had begun. The insurrection was in full career.

It is now necessary to sum up the rather heterogeneous evidence of the preceding pages and try to arrive at some conclusion as to the value of the general strike as a revolutionary weapon. In particular, an attempt must be made to answer the question whether a general strike can in any circumstances provide conditions which will indirectly weaken the fighting power of the armed forces of the *status quo* government, so that an insurrection may succeed even against their opposition.

It seems clear that the general strike has certain inherent weaknesses that cannot be overcome. Its object is to hold a government to ransom by the dislocation of all economic life. If the middle classes are against the strike, this dislocation cannot be completely effected since they are competent to run skeleton necessary services. Where the dislocation is complete, after a few days the strain put upon the strike organization will probably be beyond its resources to bear. The mass of strikers must themselves be fed and maintained, and this presupposes organization and financial resources on a vast and probably quite impossible scale. Moreover, the structure of modern community life cannot survive such a dislocation for more than a few days. And if the whole structure crumbles, the resulting chaos will be a crushing liability rather than an asset. History shows that successful revolutions have invariably taken off from a springboard of properly organized community life. Whether the community life is organized in the interests of this or that class is of no moment. The point is that it is organized. It is a fallacy to suppose that revolutions are ever the offspring of chaos and foul night. Relative economic chaos may ensue for a time after a successful revolution. This may be inevitable. But no leader can afford to make the production of general chaos an instrument of revolutionary policy. During a revolution, the more smoothly the machinery runs for the neutral population, the better. In this regard, it is interesting to note a point from the abortive 1832 revolution in England. Francis Place and his friends designed and indeed had arranged for a widespread run on the banks if the King persisted in his demand that Wellington should form an anti-Reform Cabinet after the defeat of the Reform Bill in the House of Lords. According to Place, this run had two purposes. On the one hand, it was designed to bring enormous financial pressure to bear upon the Government. On the other hand, it was designed to transfer great sums of money from the banks, where it was available to the Government, into the hands of the Reformers themselves. This money was wanted so that, if a revolution broke out, the populace might be fed and maintained.[1] Place realized vividly enough what would happen to London if there were a failure of supplies even for three days. The actual plan may have been rather naïve, but the principle was sound.

A general strike, then, must succeed in its objective within the first few days. If this does not happen it will probably collapse under the weight of the dislocation it has itself brought about before that dislocation actually brings down the whole social structure. There is a third alternative: that it should transform itself into armed revolt. Granted the opposition of the armed forces of the government, such a revolt can only be successful if the conditions created by the strike prevent the troops from exerting their full strength. If the dislocation of transport and supply can be made to affect the troops, this condition might be achieved. But in modern circumstances, it is impossible to see how in practice the troops could be immobilized. They have their own motor transport for men and munitions. Over a short period they are probably self-sufficient from their own stores of provisions. It is inconceivable that insurgents would be able to hold the main stores of food —or in England, the docks—against trained troops for long enough to starve out the army. And in any case such tactics would recoil against their own supporters and against the general population.

It appears, therefore, that taking it by and large, the general strike is not a good revolutionary weapon. Its main revolutionary value is as an expression of working-class solidarity. It can sometimes be used to create artificially a revolutionary situation, but unless such a situation can be used as the taking-off point for an already planned insurrection, whose chances have been calculated, it is a useless expenditure of enormous energy. As an actual instrument of policy, it is more wasteful of energy than a straight insurrection, and its failure is more likely to set back a working-class movement than the failure of an insurrection. It has not the same sentimental appeal; it creates no tradition, no sense of a cause for which men have heroically died. In particular, the general strike cannot create conditions which will seriously interfere with the fighting capacity of a modern army.

[1] Letter from Place to Hobhouse, the outgoing Whig Minister for War. Quoted by Graham Wallas, *Life of Place*, p. 315. 'Go for gold, it is said will produce dreadful evils. We know it will, but it will prevent other evils being added to them. It will *stop the Duke*. Let the Duke take office as premier, and we shall have a commotion in the nature of a civil war with money at our command. If we obtain the money he cannot get it. If it be but once dispersed, he cannot collect it. If we have money we shall have the power to feed and lead the people, and in less than five days we shall have the soldiers with us.'

5

THE ATTITUDE OF THE ARMED
FORCES

Armed support of fighting forces not necessary for a successful insurrection—striking power of an existing government
can be paralysed by fear of disaffection—this method likely
to operate through the officers rather than the rank and file—
possibility of its use as a basis for fascist revolt—unbridled
power of an officers' corps under a weak government and
consequent danger of political anarchy.

In the preceding chapter an analysis has been attempted of those rare
situations in which an insurrection can be carried through against the
opposition of regular armed forces, because these are for one reason
or another prevented from making use of their full resources. We must
now discuss that type of situation where the armed forces do not openly
join a revolutionary outbreak, but where their attitude as a whole, or the
attitude of key groups among them, suggests to the *status quo* government
that no effective reliance can be placed upon them to defend the existing
regime. If revolutionary leaders can develop such a situation, they will be in
a position to launch an insurrection with fair hope of success. The effect is
to produce a condition of nervousness on the part of the existing government so that its striking power will be in practice paralysed or at least
decisively weakened. This impotence may be out of all proportion to the
actual weight of disaffection among the armed forces. It is largely psychological; but experience shows that it may be none the less conclusively
effective.

At the opening of the Revolution of 1688, the British Navy, for instance,
was not openly disaffected except for a handful of officers.[1] It is true that
there was considerable anti-Catholic feeling. Catholic chaplains who had
been sent on board several ships had been thrown out by the seamen, and a
Catholic admiral who had caused Mass to be celebrated on his flagship had
nearly brought the fleet to mutiny. It was for this reason that, a few months

[1] Cf. Powley, *The English Navy in the Revolution of 1688*, and Hannay, *Short
History of the British Navy*, pp. 455 sq.

previously, the Earl of Dartmouth, who was popular with the seamen, had been appointed Lord High Admiral. The behaviour of Dartmouth and his captains strongly suggests that, whereas they were not prepared at the start to throw in their lot actively with William of Orange, yet they were anxious not to fight him if an excuse could be found for avoiding an engagement. It was known for weeks beforehand that William was making plans for a landing. But Dartmouth deliberately stationed his fleet off the Nore, a position which several naval critics consider to have been extremely bad from a strategical point of view. King James himself, who was no unintelligent naval strategist, was clearly worried by it at the time.[1] Hannay goes the length of saying that the strategy was so obviously weak that it was probably a frame-up arranged by the pro-Orange minority.[2] Further, when it was known that William had sailed and slipped down the Channel on his 'Protestant wind', valuable time was lost in getting under sail to chase him.[3] Again, Dartmouth called a council of war off Beachy Head during the course of which he frankly demanded from his captains where their allegiance lay. At this council it was decided not to fight if an action could be avoided with honour; and, indeed, William's landing at Torbay was accepted a day or two later as a *fait accompli* and not the slightest effort was made to seize his ships or to dislodge him, though there seems to have been no valid technical reason why this should not have been done. Moreover, when Dartmouth heard of James's flight, he surrendered the entire navy to William of Orange out of hand.

There is no evidence, however, that the sailors would have refused to fight a general action if resolutely led. Nothing indicated that they would have preferred open mutiny, like the Kiel seamen when they refused to sail to search out the British fleet in the North Sea on the proposed 'death-ride' of November 1918. The whole picture suggests that the seamen were passive, if vaguely sympathetic to William's cause,[4] and the officers hesitating and uncertain like Dartmouth, or else, in selected cases, actively disloyal.[5] How far James was aware at the time of the details and political im-

[1] Powley, *The English Navy in the Revolution of 1688*, p. 60.

[2] *Short History of the British Navy*, p. 460.

[3] But cf. Powley, *The English Navy in the Revolution of 1688*, p. 81, who gives a quotation from the Journal of Captain Grenville Collins which suggests that the fleet had lost the tide when the Dutchmen were sighted.

[4] Hannay asserts, however, that numbers of sailors had already made their way across the North Sea to man the ships of the Prince of Orange under Russell and Herbert. (*Short History of the British Navy*, p. 458.)

[5] Cf. young Lieutenant Byng's ride, while on leave, to meet William after his landing and his interview with William from which he brought back a letter for Dartmouth which was placed secretly on the latter's dressing-table. (Powley, *The English Navy in the Revolution of 1688*, p. 130.)

Cf. also a meeting in London some time earlier which Byng attended where methods for making Orange propaganda in the Navy were discussed. Byng was

port of Dartmouth's various actions and inactions it is difficult to be sure, but there is plenty of evidence that he guessed the general trend of affairs in the navy and believed that he could no longer rely upon its loyalty.

The part played by the army was similar.[1] The rank and file were not enthusiastically devoted to James, even though the army was in a sense his own personal affair. There had been several incidents during the preceding months which suggested discontent. The news of the acquittal of the seven bishops, for instance, was greeted by the troops in camp on Hounslow Heath with terrific cheering. James happened to be visiting his soldiers when the news came through: 'What is that clamour?' he asked. 'Sire, it is nothing; the soldiers are glad that the bishops are acquitted.' 'Do you call that nothing?' was the King's dry comment.[2] But perhaps the temper of the troops, half-disgusted but not actively disloyal, was best shown by 'Lilli-bullero!' All through the autumn, the soldiers as one man were singing the rude anti-Papistical jingle—with that engaging capacity of the English private for feeling the major crises of his history in terms of a catchy popular song.

On the whole, this kind of protest seems to have been the limit of unrest. The troops quartered in and around London, who had felt the political temper of the city, were perhaps more seriously disaffected. But the main body of the line was definitely not prepared for mass desertion.[3] Churchill seems to have realized this in planning his own getaway to the Orange side. He waited until the eleventh hour and then deserted direct to William with about four hundred officers and troopers. It has been suggested that he took this course because he had hoped earlier on that he might have been able to coerce James into granting the country's demands by staging a large-scale army desertion. But after watching the situation develop for a few days, it became clear to him that a revolution led by the army was out of the question. In judging the actions of the English leaders it is important to remember that they had no thought-out plan either as to the ultimate function of William or as to the position of James. They hoped, perhaps, to be able to overawe the King by a demonstration of hostile strength and they wanted above all else to avoid a situation which would lead to serious civil war.

---

given the job of winning over his own captain, Ashley, and also Captain Cornwall. (Byng's *Memoirs* quoted by Hannay, *Short History of the British Navy*, p. 459.)

Cf. also Dartmouth's refusal as a patriotic Englishman to arrange for escorting the baby Prince of Wales over to France as James II desired. (Lodge, *Political History of England, 1660–1702*, p. 293.)

[1] The discussion of the position of the army in 1688 is based mainly on the account in Winston Churchill, *Marlborough: His Life and Times*, vol. i.

[2] Winston Churchill, *Marlborough: His Life and Times*, vol. i, p. 270.

[3] Ibid., vol. i, p. 294.

The position in regard to the officers is specially interesting. It is agreed, though there is, apparently, no definite proof, that the general revolutionary conspiracy had its military side and that this was developed among high officers of the army step by step with the plans of the politicians. Bishop Burnet asserted that soundings had been taken in the army:

'It was next proposed to three of the chief officers of the army, Trelawny, Kirk, and the Lord Churchill. These all went into it.'

Burnet says that Churchill also undertook that Prince George and the Princess Anne would leave the Court and come over to the Prince as soon as was possible. 'The thing', he says, 'was in the hands of many thousands, who were yet so true to one another that none of them made any discovery.'[1]

Churchill certainly had been in communication with William. He had written to him in August:

'Mr. Sydney will let you know how I intend to behave myself. I think it is what I owe to God and my country. . . . If you think that there is anything else that I ought to do, you have but to command me.'[2]

At the crisis, however, when the Royal Army was marching west to encounter William, the number of open desertions was relatively small.[3]

King James was not a coward, but Churchill's desertion seems finally to have broken his nerve. He had already been suspicious of his lieutenant's loyalty for some days, and he had even discussed with his advisers the wisdom of arresting him, but had decided that the risk was too great owing to his position with the troops. Churchill was perhaps the most popular and trusted officer in the army. Instead of putting him under lock and key, James decided to promote him, in the hope maybe that this action might please and stimulate the soldiers and revive Churchill's loyalty. When Churchill went, James threw in his hand. No doubt he was also influenced by Dartmouth's hesitations and the uncertain position throughout the fleet. News from the counties must have been coming through too, and the attitude of the militia was not encouraging.

James's flight, his capture by Thames watermen and final escape, his wanton childish action in throwing the Great Seal of England into the river, are episodes that belong to the story-books. A more serious commentary on the condition of nervous impotence to which the Stuart Government had been reduced, by the resolute action of a few officers and the hesitations of others, can be found in Feversham's irresponsible treatment of the stranded

[1] *History of His Own Time* (London, 1818), vol. ii, pp. 398, 399.

[2] Letter to William of Orange dated 4th August 1688, quoted by Winston Churchill, *Marlborough: His Life and Times*, vol. i, p. 272.

[3] Lord Cornbury attempted secretly to lead over three regiments of horse to William at Exeter but his officers became suspicious and demanded his orders. Cornbury then made off himself with only a couple of hundred men and left his regiments to extricate themselves. *Vide* Winston Churchill, *Marlborough: His Life and Times*, vol. i, p. 290.

army. After James's flight the troops were disbanded by Feversham's order, unpaid but not disarmed. They were allowed to disperse all over the Home Counties without discipline, without money, and without leadership.[1] Yet even after Churchill's desertion, Feversham had still believed that it was possible to fight and had tired to rehabilitate the failing courage of the King and his advisers. He suggested a general purge of disaffected officers. He wanted to promote the sergeants and place Catholic and French officers in key positions. It is possible that he underestimated the extent of the disaffection, but it is at least arguable that had James been prepared to make a spirited appeal to the troops and lead his own soldiers into battle, at the same time promising to summon a free parliament, a stubborn stand could have been made. Such an appeal would have bound the waverers to him and placed the open deserters in a position of extreme political difficulty. Moreover, there were 40,000 Royal troops concentrating on Salisbury,[2] more than double the number at William's disposal. The King refused to face the risk. The 'bloodless' revolution was won by creating out of passive ill-feeling and a little active disloyalty an instrument capable of paralysing a government's entire will to action.

An almost exactly parallel condition of affairs occurred in the spring of 1914, when the Asquith Government began to fear that it could not trust the army in its dealings with Ulster.[3] The Home Rule Bill was in process of being passed through its final stages in the House of Commons by a Liberal Administration held in office by the support of the Irish Nationalist Members; and across the Irish Sea more than a hundred thousand Ulster volunteers had sworn their solemn Covenant to resist incorporation in an Irish Home Rule system, even to the length of armed resistance against the government of the day. They were disciplined men, who combined in a strange fusion of race the grim fanaticism of their Covenanting Scots forebears with that unheeding valour of the Irish, whose north-east province they claimed as their own. They had been seriously drilling for months and were now secretly importing arms from abroad. And they were supported to the hilt by Conservative opinion in England.

The Conservative leaders had no hesitation in emphasizing the parallel with 1688 for the edification of the Government. Speaking in Dublin 'of all places', Bonar Law had said in November 1913:

'King James had behind him the letter of the law just as completely as Mr. Asquith has now. . . . In order to carry out his despotic intention, the

[1] Winston Churchill, *Marlborough: His Life and Times*, vol. i, p. 309.

[2] Ibid., vol. i, p. 293.

[3] The discussion of the relation between the Army, Ulster, and the Liberal Government is based to a considerable extent on the information in Sir Henry Wilson's Diaries, *vide* Callwell, *Field-Marshal Sir Henry Wilson*, vol. i, chaps. 8 and 9. I have also used Ronald MacNeill, *Ulster's Stand for Union*, and Ian Colvin, *Life of Carson*, vol. ii.

King had the largest army that had ever been seen in England. What happened? There was no civil war. There was a revolution and the King disappeared. Why? Because his own army refused to fight for him.'[1]

The question at issue for the army was posed in terms of what response should be made if troops were ordered to march against Ulster. This order was expected when the Home Rule Bill should become law. Ulster must then decide whether to implement the Covenant by resisting its application to the north-east. In the event, as will be shown, an order was given in March 1914 to the troops at the Curragh which could only be construed at the time as meaning a definite move against Ulster. The real intention of this order has never been satisfactorily explained, but it brought the crisis in the army to a head. The immediate result was the Curragh Mutiny, when fifty-eight cavalry officers who would have been actively engaged in the projected move elected to resign their commissions rather than obey their orders.[2] There seems little doubt that their feeling was shared by most of the officers in other Irish commands.

In 1914, as in 1688, the crisis hinged on the action of the officers rather than on that of the rank and file. There is no real evidence to show that the rank and file was anything but passive. It is true that during the Curragh Mutiny two battalions did apparently down their arms; and General Paget, the Commander-in-Chief in Ireland, wired to the War Office that he feared the men would refuse to move. But there is no sufficient reason to suppose that the men would in fact have refused to march had their officers been prepared to lead them. Since, however, almost all the officers had chosen to resign rather than march to overawe Ulster, it is obvious that the troops were paralysed as effectively as if they had themselves mutinied. They could only have been brought into action after a drastic reorganization of the whole Command. The evidence in regard to unrest among the officers, not only at the Curragh, but throughout the army, is overwhelming. It is clear that disaffection was keener and more widely spread even than in 1688. Again, as in 1688, discontent was very marked among the general officers. Sir Henry Wilson, the Director of Military Operations, was secretly at the centre of the officers' conspiracy and his diaries for that period are a mine of information in regard to the position of important officers. Early in November 1913 he had an interview with Bonar Law during which the position of the army was discussed and Wilson, a servant of the Government elected to power, then told the Opposition leader that if the army were ordered to coerce Ulster, there would be wholesale disaffection. It had been suggested to Bonar Law that 40 per cent of officers and men would leave the army. Wilson himself put the percentage very much

[1] Quoted by Asquith, *Memories and Reflections*, vol. i, p. 204.
[2] Ian Colvin, *Life of Carson*, vol. ii, p. 335.

lower, but still at a very serious figure.[1] In March, when opinion was at boiling point over the liquidation of the Curragh Mutiny, Wilson reports a meeting at the War Office, when all the Commanders-in-Chief and Divisional Commanders came into the Chief of the Imperial General Staff's room and told him that the army—by which no doubt they meant the officers of the army—was unanimous in its determination not to fight against Ulster. A few days later Wilson travelled down to Camberley to sound for himself the officers of the Staff College. According to his report, this determination certainly prevailed at the Staff College.

Evidence from other sources is equally startling. All through the winter Conservative politicians and journalists had been frankly urging the army to mutiny.[2] Bonar Law had a long talk with the King at Balmoral on the whole Ulster situation. Mr. Churchill was also at Balmoral and Bonar Law had gone the length of warning him that the leaders of the Unionist Party were pledged to give every possible support to Ulster, and that if they were called upon to implement this promise, it was doubtful whether the army would obey the Government.[3] Lord Roberts, perhaps the only popular soldier hero that England has ever admitted, was consulted about a commander for the Ulster Volunteer Force and had actually gone in person to congratulate Carson on the successful outcome of the Larne gun-running.[4] Carson himself, speaking in Antrim in September at an inspection of the Ulster Volunteer Force, had openly asserted: 'We have pledges and promises from some of the greatest generals in the army that when the time comes, and if it is necessary, they will come over to help us to keep the old flag flying and to defy those who would dare invade our liberties.'[5]

English Conservative opinion is always mirrored faithfully if unconsciously in the pages of *Punch*. The Conservative point of view about the army was perhaps summed up in some verses which appeared after the Curragh Mutiny.

---

[1] Callwell, *Field-Marshal Sir Henry Wilson*, vol. i, p. 131.

[2] Cf. *Daily Telegraph* of 23rd October 1913, 'The Ministry are in possession of facts which make it clear that any attempt to break the loyalists of Ulster by the armed forces of the Crown will probably result in the disorganization of the Army for several years'.

Pall Mall Gazette of 28th November 1913, 'The Territorial Army must not be allowed to shelter the transmission of Regular troops for the attack upon Ulster . . . the withdrawal of every Unionist from the Territorials . . . is a duty that becomes more self-evident as every hour of the crisis develops.'

Observer, of 30th November 1913, 'Every Unionist ought to prepare to leave the Territorials . . . and the whole of Unionist influence throughout the country ought to be used to prevent recruits from joining as long as there is the slightest threat of coercing Ulster.

Quoted by Gwynn, *Life of John Redmond*, pp. 283, 284.

[3] Ian Colvin, *Life of Carson*, vol. ii, p. 203.

[4] MacNeill, *Ulster's Stand for Union*, p. 220.   [5] Ibid., p. 162.

THE ATTITUDE OF THE ARMED FORCES

We see young soldiers, too, who serve the King
　　For half the wage a Labour Member cashes,
Prepared at honour's higher call to fling
　　Their gallant dreams away in dust and ashes.
We care a lot for any laws they break,
　　But more we care to see what sacrifices
Men still are found to make for conscience' sake,
　　Knowing how hard the price is.

The Curragh Mutiny and the events leading up to it show with particular clarity the methods by which a defeatist psychology can be built up and imposed upon a *status quo* government once that government begins seriously to doubt the loyalty of key groups among its fighting forces. It is therefore useful to discuss them in some detail. In December 1913 the War Office called a conference of the General Officers Commanding in the United Kingdom. At that conference, according to Asquith, General Paget, who held command in Ireland, was given permission to allow officers domiciled in Ulster to disappear quietly and without prejudice to their military careers before any march against the northern province should actually take place. In March events began to move quickly. Asquith received information which led him to suppose that the Unionists contemplated a serious seizure of arms. On the 11th he appointed a special subcommittee of the Cabinet to deal with Ulster, and on the same day Mr. Winston Churchill, then First Lord of the Admiralty, ordered two cruisers to lie off Lamlash where they would be at hand to deal with any developments in Ulster. A military governor of Belfast was appointed. Two or three days later the Dorsetshire Regiment, then stationed in Belfast, was moved out of the town so hurriedly that equipment and ammunition were left behind. On the 14th, Seely, the Secretary of State for War, sent a letter of instructions to General Paget in which the general was ordered to strengthen garrisons at various points, ostensibly with a view to guarding stores of arms. Paget suggested that it would be wiser to move the arms rather than increase the garrisons, as he considered that any concentration of troops might be regarded by Ulster as an act of provocation, and would, therefore, almost certainly lead to bloodshed. The suggestion was brushed aside by Seely, and Paget was called to confer in London. On March the 19th Generals Wilson, French, and Robertson met at the War Office to discuss which of them should 'run the Ulster war'. No-one cared for the job, and the burden was finally pushed on to the shoulders of Robertson. It is perhaps worth remarking that Robertson was that rare phenomenon, an ex-ranker who had risen by sheer hard work and efficiency to high command.[1]

[1] Robertson, *From Private to Field-Marshal*, p. 1. For his own account of this argument, *vide* p. 194.

THE ATTITUDE OF THE ARMED FORCES

He seems to have shared the political opinions of the other generals, but by tradition he was outside their social grouping, and the army was, therefore, for him emphatically a professional career. Wilson had already told French his view that it would be necessary to mobilize the whole army in order to crush the North, since an Ulster war would certainly mean unrest over the remainder of Ireland, and also perhaps in English industrial centres. More-over, Europe might not look on unmoved. Wilson, like Marlborough two hundred years before, was prepared to hold on to his command to the last possible minute, but there can be no doubt that had the final parting of the ways been reached, he would have made common cause with Ulster. On March the 20th Paget was back at the Curragh. He called his officers together, informed them of the impending move against the North, and, apparently, gave them all, irrespective of either Ulster or Irish birth, the option of resigning. Fifty-eight did so. These military movements coincided in time with the complete deadlock which had been reached politically, owing to the breakdown of any negotiations for the temporary exclusion of Ulster from the Home Rule Bill—'the death-warrant with a stay of execu-tion', as Carson called it. Now the Unionists believed that these movements were designed for a blockade of Ulster which must inevitably lead to violence. They supposed that the plan was to provoke Ulster to draw first blood and thus precipitate a small full-dress war which could be used as an excuse for a drastic and complete suppression of the whole Ulster movement. Paget himself seems to have taken this view of the situation, and to have conceived the extraordinary idea that ostensibly he would obey his orders to move against Ulster, but that when hostilities actually occurred he would only expect his troops, in particular his allegedly disaffected cavalry, to fight half-heartedly, and would take the first opportunity to effect a parley.[1] This notion was, of course, superseded by his more realistic decision to allow his officers a free choice of action beforehand.

From the standpoint of dealing with a difficult rebellion, the Machiavel-lian plan to provoke Ulster first, if it were indeed in the minds of the Liberal leaders, was not without shrewdness and might have emanated from the brain of a Metternich or a Thiers. It was supremely important for the Ulster leaders to keep to the full the sympathy of the army and the whole-hearted backing of Unionist opinion in England. Conversely, an event which should weaken this sympathy would enormously simplify the Government's position. If Ulster could be quietly provoked into an appar-ently wanton attack on the army, public opinion would react unfavourably to Ulster. There seems to be no clear evidence that these considerations had been formulated as a plan by the Liberal leaders. The point is that Paget believed there was a plan to force Ulster to open hostilities, and he effec-

[1] Ian Colvin, *Life of Carson*, vol. ii, p. 338.

tively frustrated it by his handling of his Curragh officers.[1] Faced with a commander who had given his officers a free choice of action which had resulted in wholesale resignations, any government would have been at least temporarily paralysed.

The trouble in the army was not yet finished. On March the 21st, after the news of the mutiny had come through to London, Seely actually asked Wilson to what terms the army would agree. A memorandum was drawn up, the crucial paragraphs of which read that Ulster was not to be coerced under any circumstances. Seely initialled this memorandum without the Prime Minister's knowledge. It is to the credit of Asquith's courage that when he saw the 'peccant paragraphs' he repudiated them at once in the House of Commons. Seely resigned, Sir John French resigned; Wilson, acting the part of Marlborough to the last, decided to hold his hand. But in this case there was no Feversham to press upon Asquith an entire reorganization of the army. His courage did not go beyond his House of Commons speech; and a few days later all the officers who had resigned at the Curragh were reinstated. From that day on, any plan for the coercion of Ulster was effectually finished. The revolutionary tactics had been completely successful without a drop of English or Ulster blood being shed. The Government in power had been induced to believe that it could no longer trust its armed forces and had capitulated.

Now, it is uncertain whether Asquith was aware in detail throughout the winter months of the full extent of the disaffection in the army. He himself admits, for instance, that he did not know until later about Sir Henry Wilson's activities. On the other hand, Redmond has a note[2] of a meeting with Asquith in November during which he (Asquith) said that his information from the War Office was of a serious character, pointing to the probability of very numerous resignations of commissions in the event of troops being used to put down an Ulster insurrection. Some of the authorities estimated these resignations as high as 30 per cent. It was the spectacular climax of the Curragh Mutiny that finally broke the Government's nerve. This suggests that, from the standpoint of revolutionary leaders who have a determined mass of public opinion behind them, a quite small spearhead in the shape of openly expressed military discontent among groups of officers

[1] Asquith asserts that the proposed concentration of troops was simply with a view to guarding stores, *vide Fifty Years of Parliament*, vol. ii, p. 149. Cf. Ian Colvin, *Life of Carson*, vol. ii, p. 331; Denis Gwynn, *Life of John Redmond*, pp. 286 sq.

[2] 'His (Asquith's) information from the War Office in regard to the attitude of the army was of a serious character, pointing to the probability of very numerous resignations of commissions of officers in the event of troops being used to put down an Ulster insurrection. Some of the authorities estimated the number of these resignations as high as 30 per cent.' (Notes by Redmond quoted by Denis Gwynn, *Life of John Redmond*, p. 235.)

may be sufficient for their purpose, provided that they can handle the psychology of the situation—as the Unionists did with supreme ability. The stiffening provided by the hundred thousand drilled and disciplined, if largely unarmed, Ulster Volunteers must also be taken into account. It is perhaps also relevant, in assessing the defeatism to which the Liberal Government was reduced, to remember that there was a strong and probably well-grounded fear that a serious armed clash with Ulster might provoke repercussions abroad and in the Colonies which it might not be possible to control. The European policy of Germany was hardly calculated to inspire trust; and an English embroilment in Ireland might have been more than welcome to the German rulers.

The Spanish officers' rebellion which developed into the recent civil war bears considerable resemblance to this type of pressure. There is, however, one important difference. The aim of the revolting Spanish officers was more far-reaching. They were determined themselves to sweep away the existing government altogether and replace it with men who would be their instruments, and they were determined to remake the Spanish constitution according to the plan favoured by the classes from which they were drawn and on whom they relied for civilian support. And the method was to be a straight seizure of power by open revolt in every town in Spain. From the standpoint of the mechanism whereby the striking power of an existing government can be reduced, this difference is, however, largely irrelevant.

The Spanish Government was faced essentially, as was the Stuart Government in 1688 and the Asquith Government in 1914, with a situation in which it could not rely upon the officers' allegiance and feared that the officers would be able to carry with them a large proportion of the rank and file. The Spanish officers were not being asked, as the Curragh officers were asked, to perform a specific action which they disliked, but they were being asked, as James II's officers were asked, to serve a government whose whole tenor they feared and hated. Basically, their reaction in all three situations was similar, and the problem of defence which they put up to the existing governments was essentially the same. Had it not been for the spontaneous rising of the Spanish workers in the great cities to defend the Republican Government, it is probable that it would have been scared into surrender just as James II and Asquith were scared. But the heroism and determination of the workers forced the Government to take up the challenge and face without flinching the consequences of the revolt of its officers' corps. Nevertheless, despite the magnificent defence put up by the workers, despite the fact that the greater part of the air force, both officers and men, and the rank and file of the navy held loyal to the Government,[1] the history of Spain during the opening phases of the rebellion can only emphasize how serious a widespread officers' revolt can be, provided it can raise any real

[1] Duchess of Atholl, *Searchlight on Spain*, p. 87.

support among influential sections of the civilian population and provided it can succeed in carrying with it at any rate a proportion of the rank and file. It is important to emphasize this point. The earlier phases of the Civil War were undoubtedly critical for the Government; and at that time the situation was not dominated by German and Italian aid. Yet the Government won through these opening phases only with the greatest difficulty. In a later chapter it will be shown how the construction of a modern army favours a passive attitude on the part of the rank and file and places politically the military weapon in the hands of the officers.

The political inference to be drawn from the English experiences of 1688 and 1914 and the Spanish of 1936 is of frightening import. In all three cases, the corps of officers was accepted as the linchpin of the army, and when the linchpin was withdrawn, the wheels ceased to revolve. In the British cases, the result was surrender; in the Spanish, a bitter and protracted rebellion culminating at last in the rebel success. The men remained passive or, as to a considerable extent in Spain, blindly accepted their officers' lead. Now it is obvious that where an officers' corps is recruited exclusively, or even mainly, from the propertied ranks of the population, an officers' revolt will only be used in a counter-revolution against a progressive system or in an insurrection of fascist type. It is not difficult to visualize a situation in which key groups of officers could render decisive support to a fascist bid for power, either by a refusal to carry out their orders on the lines of the Curragh Mutiny, or by an open military revolt linked to a political fascist drive on the lines of the Franco Rebellion.

This raises a question of the most serious and immediate concern not only for Opposition Left parties who may one day, thanks to an electoral majority, find themselves in the position of a government pledged to a reform of the existing social system, but also for all democratic governments. It is not fanciful for instance to foresee a situation in this country in which the British Labour Party, returned to power on the tide of some popular turn of feeling, found itself held to ransom by the officers of its armed forces when it came to translate a serious socialist policy into action. It would then be faced with the choice of abandoning its mandate or proceeding to a reorganization of the fighting forces in the teeth of a threat of civil war. It is hardly less fanciful to envisage a decline of democratic courage and enthusiasm in this country, owing perhaps to severe economic depression or to the exigencies of war, which would enable the fascist elements to combine and induce the officers' corps to act as their spearhead. Such dangers can only be averted by a reorganization before trouble occurs of the system on which most modern armies are based. This will be discussed in more detail in a subsequent chapter.

The situations just discussed prove how ruthlessly an officers' corps will use the military weapon when political passions are deeply stirred. The conception of the army as a passive instrument in the hands of the government of the day works only to the extent that that government can command the goodwill of the officers' corps. It is a conception perhaps better fitted to adorn the pages of books on political theory than to stand up to the buffetings of real life. And in countries where the government of the day is neither firmly rooted in popular consent nor grounded on a strong and virile governing group, the theory will almost certainly break down altogether. The result will be anarchy; the sanction of force being concentrated in the hands of one military set after another who will use it unashamedly to further their own political or even personal aims. The history of Spain throughout the nineteenth century has been made largely in terms of the political weight which the corps of officers could throw into the scale of whatever party they considered would further the political (or personal) interests for which they stood at any given time. The Franco Rebellion is simply the last and most terrible of a long series of attempts on the part of the army officers to mould the government of the country to their own liking either by intrigues with the political parties or by isolated military action.

When Ferdinand VII[1] came back to Spain after the expulsion of the French in 1814, he swore to observe a constitution which was very broadly liberal in its outlook and which had been promulgated during his exile. Within a few months he showed that he valued his oath only in so far as it would help him climb back to power. At every point where the constitution clashed with his interests, he successfully thrust it aside. Making nonsense of its provisions for representative government, he embarked at will on a course of utterly brutal repression and persecution of its champions. Civilian political organizations were either non-existent or at far too embryonic a stage to exert effective pressure on the King. The progressive elements in the country had neither party unity nor any real mass backing. The peasants were politically uneducated and steeped in old tradition; the Industrial Revolution had as yet scarcely put any mark upon Spain and there was no real growth of a proletariat in the towns.

In the national life two organizations only showed coherence and a capacity for disciplined action. These were the Church and the Army. As a champion of rising liberalism the Church was naturally ruled out. There remained the army, many of whose officers had been sincerely infected with liberal ideas through contact with the French. It was, therefore, inevitable that the weak progressive civilian elements should turn to the army for leadership and that army officers should frequently take charge of, even where they did not initiate, any movement for reform. These pushes always

[1] Histories of modern Spain in English are meagre. The following summary is sketched from the *Cambridge Modern History*; David Hume, *Modern Spain*; and J. A. Brandt, *Towards the New Spain*.

took the form of direct action, partly, no doubt, because direct action is the natural resort of soldiers, but also because effective constitutional pressure was outside the range of practical affairs. Hence it came about that army officers acquired the habit of staging a revolt, or of sponsoring somebody else's revolt whenever they wished to influence policy. Sometimes these revolts were purely military, the officers influencing the troops under their command. In other cases they were combined with crowd action in the big towns and with movements by the National Militia.

As the century advanced and the habit of revolt increased, the political character of the rebellions became more complicated and inconsistent. Generals and officers might rebel out of genuine disgust at the inefficiency and utter disregard of popular rights and aspirations displayed by the Bourbons and their reactionary ministers; or they might rebel out of disgust at the continued practical inefficiency of government during the rare interludes when the monarchy had been forced to take on a relatively liberal ministry; or they might rebel out of sheer personal animosity. In spite of its absolutist pretensions and its power to persecute the Liberals, the monarchist system was far too weak and ineffective to exercise any sort of control over its army officers. And these revolts were quite often successful in so far that the ministry, which had incurred the odium of the revolting generals and their followers, was overturned by direct action and not by constitutional pressure in the Cortes. More than once they were successful in wringing a new constitution, either more or less liberal on paper than its completely abortive predecessor and after a few months equally abortive itself, from the obstinate monarchy which acknowledged no influence except superior force. On one occasion the generals overthrew a regency, on another a king, on a third a republic.

Sir Henry Maine, in his *Popular Government*,[1] gives a caustic summing up of this position:

' My calculation is that between the first establishment of popular government in 1812 and the accession of the present king (Alphonso XII) there have been forty military risings of a serious nature, in most of which the mob took part. Nine of them were perfectly successful, either overthrowing the constitution for the time being or reversing the principles on which it was administered. I need hardly say that both the Queen Regent Christina and her daughter Isabella were driven out of Spain by the army or the fleet, with the help of the mob; and that the present king, Alphonso, was placed on the throne through a military pronunciamento at the end of 1874. It is generally thought that he owes his retention of it since 1875 to statesmanship of a novel kind. As soon as he has assured himself that the army is in earnest, he changes his ministers.'

The result of this fantastic licence to take direct action on any and every

[1] Preface 1885, p. 16.

issue that interested them, which the army officers permitted themselves, was an instability of policy, a bewildering change and alteration of ministries and governing personalities, a welter of sporadic insurrections, a major and chronic dynastic civil war, and an irresistible invitation to other European Powers to fish in troubled waters. Surely a unique chapter in the annals of a settled and civilized nation.

The history of the period is too intricate and confused to trace in any detail here; but it is impossible to picture the position at all vividly without summarizing the main points and making use of at least a few picked concrete illustrations which may show up the crazy road on which Spain was travelling.

In 1820, when Ferdinand had forced the Progressives to put up with eight years of arbitrary and persecuting rule, an insurrection led by General Raphael del Riego, which had considerable popular support, coerced the King into reaffirming the Constitution of 1812. Before that date there had been at least four unsuccessful attempts led by army chiefs to force the King's hand. The success of del Riego's revolt was, however, short-lived. The more reactionary European monarchs took fright at this victory for liberalism and, fearing that Ferdinand would not be able to climb back into his absolutist saddle by himself, they decided to hoist him up again themselves. In 1823 a French army marched into Spain. Thanks to the threat of French bayonets, Ferdinand was reinstated in all his old arbitrary power and a further period of ruthless repression began. No less than sixty-three deputies of the Cortes were condemned to death as rebels.

In 1833, Ferdinand died, and by his death contributed indirectly to a considerable increase in the political power of the army. Ferdinand had no son and Spain was subject to the Salic law of succession. His daughter was, moreover, a child of only three. According to the traditional law, the succession should have gone to his brother, Don Carlos, a reactionary Conservative. Ferdinand, no doubt, was not inimical to his brother's political views but, egged on by his queen, he became determined to secure the throne for his own child. He therefore swept aside the Salic law by a special decree which gave the succession to his daughter. At his death the effect was to split the Monarchists between the followers of Don Carlos and the followers of the Queen Mother Christina and her daughter Isabel. The Carlists took up arms and continued their efforts to secure the throne for their candidate throughout forty odd years of ebb and flow of rebellion. As a result of this chronic disease of civil war, the army naturally increased in political importance, so that the fiat of a successful general could strike terror into any government. This situation is well illustrated by the pronunciamento of General Espartero in 1840. The previous year Espartero had successfully liquidated the current phase of Carlist rebellion after much difficult fighting. He had therefore become the most powerful figure in Spain.

THE ATTITUDE OF THE ARMED FORCES

In 1840, a law was pushed through the Cortes which gave the Queen Regent power to appoint mayors and sub-mayors for all muncipalities throughout Spain. This was simply a cunning move to destroy the growing power of the Progressives in the cities. Barcelona rose in revolt. When the insurrection broke out, the Regent was in the town. She sent in hot haste for Espartero to break the rising. But Espartero refused to coerce the people. He demanded the retirement of the ministry and the revocation of the hated law before he would give any help. The Queen could stick to no consistent policy. She forced the resignation of her ministry and then appointed another equally reactionary in its stead. The people of Madrid, aided by the National Militia and the municipality, rose in angry insurrection. Most of the troops fraternized with the insurgents, the Captain-General of Madrid fled, and the Civil Governor was imprisoned. Then the Queen had to bow to the storm of popular feeling and appoint Espartero Prime Minister. Espartero at once presented to her a programme of reasonable reform. Sooner than accept this, Queen Christina threw up her regency and retired across the frontier to France. The general took her place as regent, with the chance before him of enormous personal power to govern, so long as he could hold his place. But two years later, he was himself ousted. His regency had produced neither a strong central government nor an improvement in general conditions throughout Spain; and in 1843 a combination of Progressive and Conservative generals, led by Narvaez, launched a revolt and forced their way to Madrid. Espartero fled to England and the young Queen Isabella was declared of age.

These two pronunciamentos are picked out merely as two typical samples from the string which adorns Spanish history during these decades. The succeeding period is dominated in seesaw fashion by the ascendancies and eclipses of Narvaez, Espartero, and Leopold O'Donnell; until the more serious and considered rebellion led by General Prim and Admiral Topete in 1866 overthrew the Bourbon dynasty and issued after five confused years in the ill-starred Republic of 1871.

Prim had come home from Mexico about 1864. He at once began to assess the political situation in its true proportions. He realized that the expulsion of the Bourbons was the one hope for Spain and he began to win over the army, regiment by regiment. In 1866 he pronounced against the Bourbon dynasty, but the revolt proved ineffective and he fled to Portugal and later lived in exile in England. In 1868, believing from his information that his time was now ripe, he sailed from London disguised as a servant. Five days later he boarded the flagship of Admiral Topete, who at once joined the revolutionary cause and issued a manifesto demanding a constituent Cortes. Then the general and the admiral landed at Cadiz and raised the town. Seville followed Cadiz. Prim and Topete gave General Serrano command of the land forces and he at once marched for Madrid, which he entered on October the 3rd, after fighting and beating the Monarchist troops in a battle on the Guadalquiver. Isabella fled with her entourage to France; and Bourbon rule was at an end.

The revolutionary settlement, after the overthrow of the Bourbon dynasty, was rendered precarious from the very start by the hopeless disunity of political parties throughout Spain when it came to the performance of positive tasks of reconstruction. The more moderate Liberals and the Republicans had combined to make the revolution; but the Liberals succeeded in pushing the Republicans into the background during the shaping of the post-revolutionary settlement, of which they took charge themselves. The Republicans were, therefore, disgruntled and ready to join up in factious opposition with any party of malcontents in the Cortes. So the progressive elements were badly split and further weakened by the constant menace of Carlism. The Carlists' strength was formidable and ready at any moment to flare up in one of the periodic bursts of rebellion. They commanded support among the clergy who still influenced the rural population throughout Spain. Finally, there were the Alphonsists, the partisans of ex-Queen Isabella's baby son. They were still weak and their policy was a waiting one. In these circumstances, the settlement had no possible strong point of support except the army whose effective chief was Prim. Moreover, if Spain were to remain a coherent nation, a strong and acceptable central government was essential. Whether Prim would have liked a republic or not himself is a matter of indifference. The country was not ripe for one; and Prim set out on a search throughout Europe for a monarch who should be agreeable to the Great Powers and who would be prepared to govern Spain on a firm basis of constitutionalism.

If Prim had been able to find a suitable king at once and set him without delay securely on his new throne, the country might have settled to a stable regime, but his search proved ignominious and disheartening to a degree. It took him two years to find a candidate whom the European Powers would endorse and who would himself accept the thankless and invidious task of ruling Spain. Finally, he induced Amadeo of Savoy, a prince of fine character and liberal tendencies, to take over the vacant throne. But the very day on which Amadeo set foot in this new territory, Prim was assassinated. He was the one man who could have held the army together in united support of the new king and the new regime. He was popular with the rank and file and had a personal following among the officers.

Amadeo shouldered a burden which had been weighted by circumstances impossibly against him. He endured it for three years and then abdicated out of sheer disgust and weariness at the futility of his position. His desire to abide by the Liberal settlement and rule constitutionally resulted only in increasing political chaos, and at length the army chiefs told him that he must rule by the sword. Amadeo refused and resigned his throne. The

THE ATTITUDE OF THE ARMED FORCES

Republic was thereupon proclaimed. It had perhaps as much chance of taking root as a tree planted upon rocks. The simmering disorder in the country boiled up at once in crossing currents of violence. General Gaminde, who was in command in Catalonia, concentrated his troops at Barcelona and tried to counter the Republican proclamation by inducing the soldiers to proclaim young Alphonso as King. But the soldiers were counting on the new Republic to abolish conscription—one of the most hated features of Spanish life—and they refused to rise. Gaminde and most of his officers fled, and the army at least partially fell to pieces. This left the country at the mercy of the Carlists who leapt to their opportunity. In a short time they had 75,000 men under arms and had won complete control, military and administrative, over a compact block of country in Navarre and the Basque Provinces. Throughout the rest of Spain they waged a nagging guerrilla warfare.

The general chaos was further increased by the deep-seated federalist desires of various provinces which now broke out into direct action. Barcelona and the towns of Andalusia and Murcia, for instance, assumed practical independence of the central government in Madrid. At Cartagena, the centrifugal elements seized the fleet and completely disorganized the navy. To any observer, it must have appeared that Spain as an integrated nation was breaking up altogether.

The Republican leaders sent a small but reliable force under General Pavia to Andalusia. He suppressed the unrest of the troops at Cordoba and crushed the cantonalists and federalists of Seville. Pavia's success suggested that the army, but the army alone, might still be capable of saving Spain. But if the army were to undertake this task and carry it through, it was clear to the civilian politicians that the generals would reassume their old predominance and arbitrary influence. The leaders hesitated. Finally, their fear of renewed militarism overcame their fear of anarchy and they stopped Pavia in the full career of his victories over rebellion and disorder. There was, however, a strong and realistic group in the Cortes who dreaded anarchy even more than it dreaded the rule of soldiers. These men overthrew the first Republican leaders, replacing Salmeron by Castelar whose commission was virtually to pull the country together and hold it by force. This commission in itself could only be construed as an acknowledgement of the failure of the Republic.

Castelar began by raising a compulsory levy of 120,000 men. The levy, no doubt, gave him the necessary troops to restore law and order. Cantonalism was broken up and central authority reinstated and a serious start made to clean up the Carlist war. But in effect the new application of compulsory military service gave the Republic its *coup de grâce*—or perhaps it might be more accurate to say, one of several *coups de grâce*. Freedom from the blood-tax was the only interest that the common man or the private soldier had found to bind him to the Republic. It was too much an affair of the intellectual middle classes and too little an expression of the feelings of the common people. The reintroduction of conscription knocked away the only popular supports.

With the help of the army Castelar had indeed restored order; but the deputies of the Cortes were now thoroughly alarmed at their own action in fastening military rule once more upon their country. It became clear, on the one hand, that when the Cortes met in the spring of 1874, it would oppose Castelar's militaristic policy, and on the other hand that the generals would refuse to accept a return to any weak-kneed rule. Caught in the impact of this opposition, the Republican Cortes collapsed like a house of cards. General Pavia, acting the part of a minor Cromwell or Napoleon, surrounded the Chamber of Deputies with troops and expelled the members. The Republic, in fact if not yet in theory, was at an end; and it became obvious to anyone who chose to accept the practical implications of the situation that the restoration of young Alphonso—then a lad of sixteen and a cadet at Sandhurst—was the only solution to the impasse. Alphonso's advisers desired the situation to ripen still a little more, however, and it was not until December 1874 that they suggested that his time had come. A proclamation was issued in his name promising constitutional government and a general amnesty. The army reacted at once. Two battalions at Murviedo proclaimed Alphonso, and the troops throughout Spain followed their example. This was the last serious open military pronunciamento to change Spanish policy for many years. By one means or another Alphonso succeeded in governing with some sort of continuity and the army was relegated, if not to its correct place in a civilized and efficient state, at least to a position in which it could no longer openly control politics.

The foregoing summary has been necessarily thin and selective, but it should have made clear how in the last resort the entire political life of nineteenth-century Spain hinged on the attitude of the army officers. It is important, therefore, to make some attempt to analyse the reasons which made possible their outrageous political influence. The traditional governmental structure of Spain was the Absolutist Monarchy supported by the twin pillars of the Church and the Army. But all through the period under discussion, this edifice was rocking at its foundations and crumbling on its façade. The attacks to the foundations came from the Liberals and were opened by them with the Constitution of 1812. But these attacks were never sufficiently firm, united, and sustained to bring down the absolutist system for good. Beautiful constitutions were sketched on paper or even sometimes forced through the Cortes, but their promoters were never able to hold and develop the partial revolutions which they had made. Their political ideals were admirable but they lacked entirely the capacity for handling practical political situations to good advantage. They were further hampered by lack of mass support owing to the political and industrial backwardness of the Spanish people. Moreover, the peasants were still almost entirely under the influence of the Church; there was no chance of a jacquerie. Liberal strength was the strength of intellectuals, democratically-minded aristocrats and army officers with popular leanings, backed from time to time by popular sentiment in a few big towns. There was no solid and united industrial middle class craving for power as in England in 1832, no active revolutionary peasantry as in France in 1789, no proletariat as in Russia in 1917. Thus the Liberals could do little more than nag away at the foundations of absolutism. And their periods of partial success alternated with periods of eclipse marked by savage reaction—a seesaw of political movement which merely increased the general weakness of the country's political structure.

The façade of the absolutist edifice was crumbling owing to the division of the monarchist strength between the Carlists and the supporters of Isabella. This put a chronic strain upon monarchist sentiment, a strain which had begun before the Carlist divisions, thanks to the personal unpopularity of Ferdinand during his long reign and the horror excited throughout liberal Europe by his cruel repression of reform. Ferdinand's successors, the Queen Mother Christina and her daughter Isabella, also had their meed of unpopularity owing to the crude irregularities of their private lives; and the necessity for finding a husband for Isabella who should suit the requirements of the Great European Powers added yet another solvent to Spanish political coherence. These Powers not only interested themselves in the 'Spanish marriage'—a field in which England and France intrigued shamelessly for influence in the Peninsula, but they added to the general chaos by the barefaced abandon with which they angled the confused waters and then quarrelled among themselves over their self-seized fishing rights. We have seen how France re-fettered reaction upon the country after del Riego's rebellion.[1] England interfered in the Carlist war on the side of Isabella in much the same manner that Italy and Germany interfered in the Franco Civil War. The English Legion numbered 10,000 men and fought with conspicuous success in the north-west. During the siege of San Sebastian by the Carlists, English warships bombarded the key to the Carlist position and Espartero's ultimate success was in no small measure due to English help.[2] Finally, Prim's combing of European Royal houses for a king contributed to the various causes of dissension between Napoleon III and Bismarck which led up to the Franco-Prussian War.[3]

Yet a further solvent was at work in the break-up of the Spanish colonial empire.

[1] David Hume, *Modern Spain*, pp. 232 sq.   [2] Ibid., pp. 326 sq.
[3] J. A. Brandt, *Towards the New Spain*, p. 143. For a detailed and lively account *vide* Philip Guedalla, *The Second Empire*, pp. 408 sq.

THE ATTITUDE OF THE ARMED FORCES

Spain then presented the spectacle of a social and political structure which was obviously collapsing under the pressure of strains which it could not control and distribute. In such a condition of affairs the officers' corps of a professional army inevitably snatches a casting position. Its entry into partisan politics can only be certainly held in check where the army is in fact an almost perfect expression of one aspect of a secure popular government, as in Switzerland, and has, therefore, no temptation to independent action; or where the central government is strong enough to make the army its servant. The French have always feared the dictatorship of generals and, with the exception of the Napoleonic period, have always successfully avoided it. The whole point of view is aptly summed up in a story of a little passage of arms between Clemenceau and Foch during an inter-Allied conference in 1918. Foch launched out on an argument which was not strictly confined to military matters. Clemenceau interrupted at once in his voice of thunder, 'Be quiet,' he shouted. 'It is I who am the representative of France.'[1]

Where such a point of view can be made a reality the army becomes a guarantee of political stability. But even where a government is strong, and at the same time based on popular consent, the difficulty of maintaining this reality is apparent. It has been shown in the case of the Liberal Government of 1913–14 in this country. Where a government is weak and at the same time violent, as in the Spanish case, there is no possibility of effectively controlling the army. An absolutist government, with no basis on popular consent, can only rely upon its army when in fact it derives its own strength from military force because it is in effect the expression of the officers' corps.

---

[1] Bénoist Méchin, *Histoire de l'armée allemande*, vol. i, p. 19.

6

THE EFFECT OF FAILURE IN WAR

Disintegration of the rank and file through exhaustion and unsuccessful war.

In order to break up the resistance of the fighting forces, a revolution from the Left must rely upon the disintegration of the rank and file. This objective is far more difficult to attain than support by an officers' corps for pressure from the Right. Officers' corps have always been politically conscious where their own interests were involved. Since these interests have almost invariably coincided with the existence of a political system based on the rights of property, no effort has been necessary on the part of Right governments to check their active political sympathies. The officers have, therefore, seldom hesitated to take up a partisan political position in accordance with their own convictions. But the natural sympathies of the rank and file would not so easily go to governments based on the interests of private property. In building up army systems effort has therefore been directed to keep the rank and file politically inert and leaderless. The methods framed to achieve this end have resulted in an insulation of the rank and file from the live currents of political feeling which can galvanize ordinary citizens to action. Experience proves that on the whole the rank and file will never disintegrate on their own initiative through the impact of direct political emotion. Some other and stronger solvent is required.

The supreme solvent for the disintegration of the rank and file is an unsuccessful war. This solvent has, however, only been shown in full operation in recent times, in Austria and Germany in 1918 and, as an outstanding example, in Russia in 1917. It is a solvent of increasing potency thanks to the colossal and complex development of modern warfare.

In a long-drawn-out war the resources of the whole nation are now mobilized and the gap between the soldier and civilian, while in one way more sharply differentiated, is in another diminished. The soldier feels the extra privation and suffering which he has to bear by comparison with the civilian and this adds to his unrest, but at the same time he is no longer by any reckoning a professional. For the mass of the young manhood of the

108

nation will have been swept into the army, and he is now the civilian in arms. He has exchanged his ploughshare or his lathe directly for a rifle or machine-gun without any preliminary months or years of conditioning in time of peace to the special mental atmosphere of armies. His mentality is still that of the farm or factory from which he has been taken and his interests those of his civilian life. He has no time to develop *esprit de corps* and to enter the closed circle of outlook of the professional soldier. And as death and wounds wear down the old corps of officers, his regimental officers tend to be drawn from civilian or non-commissioned ranks and to reflect less closely the point of view of the vanished professionals. In Russia, for instance, it has been estimated that 15,500,000 men were called to the colours during the first world war and that the quota from the peasant population represented about half of the younger able-bodied males. At the outbreak of the revolution, Russia had about nine million men under arms.[1]

It is probable, therefore, that unless he is fighting for some cause which he has invested with missionary zeal, the citizen soldier will tend to crumple sooner than the professional. He has more to lose, and he has not learned the military lesson of the 'passive instrument'. In Russia the scales were weighted against the successful maintenance of the army's morale from the start of the war. The Tsar's military machine was out-of-date and in no sense fitted to contend against the modernized armies of Germany. The soldiers vaguely realized that they were pitted against a foe whose generalship, technique, and equipment were in every way superior to their own. They observed that they were a match for the enemy only when their leaders resorted to the hated and callous method of sheer weight and sacrifice of numbers. An anonymous engineer commented: 'It is hopeless to fight with the Germans for we are in no position to do anything; even the new methods of fighting become the causes of our failure.'[2] The generals, too, admitted their inferiority. Ruszky confessed to the Ministers in Petrograd: 'The present-day demands of military technique are beyond us; at any rate we can't keep up with the Germans.'[3] In addition, the Russian soldier suffered from gross neglect and inefficiency in the matter of supply. Railway transport was virtually breaking down even before the disorganization consequent on the revolution. Finally, there were political difficulties. A centrifugal tendency of nationalism made for bad co-operation and caused units to become muddled through a shifting of their personnel.[4]

---

[1] Chamberlin, *The Russian Revolution*, vol. i, p. 223. This book appears to be more objective in standpoint than any other study of the Russian Revolution that I have come across, and it is, therefore, used as a general basis for the subsequent discussion of Russia. But compare these figures with those given by Wollenberg, *infra*, p. 118.

[2] Trotsky, *History of the Russian Revolution* (Gollancz, one-vol. ed.), p. 40.

[3] Ibid., p. 40.

[4] Chamberlin, *The Russian Revolution*, vol. i, p. 230.

Moreover, the whole regime was becoming increasingly unpopular and rotten. It was said that the Tsar and the Tsarina and their entourage were given over to pro-German influences and, in high military circles, a *coup d'état* aiming at a palace revolution was freely discussed. Such talk must have filtered through to the rank and file; and in any case, the peasant soldier was beginning to realize that he had nothing whatsoever to gain for his class by fighting for the Tsarist regime. Sir George Buchanan, British Ambassador to Petrograd, and a shrewd observer of Russian affairs, quotes an interview which he had with the Tsar during the winter of 1916. 'Your Majesty must remember,' Buchanan told the Tsar, 'that the people and the army are one, and that in the event of revolution only a small portion of the army can be counted on to defend the dynasty.'[1]

The Russian Army was thus well-prepared ground for the growth of revolutionary feeling. From the standpoint of revolutionary strategy, it is simplest to regard its break-up as taking place in three main phases.

The first phase represents a gradual process of discontent and disillusionment piling itself up for months before the outbreak of the March Revolution. This discontent does not seem to have been very actively worked upon by revolutionary leaders, most of whom, after all, were still in exile, or serving sentences of imprisonment. It was internal, due to the conditions sketched above, and aggravated, no doubt, by the particular terms of service of the Russian Army. Tsarist regulations were framed so as to be humiliating and galling for the soldiers. They could not travel in street cars or enter a restaurant; they could receive no books or newspapers without their commanding officer's permission; they were disciplined by a brutal system of corporal punishment.[2] How far these regulations were relaxed during the war it is difficult to find out, but it is obvious that, in so far as they held good, they would prove peculiarly irritating to the new type of civilian soldier. Prior to the March Revolution, the unrest was showing itself in spasmodic outbreaks. At a conference of commanding officers held in December 1916, the generals admitted frankly that Riga and Dvinsk were 'misfortunes' of the northern front—two nests of propaganda. Brussilov reported disturbances in the 2nd Siberian Corps. Evert mentions riots in a regiment of the 3rd Army over the distribution of sugar, as a result of which several men were shot.[3] In October 1916, the gendarme administration for Petrograd Province reported that the mood in the army was alarming. The relation between the soldiers and their officers was extremely tense: 'everyone who comes near the army must carry away a complete and convincing impression of the utter moral disintegration of the troops.'[4] These are perhaps straws; a more serious indication of the way the wind

[1] *My Mission in Russia*, vol. ii, p. 48.
[2] Chamberlin, *The Russian Revolution*, vol. i, p. 106.   [3] Ibid., vol. i, p. 226.
[4] Trotsky, *History of the Russian Revolution* (Gollancz, one-vol. ed.), p. 44.

was blowing was the chronic and rising drain of desertion. All this unrest was reflected in the famous Order No. 1, published on the very morrow of the March Revolution. This clearly represents the climax of a growing mood of previous discontent, rather than a new revolutionary idea. Order No. 1 laid it down that soldiers should no longer salute their officers when off duty and that officers should no longer use the patronizing pronoun 'thou'[1] in addressing their men. Strict discipline was to be maintained, but the soldiers were to enjoy full political and civil rights as citizens. Committees should be elected by the rank and file in all units to look after the soldiers' rights and deal with their grievances. The orders of the Military Commission of the Duma, a body which took on the management of military affairs after the fall of the Tsar's Government, were to be executed only when these did not clash with the policy of the Soviet.[2]

The second phase of disintegration represents the attitude of the army to the March Revolution in Petrograd. During the five days of the uprising the soldiers proved conclusively, both to themselves and to the workers, that they were not prepared to fire upon their comrades in the streets at the orders of the Tsarist Government, but were indeed ripe to go over and take their place in the very vanguard of the revolution.

The March Revolution, as we have seen, broke upon Petrograd almost spontaneously. It came as the climax of a demonstration against the food shortage added to a great strike at the Putilov works which threw thousands of workers in angry mood on to the streets. So far as there was organized leadership in the movement at all, it seems to have been aimed at winning over the troops. The decisive moment came on the morning of March the 12th, when the centre of interest suddenly shifted from the rebellious workers with their amateur weapons to insurgent soldiers armed with rifles and machine-guns. On the previous day, Sunday, March the 11th, orders had come through from the Tsar for the suppression of all disturbances and certain regiments had fired upon the crowd. This attack on the crowd has been aptly described as the snapping-point of the frail cord of discipline. The mutiny started in the very unit which had inflicted the heaviest losses on the workers. During the Sunday night, the soldiers discussed the situation amongst themselves and decided not to shoot again. In the morning, after vain appeals from their officers, they poured into the street and made for the Viborg quarter, the great working-class district, where they fraternized with the people. One after another, the other units of the garrison joined in. By the night of the 14th it had become obvious to the authorities

---

[1] Readers of Gogol will remember the passage in *Dead Souls* where the young landowner Tientietnikov takes bitter offence and leaves the house of the girl he is courting for good because her father addresses him in the second person singular.

[2] Chamberlin, *The Russian Revolution*, vol. i, p. 86.

that the Petrograd garrison must be written off entirely as a force able to defend the old regime and that it was futile to think even of sending troops from the front to suppress the rising. General Ivanov tried to bring a body of Cavaliers of Saint George into Petrograd, but even these hard-boiled Tsarist warriors broke their discipline and melted away when they came into contact with the infected regiments stationed at Tsarskoe Seloe. Hitherto, the issue as between soldiers and people had always been in doubt. The hesitation of the demonstrating workers, questioning whether at long last they could rely upon support from their comrades in the army, has been described by Trotsky in one of the most dramatic passages of his history:

'A new relation of forces was mysteriously implanting itself in the consciousness of the workers and soldiers. It was precisely the Government's offensive, called forth by the previous offensive of the revolutionary masses, which transformed the new relation of forces from a potential into an active state. The worker looked thirstily and commandingly into the eyes of the soldier and the soldier anxiously and diffidently looked away. . . . The worker approached the soldier more boldly. The soldier, sullenly, but without hostility, guiltily rather, refused to answer. . . . Thus the change was accomplished. The soldier was clearly shaking off his soldiery.'[1]

The events of March the 12th and the subsequent days showed conclusively that the soldier had decided on his answer and was indeed shaking off his soldiery like an infected garment.

It is clear that this second phase of the army's break-up, although of decisive importance, was simply an acceleration and a definition by an outside event of a general process at work. At this stage it was not closely related to a definite and constructive political aim, nor was it controlled by any of the revolutionary parties. It was part of the general protest against the war with its attendant sufferings and against the oppressions and the incompetences of the old regime. Political definition and control came later. Various points, however, are worth emphasis. In the first place, the spontaneity of the decisive break-up is remarkable. The army dropped from its place in the State like rotten fruit from a tree. It was not necessary to try to organize the disintegration, all that was needed was to catch the fruit as it fell. This happened as it were naturally, as the soldiers fraternized with the workers and became absorbed in their emotions. Again, the Government's method of handling the situation gave every advantage to the revolution and this cannot altogether be discounted in reckoning up its easy success. Military preparations against disturbances in Petrograd had not been omitted, but the Government intended to use troops only as a last resort. If disturbances should occur, the first plan was to suppress them with Cossacks and police. The morale of the Petrograd garrison had there-

---

[1] *History of the Russian Revolution* (Gollancz, one-vol. ed.), p. 135.

THE EFFECT OF FAILURE IN WAR

fore been neglected. Further, the garrison was swollen beyond reason (it consisted of no less than 150,000 men) and was made up of the most unreliable elements, from a disciplinary point of view, on which the Government could have laid hands. Sir George Buchanan has conclusively shown up this weakness:

'The initial mistake', he says, 'lay with the military authorities who ought to have left a small body of disciplined and reliable troops to keep order in the capital. As it was, the garrison, some 150,000 in all, was composed solely of depot troops. *They were all young soldiers fresh from their villages* (italics mine). The corps of officers entrusted with their training was far too small to handle so large a body of men. It consisted of men who had been invalided home or of inexperienced boys.'[1]

Yet, when the revolution broke, the Government made no attempt to rectify this situation. Whether the situation could indeed have been saved must be a matter for historical conjecture. But at least the Tsarist Government could have tried to save it by methods which had proved successful in combating other revolutions.

Within twenty-four hours of the outbreak of the Paris Commune, Thiers had withdrawn every regular soldier from Paris lest he should be infected by the insurgent populace.[2] Somewhat similar tactics of complete withdrawal from the insurgent area were used by Radetsky after the 'Five Days' of Milan in 1848, when he left the town in the hands of the Italian rebels and, retreating behind the forts of the Quadrilateral, awaited reinforcements from Austria, reorganized his army, and finally advanced to clean up the north of Italy by open warfare. Vienna was also reconquered for the Empire after its insurrection in 1848 in the same way. The troops were withdrawn from the insurgent city, re-formed outside, stiffened by a reinforcing army, and finally brought back again to invest the capital and retake it after a bitter siege whose ultimate success was assured by the preponderance of men and material which had been accumulated on the Imperial side.[3] The historical precedents for withdrawal were, then, pretty conclusive, and yet it does not seem to have occurred to the Petrograd Command that such tactics would give the only possible chance of restoring discipline and morale. They were required even more in the interests of the nascent bourgeois Provisional Government than in those of the doomed Tsarist regime. After the February Revolution of 1848 in France, the entire Paris garrison, although it had favoured the setting up of the Provisional Government, was nevertheless withdrawn to points well away from the city. This was done

[1] *My Mission in Russia*, vol. ii, p. 62.
[2] Cf. *infra*, p. 155 sq.
[3] Short accounts of the Italian and Viennese tactics are given in the *Cambridge Modern History*, vol. xi, pp. 81 sq., 186 sq.; see also Bolton Paul, *History of Italian Unity*, vol. i, pp. 216 sq., 227 sq.

by Lamartine and his friends in order to keep the army politically sterilized and to prevent its falling under the influence of the extremists.[1]

But all through the spring and summer of 1917, the enormous Petrograd garrison was allowed to remain a seed-bed and focus for military and political discontent. The Provisional Government was terrified of it, but yet made no serious effort to control it; and the Soviets gained a sure footing in the barracks, with admirable results for the revolutionary Left. When the Bolshevik Revolution broke in November, there was not a soldier in the capital willing to fire a rifle in defence of Kerensky's regime. The use to the Left of the garrison is shown by the fact that, when suggestions were made in the summer for the withdrawal of considerable bodies of troops from Petrograd, the scheme was severely attacked by the extremists on the ground that the Government wanted to remove from Petrograd one of the strongest guarantees of the revolution.

The third phase of the break-up of the old army represents the period between the March Revolution and the Bolshevik seizure of power in November, after which the army fell to pieces altogether and simply passed out of existence as part of the structure of the state. This phase is marked by active revolutionary organization. The problem was to control the disintegration of the army and to complete it in the interests of the advanced wing of the revolution. As the summer months went on, the cleavage of interests as regards the army between the moderates and the advanced wing became increasingly apparent. The moderates were in favour of fighting the war against Germany to a victorious close in conjunction with the Allies. They considered that revolution in the army had gone far enough and were only too anxious to restore discipline and fighting capacity. In the units at the front they were represented by the commissars, who had been appointed to act as a link between the troops and the Government after the March Revolution, and to a lesser extent by the various regimental committees which had sprung up everywhere and were composed partly from the rank and file and partly from the more liberal-minded officers. The advanced sections of the Left, among whom the Bolsheviks were gradually gaining the leadership, realized, on the other hand, that the disintegration of the army must be made far more complete in the interests of any revolution further to the Left than a bourgeois-democratic settlement. As the Russian stage was then set, the Left was in a much stronger position than the moderate parties from the outset of this third phase. Discipline was declining every day by a sort of natural process without the necessity for inserting Bolshevik solvents. The army at the front passed the spring and summer in wholesale desertions, continuous disregard of orders, attacks on and even murders of unpopular officers, endless committees, fraternizations with the Germans, and blank refusals to go into an attack. Pacifist

[1] Cf. *infra*, p. 224.

sentiment was running rife. General Alekseev wrote to the Provisional Government at the end of April: 'With great surprise I read the reports of irresponsible persons about the splendid sentiment of the army. To what purpose? We don't deceive the Germans and for ourselves, this is fatal self-deception.'[1] Kerensky's whirlwind campaign at the front for an offensive collapsed in ignominious failure before the sullen indifference and hostility of the troops. In Petrograd, the universal desire of the garrison to stay put in the city and avoid dispatch to the front provided a superb field for revolutionary manœuvre.

The moderates, saddled with this policy of continuing the war, had every sentiment of the Russian soldier against them. He longed only for peace. He realized that his comrades back in the villages were already seizing the land far and wide, and he naturally wanted to get back home to take his share in the scramble. This state of mind, the extreme Left, led by the Bolsheviks, was able to exploit to the full. When Lenin returned to Petrograd from exile in April, he realized the implication of the situation at once. The Bolshevik slogan 'Peace, bread, and land!' was developed throughout the summer and proved irresistible. It was a burning-glass to focus the soldiers' discontent and it was used ruthlessly to fire the entire army against the Provisional Government. Moreover, here was a foursquare and uncompromising position which everyone could understand; whereas the moderates, torn between their desire to reorganize the fighting strength of the army and at the same time to avoid any action which might give a footing for counter-revolution, were obviously planted on shifting sands. Sir George Buchanan, writing to the Foreign Office in September, reported a conversation he had had with Kerensky: 'He (Kerensky) could not deny that there might be an eventual collapse owing to the breakdown of railways and the scarcity of supplies, while the fear of the army being one day used to carry out a counter-revolution makes him hesitate to go all lengths to restore efficiency and discipline.' Buchanan saw the position clearly: 'A well-disciplined army was regarded by the majority in the Soviet as a dangerous weapon that might be one day turned against the revolution, while the Bolsheviks foresaw that the break-up of the army would place at their disposal a mass of armed peasants and workmen who would help them to rise to power.'[2] The uncertain standing of the moderates was, however, summed up most sharply perhaps by Brussilov who had been appointed Commander-in-Chief in the spring: 'The position of the Bolsheviks I understood, because they preached down with the war and immediate peace at any price, but I couldn't understand the tactics of the Social Revolutionaries and the Mensheviks who first broke up the army as if to avoid

---

[1] Chamberlin, *The Russian Revolution*, vol. i, p. 107.
[2] Buchanan, *Mỹ Mission in Russia*, vol. ii, p. 108.

counter-revolution and then at the same time desired to continue the war to a victorious end.'[1]

It is worth considering in more detail the actual methods used to break up the old army discipline. The oustanding feature was the system of regimental committees. These cropped up in every possible niche in the army on the very morrow of the March Revolution. They were flexible both as regards their functions and their personnel, and they immediately took such hold that Alekseev and Guchkov were forced to legalize their existence. Roughly, it was laid down that their functions should be to control supply and to take legal measures in the event of any abuse of authority, to settle misunderstandings between officers and soldiers, to maintain discipline and order, and to prepare for the elections to the future constituent assembly. As regards membership, they consisted of four-fifths soldiers and one-fifth officers. The men elected to serve on them were apt to be the intelligent non-commissioned officer, the less aristocratic war-time commissioned officer, and the non-combatant employed in one of the various auxiliary services. These committees were at first obvious agents of disintegration. They were in no sense imposed upon the troops by the revolutionary parties, but from the standpoint of tactics they were in fact essential, since only thus could the soldier be given a focus for his own revolutionary sentiment and a sense of community with the revolution at large. Committees such as these are, of course, a classic and natural expression. They first found form in the opening phases of the French Revolution. Here their activities were almost exactly similar, and their success as a disintegrating factor can be attested by the numerous complaints and jeremiads in regard to them indulged in by officers of the old regime who had retained their posts. They will be discussed in more detail when the swing-over of the old French Royalist army to the Revolution comes to be analysed. As the Russian Revolution developed, the committees, however, seem to have begun to act as a brake, and the Bolsheviks did not use them. This political lag is not surprising. Opinion in Petrograd was moving consciously to the Left far more rapidly than opinion at the front and, in addition, the committees, being in some sort official bodies, reflected the temper of the Government parties rather than the view of the advanced wing. The Bolsheviks relied on going, as it were, below the committees to get under the skin of the individual soldier. They did not expect him at once consciously to accept and understand their aims, but they realized clearly that sooner or later the pressure of events, as they would interpret these for him in their simple and masterly slogans, must sweep him into their following. This process they accelerated by their military organization. They introduced newspapers into the trenches urging the soldiers to take control of their own committees and they advocated organized fraternization with the

[1] Chamberlin, *The Russian Revolution*, vol. i, p. 152.

THE EFFECT OF FAILURE IN WAR

Germans at the front and the popular seizure of estates by the peasants in the rear. They ran a soldiers' club in Petrograd where men from the front could meet their more politically educated fellows from the Petrograd garrison, and they arranged delegations of soldiers to the factories where they could mix with the advanced workmen and learn politics from them. The hold of the advanced wing on the soldiers of the Petrograd garrison was always surer, and in the late summer a close liaison was brought about between the representatives of the garrison troops in their barracks and the Petrograd Soviet, which was by then under Bolshevik control.

In addition to the committees, the old army system was shaken by the appointment of civilian commissars to the various units, whose function was to link the fighting troops with the Government and to see that the spirit of the revolution was carried through to the army. Here again, the method had been invented by the French more than a hundred years before, but whereas the French Representatives on Mission proved themselves to be an indispensable part of the machinery for the turnover of the army to the Revolution, the Russians, through their identification with the Provisional Government, acted as a brake rather than an accelerator. In practice, their influence on the Russian Army can be largely discounted, but a reference to them is necessary, since an organization of this kind has become an accepted strategy for controlling the turnover of the armed forces of an old regime to a new political dispensation. And properly used, its influence is very great.

In accounting for the final break-up of the Tsarist Army, there are two more points to consider. The Kornilov Push in August, the only serious attempt made by the Right to effect a counter-revolution, as distinct from the efforts made by the moderates to hold up the revolution at the bourgeois-democratic stage, was decisively damaging. It broke the influence of the moderate committees and drove the soldiers into the arms of the extremists. Stankevich, Commissar for War in the Provisional Government, wrote of its results with disgust: 'The authority of the commanders was destroyed once for all. The masses of the soldiers, seeing how a General Commander-in-Chief had gone against the revolution, felt themselves surrounded by treason on all sides and saw in every man who wore epaulettes a traitor.'[1] The second point regards the position of the corps of officers. Noullens, the French Ambassador, reckoned that there were no less than 10,000 officers in Petrograd when the Bolshevik insurrection took place in November. These officers made no real attempt to organize and defend the moderate régime, because they would not support Kerensky.[2] After the insurrection they disappeared underground. In Moscow, where the officers organized a serious and gallant defence, the rising

[1] Chamberlin, *The Russian Revolution*, vol. i, p. 236.
[2] *Mon Embassade dans la Russie Soviète*, p. 125.

117

was held for several days, but the net result was similar since, when Moscow finally fell to the Bolsheviks, the liquidation of the officers' corps became a fact accomplished by fighting and flight. Thus the last stage of the break-up of the old army was the total elimination of its officers' corps.

It is perhaps not irrelevant to note the proportions of officers to men in the Tsarist forces compared with certain other armies. It has been estimated that the number of men serving in the Tsarist army in 1917 was somewhere about 12,000,000 and the number of officers when the army collapsed is given as 500,000. This produces a proportion of 1 in 24. At the opening of the great offensive in March 1918, the Germans had some 4,600,000 men under arms in the fighting forces, and about 177,600 officers, thus also giving a proportion of about 1 in 24. At the outbreak of the French Revolution, the regular army numbered 172,974 and the militia over 55,000 on a peace-time footing. There were about 10,000 regular officers. The proportion of officers to men is thus roughly 1 in 19. In 1930, the last year of the Spanish monarchy, the budgetary effectives for the home forces in Spain were 12,702 officers and 101,951 men, thus giving the very high proportion of 8 to 1. In 1932, after a year of Azana's government, the officers on the active list had been reduced to 7,902. The rank and file had been raised to 111,308, thus giving a rough proportion of 1 in 14, still abnormally high; and a significant comment on the ease with which the officers' corps could force a major rebellion. Azana's axe, moreover, was not thorough. Those officers who were retired were permitted to form a reserve and keep up close contacts with the active army.[1] From the standpoint of a Left revolution, the advantage of an army where the proportion of officers to men is relatively small is obvious. Such figures, however, can only be taken as rough indications of this sort of advantage. To assess it accurately, it would be necessary also to discuss the status of the N.C.O.s, as between the different armies. In some armies more than in others the system identifies the interests of the N.C.O. with the officers rather than with the rank and file.

In 1917 the Russian Army, as we have seen, generated internally its own solvents. It is of interest to try to analyse why, in 1905, given broadly speaking equivalent conditions, the army held together and thereby doomed the revolution to failure. In 1905, as in 1917, the army was engaged in fighting an unsuccessful war with a political background at home of rising revolutionary agitation. Mutinous incidents were frequent. There were disorders in Kiev, a small mutiny in St. Petersburg, sedition reported from Warsaw,

---

[1] The figures for Russia are taken from Wollenberg, *The Red Army*, p. 72; for Germany from the *Statistisches Jahrbuch des Deutschen Reiches*, 1924; for the French Army of the Old Regime from the *Cambridge Modern History*, 'The French Revolution', p. 401, and from Spencer Wilkinson, *The French Army Before Napoleon*; for Spain, from *The League of Nations Armaments Book for 1933*. *Vide* also p. 232.

unrest at Voroneszh. And the navy was saturated with discontent. There were two riots of sailors in Kronstadt in October 1905, a mutiny at Sevastopol and, of course, the spectacular mutiny in the Black Sea Fleet led by the seamen of the battleships *Potemkin* and *Ochakov*.[1] Yet these mutinies never coalesced into a mass movement.

There are certain fairly obvious circumstances which distinguish 1905 from 1917. In the first place, the war, though even more bitterly unsuccessful, had been of much shorter duration, so that the army had not become in the same sense a civilian army, and the number of troops in the field, compared to 1917, was relatively small. The term of service with the colours was five years[2] thus the proportion of men whose minds had been thoroughly moulded by the army system would still be large. In addition to these general considerations there were other more particular ones which undoubtedly helped to hold the army intact. Unlike their successors at Petrograd in 1917, the Government had seen to it that the most politically reliable troops were kept at home to deal with disturbances, and in the actual handling of unrest various devices were used. Rural troops were employed in towns and urban troops in the country. Regiments belonging to one gubernie were used to suppress revolts in another, and where possible soldiers of one race were used against insurgents of another. 'The utmost advantage was thus taken of natural antagonisms.' In addition, the grievances of the soldiers, which were largely of a practical nature, were met during the crisis by the authorities in a conciliatory spirit. They enjoyed improved treatment, their pay and their allowances were raised, and a special rate of pay arranged to bribe them for police duties.[3] Finally, the revolutionary political handling in 1905 was uncertain, spasmodic, and without integration. Practical revolutionary objectives, expressed in clear and telling slogans, which the soldier could appreciate and relate to his own life, slogans which must at least awaken his interest, were obscured in a haze of agitation for abstract political rights and responsibilities. No advantage was directly offered to him by the revolutionary parties which should bind him irrevocably to their cause. The contrast between these nebulous methods and the clear-cut simple objectives offered by Lenin cannot perhaps be over-emphasized.

The break-up of the Russian Army in 1917 provides cogent examples of almost all the conditions which make for the disintegration of armed forces through unsuccessful war. It is not, therefore, proposed to discuss in detail the crumbling of the Austrian and German armies which took place a year later. It is, however, worth isolating one or two points of difference, at any rate in regard to the German Army, which proved to have an important

[1] *Vide* Mavor, *Economic History of Russia*, p. 504.
[2] *Encyclopaedia Britannica*, 11th ed., s.v. Russia.
[3] *Vide* Mavor, *Economic History of Russia*, pp. 505, 508.

bearing on the development of the German Revolution.[1] In Germany, the action which resulted in disintegration came primarily and directly from the armed forces themselves. It was a consequence of their own initiative, and the civilians followed suit. The revolt of the Kiel sailors at the end of October 1918 finally broke the morale of the German forces. It was known throughout October that the war was in fact lost, and rumours that feelers were being put out for an armistice were running rife. Moreover, during the last weeks of October, a fundamental shifting of political power had taken place. The absolutist rule of the Kaiser had been wound up and Germany found itself a constitutional monarchy based on the parliamentary supremacy of the Reichstag. This shift can hardly be called a revolution, since the transference was made inevitable by the Supreme Command when it decided to resign its political powers. It was not made as a result of initiative and struggle on the part of the Reichstag; rather the Reichstag found itself in the position of the individual who is left holding the baby. The effect on the psychology of the fighting forces was, however, decisive. The sailors and soldiers believed that the first function of the new government would be to get Germany out of the war with the least delay and suffering possible and to negotiate a peace. When, therefore, the Kiel sailors were ordered by their officers to put to sea for a grand-scale raid upon England, a proceeding which could not conceivably alter the course of the war or the prospects of a favourable peace and must result only in useless loss of life, they refused to sail. Theirs was the realistic opinion of Sir Richard Grenville's crew after the *Revenge* had been shot to bits in the Azores battle and her commander wanted to blow up the ship rather than surrender:

> Sink me the ship, master gunner, sink her, split her in twain!
> Fall into the hands of God, not into the hands of Spain!

. . . But the seamen made reply:

> We have children, we have wives, and the Lord hath spared our lives.
> We will make the Spaniard promise, if we yield, to let us go;
> We shall live to fight again and to strike another blow.

The mutiny involved a hundred thousand men and it spread like a wind-blown fire throughout the troops stationed in Germany itself. The soldiers and sailors, in spite of their lack of political aim, rapidly formed councils on the Russian model to which the workers' councils, forming at the same time all over Germany, united themselves whole-heartedly. The Kaiser was pushed into abdication and the October Government resigned in favour of

[1] The following discussion is based on the accounts given in Rosenberg's *The Birth of the German Republic*, chap. vii; and *A History of the German Republic*, chaps. i, ii. Cf. also *infra*, pp. 227 sq.; Louis Fischer, *Soviet in World Affairs*, vol. i, p. 163.

a government led by the Majority Socialists under the presidency of Ebert. On November the 11th, this Government signed the armistice and the war was over. The extreme Left, spurred on during the autumn by the example of Russia and the general unrest throughout Germany, and regarding the October Constitution as a mere sop, had secretly planned an armed rising in Berlin for a date in November. This rising, coinciding in time with the spontaneous naval and military mutiny, was engulfed by the flood of undirected revolutionary emotion which the mutiny released, and its leaders were not strong enough to take control of the general movement. They too were engulfed by the tide of events. Had they been able to lead, it is possible that the subsequent history of Germany might have been made to a more radical pattern. The armies at the front, under Hindenburg's command, though they never broke discipline to the extent of actual disintegration, supported their comrades in the rear, and by their attitude forced the High Command to put itself at the disposal of Ebert's Government. So soon as the armistice was signed, the Government proceeded to bring back the troops from the front and to arrange for the demobilization and disbandment of all the armed forces, lock, stock, and barrel. This was pretty well completed by Christmas. These circumstances make the second main point of difference between the disintegration of the German and Russian armies, the first being that in Germany the initial revolutionary drive came from the soldiers and sailors themselves. It would seem that they had an important bearing on the very different development of the two revolutions.

A further important difference lies in the fact that in Germany the government formed after the Kaiser's flight ended the war at once; whereas in Russia the Provisional Government which took the Tsar's place strove to continue the war in spite of its unpopularity. Thus, in Russia, the Left had as it were the free gift of a propaganda weapon of immense value to use for deepening the process of disintegration among the armed forces in the interests of a future second and more fundamental revolution. In Germany, the virtual disappearance of the armed forces on the morrow of the moderate November Revolution prevented the use of such a weapon. But even had the army been retained, it is extremely doubtful whether the Left could have made much headway among the troops once peace had been declared. A large proportion of the soldiers were peasants just as in Russia, but whereas in Russia the land hunger of the peasant troops could be used as a second valuable weapon in the propaganda campaign for bringing over the army to the views of the Bolsheviks, in Germany there was no urgent problem of the land-hungry peasants, except in the great estates of the north-east. The campaign for peace and land throughout the spring and summer of 1917 made the ultimate support of the Bolshevik Revolution by the army practical politics. In Germany the peace weapon was knocked at the outset from the hands of the Left, and the land weapon never existed.

Moreover, the German soldier was not on the whole a theoretical socialist. Thus the Left, because it was inevitably prevented by the circumstances of the German situation from continuing propaganda among the troops, had no effective lever against the timid Government of Ebert. Again, had the first initiative for the revolution come from the workers rather than the soldiers and sailors, and had the latter been won over through the necessity of making a choice between joining their civilian comrades and suppressing an insurrection by force of arms, it is possible that the movement in the armed forces might have assumed a more definite political complexion. The Left, even in the short time at their disposal, might then have been able to some extent to influence the course of events through the medium of the army before its final disbandment. Such a theory, however, can only be put forward with caution.

The peculiar difficulty and danger of carrying through a revolution past the initial upheaval when a country is engaged upon external war cannot easily be discounted. Revolutionary leaders will be faced immediately by two alternatives both carrying the seeds of likely disaster. Either they must submit at once to a dictated peace and overcome as best they can the disgust and loss of prestige which that entails; or they must set themselves to the superhuman task of reorganizing an army which is in dissolution, partly through their own efforts, and which must now be reoriented and reshaped to a fighting machine with no respite or shelter from the storm of enemy attack. The Bolsheviks realized that for them the first alternative was the only possible one. So did the Germans. And it is an interesting comment on the difference of mentality between Russia and Germany that the Bolshevik regime never suffered serious loss of internal prestige from the humiliating terms of the Treaty of Brest-Litovsk, whereas the Weimar Republic carried to its dying day the wounds inflicted at Versailles, and indeed was sped to death largely on account of the disgust felt by the German people at these scars.

As regards Germany, it has been cogently argued in perhaps the most interesting book that has appeared on the attitude of the German Army to the revolution[1] that this humiliation might have been avoided had the negotiations for the armistice been differently conducted. The Allies concluded the armistice with a delegation of civilians nominated by the Provisional Government in Berlin and headed by Erzberger. They should have insisted on treating with negotiators from the old Imperial General Staff. If Hindenburg had come himself to deliver his sword to Foch it would have been made clear once and for all that the Imperial German Army was broken. But in agreeing to negotiate with Erzberger they allowed the General Staff an immunity from the shame of defeat which was rapidly turned to political account. The young republic had to shoulder single-

[1] *Histoire de l'armée allemande* (Bénoist Méchin, vol. i, p. 61).

handed the bitter task of concluding terms, and the officers' corps was left free to develop the legend that it had never been defeated in the field but rather had been stabbed in the back by the civilians of the rear. As time went on and the legend grew, it was easy for all the opponents of the Weimar Republic to fasten the odium on the struggling new regime.

This difference in psychology was a gift to the Bolsheviks, but it is of practical revolutionary importance to try to find out whence it arises. It is perhaps partly due to the difference between a loosely knit nation of many varying races and a disciplined people with a strong sense of martial pride. But there are other more specific causes. Russia was lacerated by civil war within a few months of the Bolshevik humiliation at Brest-Litovsk. Her people's energies were engaged to the full in partisan action; there was no leisure and security in which to incubate a festering sense of national dishonour. Moreover, the ultimate defeat of Germany by the Allies reduced many of the actual terms of the treaty to mere abstractions. Again, revolution meant much more to the Russians than it did to the Germans; they were prepared to buy it at a heavier price. And the enormous peasant population in Russia on whose support, whether bought, forced, or spontaneous, the Bolshevik regime ultimately rested, cared little about national defeat so long as they had their land, and cared even less when their anger was aroused by interference with their newly won freedom. Finally, Russia was a land of undeveloped spaces and economic resources, whereas Germany had felt the need for expansion even before she was shorn of colonies and border territories and crippled by a preposterous indemnity.

Once the civil war was liquidated, the Russian people could find full employment for their mental and physical energy in the development of their country, whereas the energy of the German people was cramped at every turn and went sour within them. In this connection it is worth remembering the experience of the Third Republic in France during the difficult years of reconstruction after the Franco-Prussian war. There can be little doubt that one important factor making for the stabilization and success of the new regime, despite the humiliating circumstances of its birth, was the outlet for surplus French energy in the African colonies.

The outstanding example of the second alternative, that of carrying through a revolution on the home front and at the same time reconstructing the armed forces so as to fight a large-scale foreign war, is provided by the French of 1789–94. The French methods of military reconstruction, and the special circumstances which made it possible to reorganize without the necessity for a clean break in organization and personnel between the army of the old regime and the army of the new, will be analysed later and contrasted against the much heavier task of creating an entirely new army which the Russians had to undertake. It is almost certain that under modern conditions revolution and a serious foreign war can only be carried through simultaneously with success where conditions obtain similar to the French. The task becomes an impossible one if the basic military framework has crumbled so completely that it requires rebuilding from fresh materials. Moreover, in comparing France and Russia, it must also be borne in mind that the genesis of revolution in the French Royalist Army was not revolt against an unpopular and ill-conducted war. French arms were only engaged after the initial stages of the revolution, and they were engaged in defence of the new ideals. The perilous defeats in the second period of the war showed the necessity for drastic military reorganization on revolutionary lines and forced the pace at which this was achieved; they quickened the *tempo* of the revolution in all its aspects, civil and military; but they were not causes of the revolution. Thus the revolutionary function of war as between France and Russia was radically different. The Bolsheviks used the war against Germany as a solvent to disintegrate the Tsarist Army. The French used their war against the Allies as a welding-iron for the fusion of the old and new military elements into a strong and tempered revolutionary weapon. Finally, the Russians in withdrawing, however ignominiously, from the war with Germany were not abandoning a revolutionary task, but the French Revolution was at bay. The French had to win their war or lose their revolution altogether.

The fact that all the great armies which were defeated in the First World War broke up in the end, either directly or indirectly, owing to the long-drawn-out strain and ultimate failure, suggests that in modern times an unsuccessful war is an almost certain agent of dissolution. Even the victorious armies, wearied too by the fearful strain to which they had been subjected, turned their weakened morale to some extent to political account. In Britain, Sir Henry Wilson openly admitted that an unpopular order could not be given to the troops since discipline was a thing of the past. And the French were warned by serious disaffection among units sent to the Black Sea to support the White Russians that the temper of the troops was far too explosive for any government to dare engage them on an unpopular enterprise.[1]

The Russian and the German pre-war armies were both armies in which the twin processes of divorcing the soldier from civilian interests and building

[1] Chamberlin, *The Russian Revolution*, vol. ii, p. 166.

So far as British working-class sympathy was concerned, Mr. Lloyd George asserted at the Peace Conference in 1919, 'If a military enterprise were started against the Bolsheviks, that would make England Bolshevik, and there would be a Soviet in London'. (Quoted by Louis Fischer, *Soviet in World Affairs*, vol. i, p. 163.)

In regard to the Polish war, a Labour delegation saw Mr. Lloyd George, and Mr. Bevin, speaking for the Transport Workers, said, 'If war is carried on directly or indirectly in support of Poland there would be a match set to explosive material, the result of which none of us can foresee.' (Quoted by Louis Fischer, ibid, p. 266.)

up a corps of officers whose interests coincided with those of the ruling class had been carried to high degree. In Germany, for instance, shortly before 1914, it is significant that the Emperor refused to create three reserve army corps on the ground that finding officers for them would necessitate introducing bourgeois elements into the officers' corps.[1] Before armies of this type will disintegrate, their character must be radically altered. The isolation of the rank and file from civilian life must be broken down and the power of the officers' corps to hold the rank and file must be swept away. It is probable that unsuccessful modern war is the only external agent strong enough to produce these alterations in character. Grand-scale modern war inevitably disarranges entirely the carefully built-up relationships of the military machine. The first necessity is to fill the gaps created by the enormous wastage, both as regards men and officers. This must be done rapidly and, as we have seen, there will be no time or spare energy to give to the psychological job of 'conditioning' the rank and file. The rank and file will become soldiers only in a technical sense. They will be subject like other men to civilian waves of emotion. Parallel with this fundamental alteration in the character of the rank and file comes a no less fundamental and important alteration in the character of the corps of officers. Wastage again must be made good, and this can only be done by giving up the position that officers must be drawn from the ruling classes. The longer the war continues and the greater the scale of wastage, the more will the gaps in the ranks of the officers' corps come to be filled by men whose background and interests have nothing in common with those of a traditional professional officer class. There will be an increasing necessity for promotions from the ranks and an increasing influx of war-time officers who are by their tradition civilians. By this means the homogeneity of the officers' corps will be entirely spoilt and the influence of the officers over their men undermined. It will be undermined from two directions. On the one side, because the isolation of the men themselves has been broken down so that they will no longer be subject to military influence in the same way. On the other side, because the officers' corps in itself will be no longer capable of exerting that influence. Moreover, protracted war produces its own discontent and unrest. When failure is added, the cup overflows and the conditions for disintegration are made.

It is hard to see what solvents other than exhaustion in war could prove strong enough to weaken the officers' corps sufficiently, or to awaken the common soldier to independent action. It is true that the French Army of the Old Regime broke down without an unsuccessful war. But there are special reasons for this which will be discussed in a subsequent chapter. It is, however, here important to note that one reason was that the officers were to some extent politically discontented at the start of the revolution

[1] Bénoist Méchin, *Histoire de l'armée allemande*, vol. i, p. 30.

and encouraged their men. If this had not been so it is possible that the army could have been used effectively to crush the revolution.

If the lesson of the First World War suggests that no army will come out of a grand-scale modern contest with its morale unscathed and that defeated armies may reasonably be expected to break altogether if the war drags on long enough, it does not necessarily indicate with the same certainty how the disintegration will work out in terms of political alinement. We are apt to assume that a disintegration of the rank and file, as distinct from the officers, accrues to the advantage of the Left. It is, of course, true that in Russia, Germany, and Austria, the disintegrating army did turn in greater or less degree to the Left. But in all three cases, the Left represented at the critical time the protest against the sufferings incurred by the war. Given the state of our present Europe, it is not far-fetched to assume conditions in which the democracies, wearied out by fighting, might find that the protest was being sponsored and used for political ends by a reactionary party successfully fishing in troubled waters. The triumph of the Nazis in Germany has shown how weariness and economic suffering and a sense of frustration can breed fascism, the monstrous changeling for true social revolution. In the democracies, it is not difficult to see how Fascist elements could cash in at the last on the suffering entailed by a long-drawn-out war against the Dictator States. No war government is popular until it can brandish the flashing credentials of victory; but the peace which follows victory is apt, as our experience has proved, to be a time of disillusionment almost as bitter as the peace which follows defeat. On any showing, therefore, the chance of revolt against a democratic government, either towards the end of or after a gruelling war, is considerable. And in the circumstances of war against the Dictator States, it would probably be easier for the revolutionary Right than for the revolutionary Left to influence and control subversive elements and exploit the possible disintegration of the armed forces. For, in the nature of the case, the Left must have identified itself with the prosecution of such a war to its utmost limits. During the war, the Left could only make a revolution by successfully urging, on the one hand, the military incompetence of the existing government and, on the other hand, by undertaking to carry out a complete reconstruction in the manner of the French Left during the wars of 1792–4. And this would mean, not only that the Left was actually capable of carrying through an administrative reconstruction of the fighting machine, but also that it was able to imbue both troops and people with a crusading zeal as ardent as that of the French soldiers who bore the arms of the Republic to ultimate victory. *Ex hypothesi*, the Left would be debarred from exploiting a will to peace. In the period of disillusionment following the war, the Left would still be at a similar disadvantage. It might win through, but it is not unreasonable to forecast that the Fascist Right would be found to hold better cards for playing the revolutionary game. It would, moreover, have the natural support of a majority of officers, even after the alteration in the character of the officers' corps due to war. There are few groups more difficult to re-absorb into a community about to take up again the avocations of peaceful workaday life than the discharged officers with no place of their own and no training for civilian citizenship, and with little prospect of finding jobs which at all square with their conceptions of themselves as ex-officers.

This is an urgent problem whose solution we should do well to ponder.

7

ARMED FORCES AND THEIR OWN
DISCONTENTS

Practical grievances among troops as agents of disintegration.

Although it can be predicted that the rank and file of a modern army of professional type will as a general rule hold firm against the emotions of revolution, unless the uprising is coupled with the disintegrating conditions of failure in war, yet there remains the question whether there is any internal solvent which may be derived from the character of the armed forces themselves, and which would be strong enough to act, in some measure, as a disintegrating agent. If a solvent of this kind should exist, it might be exploited with the help of special circumstances in the interests of a revolutionary uprising and used to transform the political indifference of the troops into revolutionary enthusiasm.

There can be little doubt that practical grievances among soldiers regarding their conditions of service make an underlying basis of discontent in most armies and, where these grievances are really widespread and deepseated, the disintegrating effect is considerable. Even where the disintegration comes primarily as a result of failure in war, the specific grievances of the soldiers may make an important contributing factor. It has been shown, for instance, how discontent with their conditions of service had given a background of unrest to the Russian Army in 1917 and a pitch for revolutionary propaganda quite distinct from the grievances of the war situation.

Practical grievances act upon the morale of an army in two ways. Either they make for a more or less chronic condition of discontent, so that the ties of loyalty and discipline which bind armed forces to a *status quo* government are weakened over a period of years and may come apart altogether at the impact of a serious political crisis; or they issue suddenly in an internal explosion—a mutiny which may or may not have a political aspect, but whose basic character is protest against specific grievances. It will be shown in this chapter how the attitude of the King's Navy at the outbreak of the Parliamentary Wars is an example of the first case. The longstanding discontent of the seamen robbed them of any enthusiasm to support the Royalist cause once hostilities had been opened and so allowed the Parliament to win over their allegiance. The French Army of the Old Regime provides another and greater example. Here the practical grievances of both officers and men, combined with disgust on the part of many officers at the incompetence of the royal administration, drew the army away from the Royalist Government during the opening phases of the revolution. Conditions of indiscipline and disloyalty were thus created in which the seeds of enthusiasm for the revolutionary cause could germinate rapidly among the rank and file. The fraternization of the soldiers with the people during the insurrection which culminated in the fall of the Bastille shows how quickly and effectively professional discontent may be directed to a political channel and transformed into a political force. The break-up of the forces of the Old Regime has, however, many special points of interest and is in many ways unique in its process. It will therefore be more useful to try to analyse it in detail as a whole rather than wrench out particular aspects from the general context. This will be done in Chapter 8.

Examples of the second case, where practical grievances explode suddenly into mutiny unrelated to any revolutionary outbreak among the people, are the British naval mutinies at Spithead and the Nore in 1797, which will be discussed later in this chapter, and at Invergordon in 1931. The Invergordon mutiny was in character solely a reaction against an alleged unjust decision regarding the men's terms of service, and it is of importance only as showing the lengths to which men, trained even in the traditions of a modern armed force, will go in defence of their rights. It shows that, given certain conditions, mutiny is a practical possibility among modern troops in peace-time.

In 1642, the Navy supported the Parliamentary forces almost to a man.[1] This support was active and has no analogy with the passive support which the seamen gave to the Revolution of 1688. So early in the development of events as January 1642, 2,000 seamen had spontaneously offered their services and protection to the harassed Parliament. In July, King Charles appointed Admiral Pennington to the command of his fleet. Parliament countered by appointing the Earl of Warwick. Pennington was a popular officer who had in previous years made very considerable personal efforts to improve the appalling conditions under which the seamen lived and worked. Yet, with the exception of the small *Providence*, every ship seems to have followed Warwick, and Royalist officers were put ashore and the crews took charge. That Warwick himself trusted the political alinement of his

[1] For an account of the Navy during the Parliamentary Wars, *vide* Hannay, *A Short History of the Royal Navy*, *The Navy in the Civil War*. Oppenheim also throws considerable light on the attitude of the seamen in his *Administration of the Royal Navy*.

men is shown by the proclamation he issued to the fleet, forbidding the sailors 'to obey the commands of their superior officers if the same tend towards disloyalty to the Parliament'. Such a proclamation would obviously have been foolhardy if there had been any serious doubt as to where the sympathies of the men lay.

Now, the labouring classes of England took small interest on the whole in the Great Rebellion. It was never a people's revolt like the great Peasants' Insurrection of 1381, but rather an affair of the squirearchy and rising commercial classes who, in the one case were anxious to liquidate the last vestiges of feudalism, and in the other were desperately concerned to see that an absolute monarchy on the Continental model, with all its contracting economic influences, did not take the place of the old feudal regime. These men built parliamentary government firmly and enduringly into English life, but they did not lay the foundations of working-class freedom. Take, for example, the Act of Settlement, which went smoothly through the Cavalier Parliament in 1662.[1] This act gave local authorities power to prevent men changing parishes in much the same way that the United States uses its immigration laws. In effect, it bound the labourer to the land. It remained in force for a hundred and thirty years.

The sailors, therefore, had no special political reason for supporting Parliament against the King. Their support can only be explained in terms of the practical interests of their own profession.

For many years before the outbreak of the Great Rebellion, the navy had been grossly neglected by Stuart governments, both as regards its fighting efficiency and its conditions of service for the seamen. The plight of the sailors was wretched almost beyond description. Most of them were men who had been arbitrarily called away from civilian jobs in the fisheries and on board trading vessels to man the royal ships, where they were forced to spend long periods away from home and to submit to living conditions so bad that they sickened and died like neglected animals. Reports on the ignominious homecoming of the Cadiz fleet in 1625 show up the miseries of the men's situation.[2] Pennington wrote of the homecoming crews that 'the greatest part of the seamen were sick or dead, so that few of them have sufficient sound men to bring their ships about'. St. Leger asserted that the men could not be moved off their ships until they had recovered some strength: 'they stink as they go and the poor rags they have are rotten and ready to fall off'. Another officer deposed that the dried fish rations had become so rotten that 'the very savour thereof is contagious'. A later report from Portsmouth, in 1628, described how 'the men lodge on bare decks ... their condition miserable beyond relation; many are so naked and exposed to the weather in doing their duties that their toes and feet miserably rot

---

[1] Trevelyan, *England Under the Stuarts*, pp. 521, 522.
[2] *Vide* Oppenheim, *Administration of the Royal Navy*, pp. 223, 232.

and fall away piecemeal, being mortified with extreme cold'.[1] In addition to the physical conditions on board the royal ships, there was the press-gang method of recruitment, whereby men were forcibly taken, not only from seaport towns, but also from inland towns and the countryside to serve in the navy, and taken without any guarantee as to how long their term of service might be. Press-gang recruitment inevitably makes for discontented crews without professional *esprit de corps*, whose interests and sentiments pull them always back towards the civilian jobs and the families from whom they have been wrested. Further, the sailors had a particular grievance against Charles in that he had run counter to the traditions of the navy in his method of appointing officers. In the golden days of the navy, when Elizabeth and her captains had hammered out a rule of rough manners and prowess and self-respect, it was the custom to draw officers from seafarers who came from social strata well known to the men. Charles had introduced a sort of cadet system for training young officers who were landsmen and even courtiers by upbringing.

It was therefore small wonder that these seventeenth-century seamen had no love for their Stuart master and were ready and flexible material for the use of any possible alternative political regime. A clear-sighted critic, commenting on their conditions of service, has summed up the political repercussion of their situation sharply:

'Naval historians have usually considered the condition of the seaman, a mere pawn in the game, as of little account compared with graphic descriptions of sea-fights and the tactics of opposing fleets. He had, however, not only existence but memories, and an examination of his treatment under the government of Charles I . . . may go far to explain why the Royal Navy "went solid" for the Parliament in 1642.'[2]

A final but important factor may be regarded as a purely accidental gift to the Parliamentarians. It so happened that those parts of England from which the seafaring population came were predominantly Puritan. Accidental factors such as these play a considerable part in most revolutionary situations, and able leaders will be likely to realize and exploit them to the full.

It is worth emphasizing that the loyalty of the seamen to Parliament was almost continuous throughout the years of the Civil War. This continuance was ensured by paying the sailors proper and punctual wages, by clothing them adequately, and by abolishing so far as was possible the hated press-gang. Moreover, since every considerable seaport was in the hands of the Puritans until Prince Rupert took Bristol, it is at least probable that wastage was made good by a suitable picking of recruits. Sailors with Royalist sympathies would hardly get berths on the Parliament's ships.

We may now take a look at the two naval mutinies off Spithead and the

---

[1] *Vide* Oppenheim, *Administration of the Royal Navy*, p. 226.
[2] Oppenheim, *Administration of the Royal Navy*, p. 222.

Nore in 1797.[1] Here again the complaints of the mutineers, in particular at Spithead, were concerned with their own professional interests. Sea reform had not kept pace with land reform, and the men no doubt felt that they were being differentiated against by a harsh and ungrateful government. At Spithead the most prominent place in their demands was allotted to an increase in wages. No wage increase had been given since the Restoration, yet the cost of living was up by a third. Again, the actual payments were irregular, and the position further exacerbated because the pay of the lieutenants had just been raised. The men complained too that bounties were only given to volunteers, an unfair discrimination against the regular seamen. At the Nore the mutineers complained that they did not get a proper share of prize money. After wages, bad food took pride of place in the list of grievances. Out of six demands made by the Spithead men, two related to their rations. There were complaints also about the savage discipline meted out by certain officers; the accounts of eyewitnesses suggest that floggings were not infrequently sadistic in character.[2]

The conduct of the Spithead Mutiny bears out the contention that the sailors' discontent was based on their own particular grievances. It was essentially peaceable and orderly and, indeed, bears all the marks of an ably led and successful strike rather than of a political explosion. It was called off so soon as the men's demands were granted and embodied in a bill before Parliament. This took a little time and accounts for the fact that there were in a sense two separate outbreaks. The original mutiny simmered down once negotiations had been started and then unrest suddenly surged to boiling point again because the men got the idea that their complaints were not after all being fully dealt with.

The situation at the Nore was more complex and was strongly influenced by undercurrents of political feeling, so that the whole outbreak assumed a more obstinate and angry character. The mutiny began a few days after the first upheaval at Spithead and seems originally to have been made with the object of backing up the Spithead mutineers. But the Nore sailors refused to accept the terms which satisfied the Spithead men and which were also offered to them. They hurled further demands at the Admiralty and their mutiny dragged on, deriving from each day's delay in effecting a settlement a more bitter and revolutionary twist. The mutinous crews, for instance, blockaded the river in order to bring pressure to bear on the Government;

[1] For a detailed account of the naval mutinies of 1797 *vide* Gill, *The Naval Mutinies of 1797*. Cf. also Dobrée and Manwaring, *The Floating Republic* (Pelican Books).

[2] In August 1795 the men of the *Weazle* sloop wrote that their lieutenant, who frequently came on board drunk, amused himself 'by making us strip and ceasing (seizing) us up to the riggin and beating us with the end of rope till we almost expire'. Quoted by Dobrée and Manwaring, *The Floating Republic*, p. 19. Cf. also ibid., pp. 66 sq.

within four days more than a hundred merchantmen were queued up at the Nore unable to get through to the Port of London. There was, too, a definite suggestion that the sailors should take their ships across to France and hand themselves over to the Directory as being the only government fit for decent men to serve under. Even at Spithead where, as it has been said, the political weighting was almost negligible, the idea of running to France was mooted. More than eighty men of the *Pompée* conspired to sail their ship to Brest and desert to the French. It is worth pointing out that neither at Spithead nor at the Nore did the officers offer physical resistance and in return they were not personally molested. They were allowed to abandon their ships without interference and the mutineers took charge.

The blockade of the Thames was raised before it could have attained anything like maximum pressure, and the plan to run the ships to France never materialized. This can only be attributed to the half-heartedness of the men who, like their comrades at Spithead, were fundamentally concerned with their own grievances, and refused to be worked up into a state of sustained and politically aimed revolutionary feeling by those few leaders on board who realized the possibility of turning the mutiny to the account of a wider movement. The political flame spurted uncertainly and then went out.

It is probable that had the political leadership of the mutiny been abler, more determined, and more clear-sighted, the revolt would have gone further and involved a grave and general repercussion on the political situation in England. It is unlikely, however, that the Nore Mutiny could have been made into the spearhead of a general revolution. The amount of directed discontent and unrest in the country hardly warrants that assumption and it is, perhaps, a significant 'straw' that the troops stationed at Sheerness refused to come in with the mutineers because they had just had a rise in pay. Whether this be so or not, the deduction from the kind of situation created at the Nore is clear. Given the support of other circumstances, such a situation could be used as the touch train for a general explosion; but it must be studied and assessed at once, not only in regard to the weight of revolutionary feeling among the mutineers, but also, and perhaps more essentially, in relation to the opportunity for using it to explode civilian unrest into an active outbreak.

A scheme to exploit discontent in the fleet, with a view to using it for a general revolutionary end, was in fact set on foot some time before the Nore Mutiny under the auspices of the United Irishmen. The total strength of the navy at the time was 100,000 seamen and 20,000 marines, including officers. Of these, it has been estimated that 11,500 sailors and 4,000 marines were Irishmen.[1] Wolfe Tone realized the possibilities of this Irish dilution to the full. His tactics were to get hold of the Irishmen in the fleet and educate

[1] Gill, *The Naval Mutinies of 1797*, pp. 313, 330.

them politically. A stiffening of informed leadership was to be provided by penetrating the ships with Irish surgeons who already belonged to the United Irish organization. So hopeful was he of the chances of mutiny owing to the Irish dilution that in 1796, when he was negotiating with Carnot, the brilliant war minister of the Revolution, for a French invasion of Ireland, he actually sketched out a plan to effect wholesale desertion and a transference of the fleet from the English to the Irish flag. This plan was put forward in a proclamation addressed to the Irishmen in the fleet, but it does not seem to be known in what manner the manifesto was circulated or how widely. Tone himself seems to have wildly exaggerated the numbers of the Irish. He is alleged to have told Carnot that there were 80,000 Irishmen in the British Navy. Be that as it may, the scheme was never put seriously to the test, since the proposed invasion of Ireland, with which it was planned to coincide, fell through on other grounds. It is, however, of considerable interest from the standpoint of revolutionary strategy, since it shows a definite attempt to convert discontent among armed forces to a political end, and to use it as the key to a general uprising. Had the plan succeeded, there can be little doubt that the striking power of the British Government would have been almost completely paralysed.

In 1797, when mutiny in the fleet had actually broken out and the prospects of converting it to a political end were therefore more reasonable and hopeful, the United Irishmen had no plan immediately ready for linking up the isolated explosions to a general movement. Tone understood the loss of this opportunity bitterly and acutely. At the beginning of August 1797 he wrote in his diary:

'Five weeks, I believe six weeks, the English fleet was paralysed by the mutinies at Portsmouth, Plymouth, and the Nore. The sea was open and nothing to prevent both the Dutch and French fleets to put to sea. Well, nothing was ready. That precious opportunity, which we can never expect to return, was lost. . . . Had we been in Ireland at the moment of the Insurrection at the Nore, we should beyond a doubt have had at least that fleet, and God only knows the influence such an event might have had upon the whole British Navy.'[1]

The cases of the navy in 1642 and 1797 are not isolated instances; indeed, history suggests it to be a fairly safe generalization that practical grievances are frequently a basic ingredient in the chemistry of the disintegration of armed forces. But these grievances have to be reinforced by political ingredients before they can become a final dissolving agent. They will only work as a means to launch a general insurrection if they can be adequately merged with strong currents of political unrest. It has already been shown how this happened in Russia in 1917, when the immediate rankling discontent of the Russian soldier was absorbed and sublimated by the immense

[1] Quoted by Gill, *The Naval Mutinies of 1797*, p. 337.

wave of revolutionary passion which swept over the entire country. In 1905, this process of absorption and sublimation was never completed for various reasons, as we have seen. The explosive mutiny on the *Potemkin*, for example, had a definite political background, but was touched off exclusively by an immediate grievance, a dinner of inedible maggoty soup.[1] Those who like to visualize their history as vividly as possible can see, in Eisenstein's film, a close-up of the meat, disgustingly crawling with huge maggots, as it was to be thrown into the sailors' bortsch. But this mutiny, though it involved most of the Black Sea Fleet, failed as a key to a general revolt because it was not controlled by a central revolutionary movement and used as part of a concerted strategy. Its force was therefore largely dissipated and wasted.

One obvious difficulty in using mutinies of the Spithead and Nore, or even of the *Potemkin* type, to touch off a political insurrection is that in the nature of the case they time themselves, and except by a mere coincidence cannot be synchronized with a rising tide of revolutionary unrest. Moreover, practical grievances can be rapidly redressed by a clever government and the mutinous impulse thus emasculated. So soon as the demands of the Spithead sailors were met with sympathetic consideration, they called their mutiny off. It is significant of the psychology of this kind of situation that the second flare-up came when the men sensed a hitch in negotiations and believed that they were in fact being tricked into surrender. Similarly, during the Russian crisis of 1905–6, the internal grievances of the soldiers, which might have made a firm basis for revolutionary unrest in the army, were also redressed in time, at least to some extent, and the revolutionary cause thus deprived of a formidable method of approach to win the troops.

The possibility of directly utilizing such mutinies cannot, however, be entirely discounted. Behind their imposing façade of immediate and specific grievances, the Nore mutineers, for example, concealed a core of genuinely revolutionary feeling. The promise to redress their grievances did not satisfy them. If this feeling in the navy could have been linked up to a general revolutionary movement throughout the country it might have been used as the spearhead of a mass uprising, and it would in all probability have spread to other naval centres, so that the action of the navy against an insurrection would have been effectively paralysed. It has been shown, for instance, how Wolfe Tone realized too late the opportunity for relating the Nore Mutiny to the revolutionary movement of the United Irishmen. Tone was certainly correct in the theoretical point of view that the Nore Mutiny produced the sort of situation which could be seized upon by a revolutionary movement and enlarged so as to break up the defending forces of the *status quo* government. He was probably incorrect in thinking that the particular opportunity he had lost could ever have been used to win permanent

[1] Constantine Feldman, *The Revolt of the* Potemkin (Heinemann).

success. The general revolutionary tide in England was not setting sufficiently strong during the critical period. The success of this kind of revolutionary strategy must depend upon the chance that the mutiny among the armed forces comes at a time when civilian unrest, for one reason or another, is about to pass the borderline between mere political discontent and revolutionary violence.

A soldier's grievances will always strike him more forcibly when he contrasts his own lot with the freer and fuller life lived by his civilian friends and relatives. It is significant that the seamen who went over to the Parliament in 1642 were frequently men who had begun their seafaring life as fishermen or in the mercantile marine and who had been taken from their civilian jobs to man the King's Navy. Years of service on board the King's ships only served to emphasize the contrast between the life of a naval seaman and the life of a fisherman, however hard the latter might be. Nor was it mere prejudice that made the family of a Victorian or Edwardian artisan who 'went for a soldier' lament the state of life in which their relative had enmeshed himself. They realized, if only dimly, that the soldier, once he has been drawn into the closed circle of interests of a professional military system, is apt to lose all sense of being a free and thinking citizen of his country, and that every circumstance of that system deliberately forces and encourages him to do so. 'My sweetheart no longer loves me because I have fallen soldier,' sang the Spanish conscript. 'But one day I will come back to her with my demobilization papers in my hand.'[1]

The establishment of close contacts between the army and the civilian population is therefore a method for making the soldier sensitive to his particular set of grievances. It is also the only method for keeping him politically alive. And perhaps the best proof of this latter contention is the importance which shrewd politicians of the Right have always attached to keeping him isolated from civilian points of view, particularly during times of unrest.

The policy of those who plan revolutions is therefore clear. They will work for a close tie-up between the armed forces and the civil population and, alternatively or in addition, they will bid for the future support of the troops by linking their grievances to revolutionary propaganda during the period of education and preparation for a revolt. They will exploit discontent with the practical conditions of service under the old regime by suggesting that under a new regime the grievances could be remedied.

In this last regard it is worth remarking that in Spain, during the revolutionary period between 1868 and 1874, the promise of the Republicans to abolish compulsory service if they won power caused the rank and file of the army to refuse to join a serious officers' insurrection which broke out at Barcelona immediately after the proclamation of the Republic, the object

[1] Jellinek, *The Civil War in Spain*, p. 54.

being to bring back the future Alphonso XII. When, however, it became clear to the soldiers that the Republic was not in a condition to abolish the hated blood tax, owing to the chaotic condition of the country, but must, on the contrary, call for fresh levies of men to cope with the disorder, they lost all interest in it. So, when Alphonso XII was proclaimed king in 1874, the rank and file of the army followed their officers in welcoming back the monarchy.[1]

Revolutionary leaders must also make the judgement whether, when the gift of a mutiny has been put into their hands, the general political situation warrants taking advantage of the weakening of the armed forces, owing to their own internal unrest, to force an uprising.

Conversely, a *status quo* government which expects unrest will be wise to insure itself against the danger of the practical discontents of its soldiery coalescing with revolutionary movements by liquidating their grievances in good time. The neutralization of the Sheerness troops during the Nore Mutiny because their pay had just been raised is a case in point. And it has been shown in a preceding chapter that one important factor making for the success of the Tsarist regime in holding the loyalty of the army during the 1905 Revolution was the shrewd attention that had been given to the remedying of grievances, and the special rate of pay that was given to encourage the soldier to do his police work of suppression without jibbing.

[1] *Cambridge Modern History*, vol. xii, pp. 260, 262.

8

THE FRENCH REVOLUTION

The French Revolution and the armed forces of the *ancien régime*[1]

At the outbreak of the Revolution, the army, both as regards men and officers, found itself already alienated to a considerable extent from the Royalist regime. The officers had their own particular grievances. In 1781, the Court had persuaded Louis and his minister Ségur into making a decree to the effect that in future all army officers must bear sixteen quarterings of nobility.[2] Noble birth was also required of all officers in the navy. Sub-lieutenants, it is true, might be drawn from an inferior social class, but they could never rise in the service higher than the rank of lieutenant.[3] This decree was hailed as an insult by numbers of officers who had bought commissions and by the fairly numerous soldiers of fortune who had hitherto been able to rise from the ranks. At the time of the elections to the States-General, there were 9,578 officers on the establishment; of these 6,633 were nobles, but 1,845 came from the middle classes, and 1,100 were ex-rankers,[4] that is to say men who, since the new regulations had been introduced, could not hope to rise in the service above lieutenant's rank. It is clear, therefore, that the percentage of officers nursing a serious professional grievance was large. In addition, the country gentry,

[1] The mass of literature touching on the relation of the armed forces to the French Revolution is such that I have had to pick a relatively short list of authorities. Even so, it has not seemed feasible to refer more than a selection of the statements made in this chapter to their sources without making an overload of notes. I have, therefore, confined the quotation of authorities to those statements which seemed of rather special interest or importance. Further, histories of the French Revolution, whether written by contemporaries or by historians of our own day, are almost invariably coloured by the political point of view of the writers. It is, therefore, perhaps as well to say that I have used M. Albert Mathiez's *La Révolution française* as a general background, and also Wilfrid Kerr, *The Reign of Terror* (Univ. of Toronto Press).

[2] *Vide* Spenser Wilkinson, *The French Army before Napoleon*, p. 91; also Hartmann, *Les Officiers de l'armée royale et la révolution*, pp. 5 sq.

[3] *Cambridge Modern History*, 'The French Revolution', p. 447.

[4] Spenser Wilkinson, *The French Army before Napoleon*, p. 101.

descendants of the proud d'Artagnans of France, had their own special complaint. They formed the largest class of regimental officer, but they were not eligible to be presented at Court and therefore they never got influence to win any of the high commands. Finally, up to 1787, when Brienne's Army Council had made a number of important reforms, out of a swollen total of 35,000 officers no less than 23,000 were absentees. Brienne reduced the total on the establishment and abolished absenteeism, but he did not eliminate the other causes of discontent. Thus, when the King and his ministers were fighting the *parlements* in 1788, the officers on the whole took sides with the *parlements*, or at least showed a widespread determination not to act against these curious institutions which were seriously concerned with the inefficiency of the King's Government and which, in spite of their essential conservatism and their upper-class or *haut-bourgeois* personnel, were the only channel for the expression of popular discontent available at the time. At Rennes, for instance, the officers of the commandant's guard prevented their men from firing on a mob which was demonstrating against the suppression of the *parlements*. Other regiments were imported, and in each case the officers refused to act against the people.[1]

When the States-General met in the spring of 1789, there were about 154 officers sitting in the Nobles-état and of these 33 voted with the Tiers-état in favour of joint sittings for the three estates,[2] a vote against the expressed wishes of the Court, and which marked the first fundamental cleavage of opinion between the old regime and the new men who were trying their strength for the first time in the service of the reconstruction of France. This liberal minority welcomed the fall of the Bastille, but as soon as it became clear that the revolution was sweeping through the months with an ever-growing radical impetus most of them began to regret their first enthusiasm. The corps of officers on the whole rallied firmly to the Crown. By the summer of 1791 their temper was causing serious anxiety to the Assembly, and it was then decreed that an oath (the second military oath) should be administered to all officers, by whose terms they must swear fidelity to the nation, law, and King in the order given. This oath, followed as it was a few days later by the flight to Varennes, brought the political position of the officers to a focus, and emigration now began in earnest. The officers who emigrated were mostly nobles; thus the field was left clear for the bourgeois and ranker officers who now saw the chance for a successful military career. This circumstance is of great importance in explaining the turnover of the army to the revolution, and its influence will be discussed in detail later. The immediate point to make is that, taking the corps of officers by and large, their discontent with the old regime did not go deep enough to permit them to throw in their lot with the revolution beyond its opening

[1] Spenser Wilkinson, *The French Army before Napoleon*, p. 96.
[2] *Vide* Hartmann, *Les Officiers de l'armée royale et la révolution*, pp. 90, 94.

phases; but that this discontent and its expression at the start was undoubtedly one of the factors acting as a general solvent of discipline. To some extent, at any rate, it suggested to the rank and file a revolutionary cue.

The rank and file had, of course, their own grievances. Their term of enlistment was eight years, and it is significant that, out of a peace-time establishment of 172,974, the army lost an average of 20,000 men a year by death or desertion.[1] This fact alone suggests the harsh and uncomfortable life which the soldier led. In the *cahiers* which he and his fellows drew up for presentation to the States-General along with the other groups of the French people, betterment of the physical conditions of his service was frequently emphasized. He asked for more adequate food, warm clothing, a proper system of furloughs. In addition, he suffered under an old-standing and odious system of disciplinary penalties. This system had been retained by Brienne, in spite of his other army reforms, and its injustice and barbarity were no doubt beginning to strike home to the soldier's mind. He could contrast it with the new ideas of the rights and dignity of man which were slowly but surely boring down like great drills, set in motion by the concepts of the thinkers, to break through the hardened class strata of the population. In 1790–1 insubordination ran like a fever rash throughout the army; and many officers seem to have attributed this to reaction against the old grim discipline and the cruel penalties if it were broken. Royalist officers, however, seem to have deliberately victimized those men who showed themselves enthusiastic for the new regime. The cause of unrest was, therefore, frequently a mixture of revolutionary ardour and revolt against specific punishments. Similar conditions prevailed in the navy. At the end of 1789 there had been a riot at Toulon because the Admiral of the port had dismissed two dockyard men for wearing the tricolour cockade inside the arsenal walls. The workmen and sailors rose and laid siege to the admiral in his house and finally carried him off to prison because he had ordered regular troops to fire on the rioters.[2] In September 1790, there was a serious riot at Brest on account of the punishment meted out to a drunken sailor. The popular clubs started an agitation and the Assembly actually thanked the local Jacobin club for its interference. And the hated clauses of the penal code were repealed.[3]

Particular grievances undoubtedly acted as an irritant, both to the soldiers and the sailors, during the early phases of the revolution. Yet these were transmuted with astonishing speed and success into a fervour of political emotion, so that the armed forces of the *ancien régime* present the only grand-scale example in history of the rank and file of an entire army

[1] *Cambridge Modern History*, 'The French Revolution', pp. 400, 401.
[2] Mathiez, *La Révolution française* (Collection Armand Collin), vol. i, p. 98.
[3] *Cambridge Modern History*, 'The French Revolution', p. 193.

and navy going over to a revolution without the previous disintegrating effect of a disastrous war, and against the influence of the majority among the officers. What were the special factors that can account for this unique happening?

All critics seem to be agreed that the discipline and military efficiency of the Royal Army was of a high order and, given the eight years' term of enlistment, the conditions for making an impersonal political instrument of the army were clearly favourable. Moreover, the proportion of officers to men, roughly 1 to 19, as mentioned above, was relatively high. These advantages were offset to a very considerable extent by the French soldier's environment. Unlike the modern soldier he did not live in barracks, but was billeted on the civilian population. And as regiments frequently stayed for years in one locality, he had every opportunity to forge strong emotional and perhaps economic links among the civilian population and to hold on throughout his service with the colours to a civilian point of view. Officers of the Dauphiné Regiment, for instance, pointed out that their regiment had been stationed for ten years in Provence and complained of this as a definite cause of disintegration. Indeed, Bouillé, the White French general who organized the flight to Varennes, was so impressed with this danger that he referred to it in an official letter, expressing the wish that at all costs troops should not be kept long among the same inhabitants but rather shifted frequently from one locality to another.[1] It is also worthy of note that many of the Gardes Françaises, who at the outset of the revolution proved one of the most unreliable regiments from a Royalist point of view, were married to Parisian working-class women. There was said to be a secret society in this regiment whose members were pledged to obey no orders directed against the Assembly. In other ways too the French Army seems to have had special opportunities for contact with the civil population. Soldiers were apparently allowed to go home to help with the harvest. The effect of this customary leave during the summer of 1789 on the political temper of the troops was explosive:

'Agitation became general throughout the garrisons after the October Days. Up till then the officers had succeeded in preventing the circulation of pamphlets, each more inflammatory than the other, which every post brought to the regiments. But the harvesters returning on October the 15th related to their comrades all the extraordinary things which were happening, above all in Paris.'[2]

It seems more likely that the returning harvesters would relate what they had seen in the provinces of the break-up of the old feudal estates and the frequent and exciting seizures of land by their own kith and kin among the peasants. But either the extraordinary events in Paris, or the equally extra-

---

[1] Hauterive, *L'armée sous la révolution*, p. 96.
[2] Hartmann, *Les Officiers de l'armée royale et la révolution*, p. 131.

ordinary events in the country, as painted by their comrades, would prove intoxicating propaganda.

The bearing of this question of contact with the civil population on the temper of an army was referred to in the previous chapter. It is important here to carry the discussion a little further. Since all politicians who might wish to use an army to deal with political unrest have striven hard to prevent contact, it would appear that experience shows it to be a serious disintegrating influence. Conversely, politicians of another school, jealous lest the army should be used by the government for the suppression of freedom, have insisted upon its intermingling with the civil population. Thus the English lawyer Blackstone laid it down, almost with the emphasis of an axiom, that 'the soldiers should live intermingled with the people; no separate camp, no barracks, no inland fortresses should be allowed'.[1]

It is interesting, in making this point about the importance of an 'aseptic army' from the standpoint of a *status quo* government, to compare the contemporary English position with that of France. Until the French wars, the small standing army in England was housed mainly in taverns; but when the exhilarating winds from France began blowing a contagion of political unrest across the Channel, this method was felt to be too dangerous. In 1792 the Home Office made an investigation of the temper and dispositions of troops in the manufacturing areas. It was reported that it was a 'dangerous measure to keep troops in the manufacturing towns in their present dispersed state and, unless barracks could be established for them where they could be kept under the eyes of their officers, it would be prudent to quarter them in the towns and villages of the vicinity, from whence, in case of emergency, they would act with much greater effect.' Pitt, fully realizing the truth of this contention, altered the entire billeting system and segregated the troops in barracks dotted all over England. In 1796 there was an enlightening if acid debate on the whole subject in the House of Commons. Windham emphasized the desirability of isolating troops and asserted that the Government should act on the maxim of the French comedian: 'If I cannot make you dumb, I will make him deaf.' Fox, taking him up with bitter sarcasm, suggested that perhaps foreign mercenaries who could hear but not understand might best answer the Government's purpose.[2] Close contact with the civil population is, then, by fairly general admission, a very serious danger to discipline in times of unrest, and the French Army, as we have seen, had special opportunities for making this contact, both before the revolution and during its opening phases.

The attitude of the officers at the start of the revolution must also be counted in, as already suggested, among the special factors which pro-

[1] Quoted by Hammond, *The Town Labourer* (Longmans), p. 83.

[2] For the position in England, *vide* Hammond, *The Town Labourer* (Longmans) pp. 83 sq.

moted unrest. Between March and September 1789 there were, for instance, some 300 food riots.[1] Little or no effort was made to suppress these owing, at any rate to a considerable extent, to the unwillingness of the officers at that early period to associate themselves with severe measures either against their own men, or against the populace. The effect of this policy on weakening the morale of the troops in regard to police duties, which have always been considered as one of the ultimate if unpleasant functions of an army, must have been considerable. It was perhaps enhanced by the decree of the Assembly handing over the maintenance of internal order to the National Guard and forbidding the employment of regular troops for this duty, except on the express requisition of the municipal authority. As the revolution progressed and the soldiers became more and more deeply infected with political enthusiasm, the officers found to their bitter regret that their initial slackened hold could never be tightened again under the old conditions. Indiscipline increased alarmingly, until by 1791 a condition of affairs approaching anarchy was prevalent both in the army and in the navy. The riots at Brest and Toulon have already been described; they were typical of the attitude of the rank and file, both in the army and the navy. The Assembly at this stage seems to have oscillated between attempts to protect the officers in the re-establishmeut of discipline and support of the excited soldiers. In the army, committees of soldiers sprang up in every regiment, corresponded with the political societies in Paris or elsewhere, received and distributed revolutionary news-sheets and pamphlets, and interfered in every way they could with any unpopular regimental measure or custom. The troopers of the Royal Champagne Regiment, for instance, refused to recognize a sub-lieutenant who had been appointed by the King. Men of the Poitou Regiment arrested their colonel. At La Fere and Stenay the soldiers robbed the regimental money chest.[2]

Trouble over the allotment of the regimental funds seems to have been pretty general and sometimes well justified. In August 1790, the Assembly on the one hand dissolved the regimental committees, but on the other hand appointed inspecting officers to check the accounts for the previous six years in the presence of delegates appointed from the ranks. This led to severe disorders, because the men considered the regimental funds, out of which they were paid, equipped, and clothed, to be theirs by right, and the inspection showed that there was much mismanagement and many unexplained deficits. In some regiments the officers went the length of subscribing among themselves to make good these deficits. But at Nancy an inquiry of this kind provoked a bitter mutiny. The men of three regiments

[1] But cf. p. 146 *infra*.
[2] For instances of indiscipline *vide* Hartmann, *Les Officiers de l'armée royale et la Révolution*, pp. 156 sq.; also Mathiez, *La Révolution française*, vol. i, pp. 98 sq., *La Victoire en l'an II*, p. 44.

of the garrison arrested a couple of officers who had been sent to check the accounts. Negotiations for the officers' release were followed by misunderstandings, and in the upshot Bouillé, who was then in command at Metz, marched to Nancy with 4,000 of his troops. The mutineers agreed to the terms proposed by Bouillé, but firing broke out, apparently without orders as on these occasions so frequently happens, and the men at Nancy decided that they had been betrayed. Three hundred soldiers of a Swiss regiment fought a pitched battle against Bouillé. They were of course beaten and twenty-one of them were sentenced to death or the galleys.[1] These Nancy mutineers were naturally held up to public opinion as martyrs by the revolutionary leaders of the Left.

The disintegrating effect on the old army of events of this kind was enormously strengthened by the general position in regard to the corps of officers between 1789 and the final fall of the monarchy in 1792. During that period various decrees were made, all with the nominal assent of the King which fundamentally altered the character of the officers' corps. The first of these was issued in February 1790, when it was ruled that all citizens should be eligible for all military employments, that the purchase of commissions should be abolished, and that every officer must swear to obey the constitution and wear the tricolour cockade. Later in that year the system of promotion was altered. Commissions were thrown open to competitive examination, three out of every four sub-lieutenancies being allotted in this way and the fourth as a nomination from the ranks. The higher grades of regimental officer were to be appointed by seniority, but the appointment of general officers was still left to some extent in the hands of the King. In addition, the power of the officers was further undermined by a decree made in April 1791, which expressly permitted soldiers to attend political meetings when not on duty.[2]

The whole position of the army, and in particular that of the officers, was under discussion in the Assembly during the spring of that year. By this time members of the Assembly justly suspected the loyalty to the new regime of a great proportion of the officers and, in order to hold these under the constitution, it was decreed that a new and more stringent oath should be administered. This was the second military oath mentioned above. The decree was signed on June the 15th. A week later the King himself made nonsense of this oath. By arrangement with General Bouillé, he fled from Paris during the night and made for Varennes with the intention of using Bouillé's command as a base for a drive to recover his lost powers. The consternation caused by the flight to Varennes was expressed by the Assembly in a third and yet more stringent and explicit military oath. All mention of the King was omitted and officers were required to swear to

[1] Spenser Wilkinson, *The French Army before Napoleon*, p. 110.
[2] Ibid., pp. 112, 113.

employ the arms entrusted to their hands for the defence of the country and to maintain the constitution decreed by the National Assembly against all its enemies within and without, etc. The effect of this third oath was decisive. On the one hand, those officers who were either actively sympathetic to the new regime, or cared more about their professional career than about politics, took the oath and thereby found themselves bound by a definite promise of allegiance to the revolution. This standpoint is well illustrated by a comment made later by Bonaparte whilst analysing his feeling to the new order at this stage:

'Until then, if I had been given an order to train my guns on the people, I don't doubt but that habit, development, education, the name of the King, would have made me obey. But once I had sworn the oath to the nation, I would have acknowledged the nation only.'[1]

On the other hand, those officers who could not bring themselves to take this oath had no alternative but resignation. It is perhaps worth noting that they were allotted a pension which was worth a quarter of their pay. The oath was refused by 1,500, and before the end of 1791 a further 2,000 had gone,[2] all apparently to join the émigrés' army across the eastern frontiers. The emigration continued even after war was declared, 598 leaving between April and July 1792.[3] The result in the navy was similar. In January 1792, of the officers inscribed at Brest, 361 were found absent without leave. Out of a total of 640, 210 only were actually at their posts.[4] It is therefore a matter of the simplest arithmetic to show that by the summer of 1792, the French Army had lost half of its entire corps of officers. This purge had two results of very great importance in throwing the army into the hands of the revolution.

In the first place, it opened the ranks of the officers' corps to an entirely new type of man. Since half the old-style officers had gone, the question of replacement was of course vital, and gave much anxiety to the Assembly. It was discussed in October 1791, and a decree made, which finally came into force early in 1792, by which half of the vacant sub-lieutenancies were to be filled by N.C.O.'s and the other half by National Guards. Exactly what arrangements were made to fill vacancies in the higher ranks is not clear, but in effect, during that and the succeeding year, the army came to be officered and commanded, either by convinced political adherents of the new regime, some of whom showed real talent for soldiering, by military adventurers like General Dumouriez, or by solid professional soldiers, many of them men who had risen from the ranks, whose chief care was to do their job well for the sake of their professional career. From the counter-

[1] Hartmann, *Les Officiers de l'armée royale et la révolution*, p. 292.

[2] Spenser Wilkinson, *The French Army before Napoleon*, pp. 115, 116.

[3] Ibid., p. 117.

[4] Tramond, *Manuel d'histoire maritime de la France*, p. 555.

145

revolutionary standpoint, a general like Bouillé understood well the danger of this reorganization. He had himself emigrated, because he could scarcely do otherwise after arranging the flight to Varennes, but he objected strongly to emigration on principle. He wanted the Royalist officers to remain with their regiments, no doubt so that they might be on the spot to make use of any opportunity that might arise for a counter-revolutionary drive. He probably considered, and correctly, that officers could serve the counter-revolution much better if they remained in France than if they went abroad to swell the ranks of an emigré army.[1]

The second result of the officers' purge was psychological. The émigré officers had laid themselves open to the charge of being traitors to their country, a charge which could be used with smashing effect by the propagandists of the Left once the nation was involved in war. For the soldiers' revolutionary loyalty and enthusiasm had been enormously stimulated by the fear of foreign invasion which had bred in them a new patriotism and an unquenchable ardour to defend the freshly won liberties of France. The French private realized that for the first time in his long history he was being exhorted to spend his blood in his own cause, for the sake of a country in which he and his friends and his relatives in the towns and villages all had a share, a country which at last had won the right to ask him for his life. And his answer, during those precarious years when half Europe was in arms against him and his own generals frequently failed him through inefficiency or betrayal, was almost always loyal and unhesitating. A less glorious and spectacular, but perhaps in detail hardly less important, clue to his feelings is provided by the assertion that throughout the first phases of the revolution, when anarchy reigned in the army in almost every other respect, he and his fellows performed with willing discipline the difficult task allotted to them of convoying grain to the towns, and preventing its export on the northern frontiers, as if they realized that to ensure the feeding of the populace was a primary revolutionary duty which had been laid upon them.[2]

The French Revolution was, of course, a long-term revolution and this, perhaps, is the underlying cause, not only of the swing-over of the army to the developing revolutionary regime, but also of the technique by which this transference was effected. There was no final and irrevocable parting of the ways until the storming of the Tuileries on the 10th of August 1792, more than three years after the fall of the Bastille. Until that date it had never been formally and as it were officially admitted that the King and the Revolution faced one another across an unbridgeable political breach. Louis never raised his standard like Charles I at Nottingham. He could not, therefore, become an open rallying-point for the counter-revolutionary forces, and these had to content themselves with underground obstruction

[1] Hartmann, *Les Officiers de l'armée royale et la révolution*, p. 294.
[2] Hauterive, *L'Armée sous la révolution*, pp. 72, 86.

in France, or resort to the émigré army across the eastern frontiers, an organization which Louis himself was forced officially to disclaim. This position reacted on the French Army in ways favourable to the revolution. In the first place, the soldiers were never driven by the clash of arms to an ultimate choice between King and people. During the Bastille rising they were withdrawn from Paris, and the troops who so gallantly and uselessly defended the Tuileries in August 1792 were mercenary Swiss and not Frenchmen. This meant that there was no real physical disintegration of units. The transference could be effected within the framework of the old cadres and organization. All that was needed was education in the new ideals. The army's character was fundamentally altered by the trend of events, but its continuity was never lost; and when the King was finally dethroned and the revolution committed to its ultimate course, the leaders found that the army had already been shaped, under the influence of the happenings of the previous three years, to a character suitable for the defence of the newborn republic.

It is interesting to contrast this process in France with the very different impact of events on the Russian Army of 1917. The Russian soldier and the Russian officer were faced at two separate points in time with a definite choice of allegiance, on the basis of an armed clash between an existing regime and the revolutionary people. In March they had to choose between support of the Tsarist Government and the bourgeois democratic revolution. The rank and file of the Petrograd garrison preferred open mutiny to an attack on the forces of the insurrection. The Tsarist Government fell because its soldiers had failed it, and the army at large transferred its allegiance at once to the newly formed Provisional Government. The officers, who themselves were mostly discontented with the Tsarist regime, followed suit without serious protest. Thus, throughout the spring and summer the army remained to all intents and purposes intact and at the orders of a bourgeois-democratic government. The position at this stage was not unlike the position in France before the outbreak of the revolutionary wars. A natural exuberance of indiscipline on the side of the men went hand in hand with a political marking-time on the part of the officers.

Three factors rapidly altered this situation during the course of the summer and autumn and finally rendered impossible any gradualist reconstruction of the army on the lines adopted by the French. The first of these factors was the propaganda of the extreme Left, who wanted to push the revolution at once beyond its bourgeois-democratic phase and on to a complete socialist outcome. The Left realized that this could not be done unless, at the critical time, the army was ripe to disintegrate in the hands of the Provisional Government. Unlike the French Left, it was therefore to their interest to work for disintegration rather than a revolutionary reconstruction. The second factor was the unpopularity of the war which in itself acted as a disintegrating agent; it produced a grave collapse of the army's old morale without giving any corresponding return in a new revolutionary morale. The third factor was the second deliberate choice of allegiance, in the face of armed revolt, which the army had to make when the Bolshevik Insurrection broke out in November. And here the army split as between officers and rank and file. The men went with the Bolsheviks, the officers either disappeared, as happened in Petrograd, or fought the revolt until they were beaten and dispersed as in Moscow. The upshot was that the Bolsheviks, on taking power, found themselves with an officerless army on their hands, and an army, moreover, whose morale was in such an advanced state of dissolution that nothing could be done to recast it in the mould of its old organization. The mouldering framework and the last stays of discipline crumbled away during the difficult weeks which succeeded the November Insurrection. It was thus impossible in Russia to control disintegration and combine it concurrently with revolutionary reconstruction. The Bolsheviks were therefore confronted by a task of military reorganization far more formidable than that which the French had had to face after 1792. The problem of reorganization, however, does not fall within the scope of the present chapter. It is here only necessary to show that disintegration, if it has to be carried beyond a certain point, presents a revolutionary government with difficulties which can only be solved by administrative genius and great political determination. For different reasons, as has been already shown, the German Social Democratic Government after 1918 found itself also faced with a complete physical dissolution of the old army—and proved quite unequal to the succeeding task of revolutionary reconstruction.

If the relatively slow development of the French Revolution permitted the retention of the old organization and made it possible to effect in a more or less orderly fashion an adequate change of personnel in the ranks of the officers' corps, it also gave to the revolutionary leaders an unrivalled opportunity to educate the army deliberately from the standpoint of producing a new revolutionary morale. At first, this education seems to have been undertaken unofficially and spontaneously by agents of the Jacobin Club. The soldiers flocked to join the affiliated societies of the Jacobins who deluged them with propaganda. Quarrels on this account made an added cause of antagonism between them and their officers in the first years of the revolution. As Mathiez has remarked: 'The new regime was strengthened but discipline did not fail to suffer.'[1] In September 1790 the Assembly,

---

[1] *La Victoire en l'an II*, p. 45; *vide* also p. 240 on the influence of the Jacobin Club in the army: 'The Clubs put . . . military matters in the first rank of their preoccupations. . . . The soldiers showed with pride their Jacobin membership cards; they maintained close relations with their brothers at home, and the Club read to the people the numerous letters which it received from the army.'

frightened lest anarchy was getting too firm a hold, refused the men the right to join political clubs, but six months later this move had proved so unpopular that permission to join clubs was again given. Moreover, agents from the parent club in Paris visited the regiments in person, castigated any lapses of enthusiasm, and saw to it that local disloyalty or indifference was forced upon the attention of the Assembly and the Government. Their methods are vividly illustrated by an extract from the minutes of the club for the 11th of July 1791. M. de Franqueville, who has been on tour in the east, is at the tribune:

'I took my leave of you, gentlemen, on June the 22nd, and since that time I have toured the frontiers of Lorraine and of Alsace. Patriotism is general. I have, however, one denunciation to make to you. The Chasseurs de Normandie have sworn to their colonel to obey him blindly when it becomes a question of marching on Paris to overthrow the constitution. These soldiers are only half a league from the frontiers, and I think it is important to recall from such a position men who are so disaffected.'[1]

The influence of these agents was considerable since the relations between the Jacobin Club and the Assembly were very close, though not easy to define. The part played by the local Jacobin Club after the naval riot at Brest has, for instance, already been mentioned.

It is perhaps worth noting in passing that this method of influencing armed forces during the opening phase of a revolution was also tried tentatively during the French Revolution of 1848. The clubs were even provided with secret funds for this purpose by Ledru Rollin, the Radical Minister of the Interior in the Provisional Government.[2]

As the Great Revolution developed, the activities of the Jacobin agents were enormously reinforced, and probably even to a large extent superseded, by the practice of sending round official 'representatives on mission.' This proved one of the most brilliant inventions of revolutionary method. It has been copied more or less closely in every serious revolutionary army since. The Russians, as we have seen, used it during 1917, but in their case it had an unexpectedly conservative influence, and must have contributed not a little to the causes which made it necessary for the Russian Left to work for further disintegration of the armed forces rather than for a positive resurgence of morale based on enthusiasm for the new order. The Bolsheviks, however, used the method again in building up the Red Army, and in their hands it was once more successful and of profound importance. It was also used by the Spanish Government during the civil war. In regard to its use in the Red Army and in Spain, it will be referred to in more detail in a later chapter.

The French representatives were members of the National Assembly and

---

[1] Aulard, *La Société des Jacobins*, vol. iii, p. 1.
[2] Quentin Bauchart, *La Crise sociale de 1848*, pp. 228–30.

their activities were not confined to the armed forces. They were attached to every provincial unit of administration, acted as liaison officers between the central and local governments, and were expected to see to it that the latter functioned on lines approved by Paris. In the later stages of the revolution they seem to have been responsible both to the Convention and to the Committee of Public Safety. So far as the army was concerned, their executive power was very great. In the late summer of 1792, after the fall of the King, Pache, then Minister for War, sent round commissioners with power to suspend and dismiss officers suspected of counter-revolutionary sympathies, and both he and his successor Bouchotte had their agents canvassing the soldiers in order to detach them from their old officers, and even spent public funds on supplying the troops with revolutionary newspapers. After July 1793, four representatives were appointed to each army and their activities increased. St. Just and Lebas, for instance, were with the Army of the Rhine throughout the winter of 1793. Discipline was in a bad way; the commissioners re-established it somehow. The pay of the troops was in arrears; the commissioners levied nine million francs from the rich of Strasbourg, of which six were allotted to the army, two for the improvement of the fortifications, and one for the relief of the poor of the city. The army was without adequate footgear; ten thousand boots were requisitioned from the well-to-do and delivered within forty-eight hours. Moreover, St. Just and Lebas made a point of going under fire and sharing the hardships of the soldiers; and they appear to have helped the generals, Hoche and Pichegru, with the plan of the offensive which was designed to recapture the Vosges and drive the enemy back across the Rhine. The spirit in which they approached their task is well shown in a report sent in by them to the central government:

'We have resolved to seek out, reward and promote merit, but to hunt down crimes, no matter who may be those who have committed them. All the chief officers and the agents of the government are ordered within three days to redress the just grievances of the soldiers—after this period we shall ourselves hear their complaints; and we shall make examples with a more severe justice than the army has yet known.'[1]

It is not suggested that all the representatives on mission showed the courage and ability, the stern but fair sense of revolutionary justice and necessity of Lebas and St. Just. A few failed dismally, as, for example, the couple who were sent to liquidate the Girondist disorders in Bordeaux, but

[1] Wallon, *Les Représentants du peuple en mission*, vol. iv, p. 176. *Vide* also Kerr, *The Reign of Terror*, p. 280.

For a short general description of the work of the representatives on mission, *vide* Hauterive, *L'Armée sous la révolution*, p. 318, also Phipps, *The Armies of the First Republic*, vol. i, p. 21. His view is apt to be antagonistic. The standard work on the Representatives is Wallon's *Les Représentants du peuple en mission* in five volumes. This gives a detailed picture of all their activities with the various armies.

preferred the fleshpots and gaieties of the city to their revolutionary job. Others, like the notorious Collot and Fouché, who were sent to punish Lyons in the autumn of 1793 for its rebellion during that summer, super-imposed a brutal and vindictive terrorism on the necessary severity of revolutionary justice. Others again seem to have shared all the blundering inefficiency of certain generals, interfering with tactics and strategy to the detriment of plans of campaign. But, by and large, there can be little doubt that one of the most important factors in the success of France in trans-forming the old Royalist Army into a new Army of the Republic, fit at last to fend off her external foes and quell rebellion within her borders, was due to the invention of this system of the representatives on mission.

Before taking leave of the French Army, it is perhaps worth noting one further, if minor, method used by the revolutionary leaders to break up the old allegiance of the troops and instil into them a new loyalty. This was the organization of fêtes and confederations in Paris and other towns, where groups of soldiers brought from all over France could join with their civilian comrades in enthusiastic rejoicing over the great deeds of the revolution. The confederations were associations of the National Guard and the soldiers of the regular army. They began in the south towards the end of 1789 and reached huge dimensions. In May 1790, for instance, there was a federal meeting at Lyons to which the National Guard sent 50,000 delegates. The fêtes organized in Paris were on an even larger scale. It has been estimated that more than 300,000 persons were present at the July the 14th celebrations in 1790. A critic of the army, commenting on the effect of this entertainment, has written: 'But above all, the soldiers sent to Paris for the Fête de la Fédération brought back from the capital . . . an incurable distrust of their officers; their return was the signal for general mutiny in the army.'[1]

This method seems to be peculiar to France, although no doubt the various congresses and conferences to which representatives of the soldiers' soviets were invited in Russia would have a somewhat similar effect. It was tried again in Paris in April 1848, when Lamartine brought the army back to the capital, ostensibly to fraternize with the National Guard and the people during the celebration of the Fête de la Fraternité.[2] The actual motive for this was, however, almost certainly different. Lamartine had his own private reasons for wishing to get the soldiers back into Paris. He was afraid of the Left, and probably believed that the presence of regular troops would have a stabilizing influence at that stage on the effervescent politics of the Paris populace.

It may be as well, perhaps, to sum up very shortly the various factors which made for the successful turnover of the army to the revolution. The

[1] Hartmann, Les Officiers de l'armée royale et la révolution, p. 165.
[2] Lamartine, The Revolution of 1848 (English trans., 1849), pp. 467 sq.

practical grievances of the officers and men at the start, the special chances which the French soldiers enjoyed of making contacts with the civil population, the long-term development of the revolution itself which allowed the army to swing over without utter dislocation, and gave the leaders the time and opportunity to work out methods for combining the restoration of discipline with an education in revolutionary ardour; all these diverse factors contributed their share to the astonishing result.

9

FRATERNIZATION

Conditions which favour fraternization—its effect on the morale of troops.

There is one special piece of mechanism designed to promote an *ad hoc* disintegration of armed forces, namely, fraternization. This has been touched upon and must now be discussed in more detail.

Fraternization must be distinguished from the general propaganda which goes on whenever and wherever soldiers are in contact with the civil population. It refers to definite attempts on the part of civilians to seduce soldiers from their duty when they are under arms for a specific purpose, for example, in order to suppress a riot or an insurrection. It is, of course, only an effective weapon when the troops are already hesitating in their allegiance, and if, at such times, soldiers are themselves not only hesitating but are hesitatingly led, the effect is deadly.

This is what occurred during the Paris insurrection preceding the fall of the Bastille. Bésenval, who was in command of the troops in Paris but apparently under the orders of the Duc de Broglie, had some 30,000 men at his disposal. This should have given him adequate strength to cope with an insurrection if he had taken steps in time. But he seems to have been uncertain what line of action the government at Versailles would wish him to follow.[1] He therefore decided on tactics of inactivity which the event proved anything but masterly. He concentrated almost all his troops on the Champs de Mars, where the Eiffel Tower now stands, then well outside the centre of the city. Here the soldiers, gloomy and troubled, were left with no definite job to do which might have taken their minds off political speculation. The only troops retained in the centre of Paris were the Gardes Françaises

---

[1] Accounts of the government tactics during the Bastille Rising do not tally in detail. Michelet, *The French Revolution*, is flamboyant but gives many interesting details. A clear account is in Kropotkin, *La Grande révolution*, pp. 101 sq.

For the defection of the Gardes Françaises, *vide* Michelet, *The French Revolution* (English ed., 1896), pp. 120, 127; also Madelin, *The French Revolution* (English ed.), p. 71.

and these were the very units where disaffection was most rife. They should have been withdrawn days before, away from the influence of the populace. The Gardes had special practical grievances of their own to fan their revolutionary sympathy—they had already broken out in a mutiny and this Bésenval knew—and special links with the Paris people to whose women many of them were attached. Bésenval contented himself with having them confined to barracks, a stupid precaution since being shut up together with nothing to do but talk would naturally inflame discontent, and an inadequate precaution, since they seem to have broken out of barracks whenever they wished, and to have spent their days in fraternizing with the civilian population. Owing, then, to this uncertainty as to what should be the task of the main body of troops at the Champs de Mars, the Paris populace had a free hand to influence the already dubious temper of the Gardes and win them over to open revolt. When the attack on the Bastille was launched, it was the Gardes who did most of the fighting for the insurgents and stiffened their ranks with trained men.

To withdraw from the infected area has been proved a correct procedure, but the withdrawal should have been complete and made with a view to keeping the soldiers in quarantine until it was considered feasible to reoccupy the disturbed areas by force. It was obviously absurd to leave the most unreliable troops in the heart of Paris waiting to swell the ranks of the insurgents. Bésenval in fact did little more than hand over a picked force of potential mutineers gratis to the people of Paris.

The troops were mishandled in somewhat similar manner at the outset of the February Revolution of 1848. It will be recalled that this revolution developed out of a dispute with the Government about the holding in Paris of one of those great political banquets which, owing to the prevention of more direct methods, had been organized all over France as an ingenious means of expressing discontent. The banquet was cancelled owing to the intervention of the Government, but the dispute had aroused Paris to passionate excitement. Crowds were agitating through the streets, and the revolution was finally exploded by a stray musket-shot, fired perhaps by one of the soldiers who were lined up to hold back a mass of demonstrators outside the Ministry for Foreign Affairs. Now, the Government had concentrated 55,000 troops in or around Paris. It was February and particularly inclement weather. Yet the soldiers were kept under arms in the streets, inactive, and without proper canteen or bivouacking arrangements, for forty-eight hours. When the critical hour came, they were chilled through with standing in the mud, exhausted by hunger, and in addition, harassed by political doubt. For the civil population had adopted the friendliest attitude towards them and in the conditions fraternization was developing rapidly. It was owing mainly to the hesitant attitude of Louis Philippe himself that no decision had been taken as to how or when the troops should be thrown against the massing insurgents. No doubt it is to the credit of the King's humanity that he was finally persuaded to leave Paris secretly and let his throne go by default rather than allow his generals to give orders which could only result in serious bloodshed. But from the standpoint of tactics to combat a revolution, the attitude he had imposed upon them during the critical hours was disastrous; and it is possible that by the time he took his final decision to go, it would in any case have been too late to retrieve the morale of the troops.[1]

The experience of Thermidor, though on a much smaller scale, is also worth recalling. When that insurrection broke out against the Robespierrist Government, the Paris Commune, which was loyal to Robespierre, called out those sections of the National Guard on which it could rely and collected them in the Place de l'Hôtel de Ville. There the sectionaries were left to stand about through a long afternoon and evening without orders and with no real knowledge of the cause for which they had been called out or the interests they were being asked to defend. Robespierre, who might still have rallied their enthusiasm to fever heat, for some unexplained reason made no attempt to address them, and no other of the Robespierrists, at any rate at the time, seems to have thought this important. Finally, the guardsmen, bored, hungry, and bewildered, began to drift off to their homes for supper; and when the insurgent troops of the Convention had collected and it became necessary to defend the Hôtel de Ville in arms, it was found that the square was almost empty of loyal guards.[2] From the standpoint of an existing government faced by impending insurrection, it is madness to keep troops standing to for many hours in the streets and uncertain of the use to which their arms may be put. 'Inaction', as Lamartine said, commenting on February 1848, 'is the great bane of the morale of armies.'[3] The first rule for combating insurrection is that soldiers should be given such positive tasks to perform that failure to obey orders can only be construed as open mutiny, a decisive breaking of their allegiance which many may hesitate to take.

Thiers, historian of the great Revolution and a master of counter-revolutionary strategy, understood acutely this problem of the vulnerable morale of troops who are under arms in the streets of towns in disturbed conditions. He himself explained his theory of how to tackle the problem to the Cambon brothers who passed it on to Recoully, from whose book it is here quoted. It will be seen that Thiers is taking a broad view of the proper method to combat urban insurrection in general and in particular the insurrection of a capital city:

[1] This account follows Lamartine, *The Revolution of 1848* (English trans., 1849), pp. 56–84.
[2] Kerr, *The Reign of Terror*, p. 481.
[3] *The Revolution of 1848* (English trans., 1849), p. 79.

'In his opinion, no insurrection could win the final victory, whatever its initial successes might have been, as long as there was in existence a government determined to fight it, supported by troops that could be relied upon. ... The essential prerequisite was not the capital, as Charles X and Louis Philippe believed, but the army.

'With the army it is always possible to win back the capital. But, on the other hand, when the army can no longer be relied upon, all is lost. Now a body of troops left in contact too long with the revolutionaries runs the risk of disintegrating. It must be snatched from such contact and reorganized in order to be able to engage in a victorious struggle afterwards.

'Thiers gave numerous examples of this: Charles V, Henry III, Mazarin, and lastly Louis Philippe who, in 1848, could quite easily have vacated Paris with his troops and returned later on. This is what Windischgraetz actually did in Vienna in the same year and Radetsky at Milan.[1]

Thiers, of course, had a large-scale opportunity to test his theory in action, and under special conditions rather favourable to his opponents than otherwise, in his dealing with the Paris Commune of 1871.[2] The final outcome was a brilliant if utterly ruthless vindication of his plan.

Thiers was well aware that the revolutionary situation in Paris was ripe and his first plan was to gain control of the cannon belonging to the National Guard before any outbreak should occur. From a tactical standpoint, he was badly placed at this juncture. The Confederations of the Paris National Guard were the focal points of discontent and, by the terms of the Prussian armistice, the National Guard had been allowed to retain its arms. In addition to small arms, the Guard were well enough supplied with guns. These had been founded or procured during the siege and most of them had been paid for by the Parisians themselves, and were therefore in a special sense their own property and proudly cherished. It was obviously impossible to leave parks of artillery in the hands of potential insurgents. By some means or other the guns must therefore be seized, and brought for safe custody to concentration points controlled by regular troops. Thiers had 20,000 miscellaneous troops in Paris and he counted on 18,000 loyal National Guards.[3] The regulars were mostly provincial conscripts, young and indifferent soldiers. Thiers, however, seems at this period to have believed, in the face of military advice, that he could rely on the regular troops sufficiently to march them by night through the streets of the resentful city, seize the various batteries by sur-

---

[1] *The Third Republic* (English trans.), p. 32.

[2] This discussion is based on Jellinek, *The Paris Commune of 1871*. *Vide* also Lissagaray, *La Commune de 1871*.

[3] Jellinek, *The Paris Commune of 1871*, p. 104.

prise attacks, and haul the captured guns back through the city to the concentration points he had arranged. The result conclusively proved him wrong. The National Guard throughout Paris rallied to the defence of their guns almost to a man; out of the 18,000 on whose loyalty Thiers had counted, less than 600 remained faithful to him.[1] And regiments of regulars, loathing the whole affair and sympathizing with the Guard, refused to obey orders to fire. The capture of the great battery of 171 guns at Montmartre was the tactical key to the success of Thiers's plan. His troops set out at three in the morning. They surprised the guard post and surrounded the guns without bloodshed. Then they stood to arms by their prize waiting for horses and gun-carriages which incompetently enough had not arrived. That wait was fatal. For three hours the men stood to arms in the raw dawn fog without rations. Then the Montmartrois began to come out on their daily tasks. They made friends with the soldiers and offered them breakfast. When Lecomte, who was in charge of the expedition, realized that his men were fraternizing he had a selection arrested. Then a crowd of women, children, and National Guards swept against the half-hearted troops; and Lecomte lost his head. He ordered the troops to fire. There was no answering volley. He gave the order again. Then the troops turned up the butts of their rifles and yelled 'Long live the Republic!' The crowd answered with 'Long live the Line!'[2]

Thiers managed to retrieve this initial error with brilliant decision and strength of mind. Before the troops had time to realize what had been happening to them politically during that night and morning of turmoil, he ordered a general retreat on Versailles. He gave the insurgents no time to follow up their initial advantage in demoralizing the soldiers. Before these could be effectively detached and won over to the insurrection, the bewildered regiments were trailing away out of Paris. He even ordered the evacuation of Fort Valerian, a key point on the road to Versailles, but the commander on the spot, fortunately as it turned out later for the Versaillese, deliberately omitted to execute the order. At Versailles, Thiers re-formed his shaken army, strengthened it with uncontaminated reinforcements, fed it handsomely, paid it well, and saw that it was kept completely segregated from doubtful civilian influences.[2] After a short period of intensive work on the army's morale, he felt sufficiently sure of its temper to try its mettle against Communard Paris. The city was invested in form, and for two months Thiers enthusiastically applied his soldiers to the task of reducing the capital of their own country by infantry engagements against the National Guard and by a ruthless bombardment of the suburbs and walls, a bombardment more brutal and intensive even than that of the Prussians. As the compassing callipers of the Versaillese army gradually closed about

---

[1] Jellinek, *The Paris Commune of 1871*, p. 115.   [2] Ibid., pp. 113, 114.

the centre of the city, Thiers did not hesitate even to throw his shells into its heart.[1]

There is no evidence that he had any difficulty with the morale of his troops once battle was engaged. Soldiers, like other men, so soon as they have actually begun serious fighting, are quickly sustained and made callous by the partisan relationships and emotions of 'one's own side', and less likely to be worried by heart-searchings in regard to the cause in which they are engaged than before they are in full action. This is a further psychological argument in support of the theory that rebellion is most surely, if bloodily, suppressed by massing troops away from the centre of unrest and then using so far as is possible the methods of professional warfare.

A somewhat analogous method, though on a much smaller scale, had been employed by Cavaignac with complete success in dealing with the 'June Days' of 1848, that bloody and despairing insurrection which followed on the closing down of the national workshops.[2] Cavaignac was given complete control of operations by the Provisional Government and he insisted on keeping his army intact at fixed concentration points outside the infected quarters of the city instead of attacking the insurgents piecemeal and at once in the traditional manner. This meant that, though the centre of Paris was held quite unchecked by the rebels for several days, when Cavaignac was ready, he had at his disposal fresh and uninfected troops fit to be used for strong and decisive attacks at the various tactical points. His plan had the full support of Lamartine whose vain romantic mind seems more than once to have cleared to a condition of shrewd practical intelligence during those chequered first six months of 1848.

A clear and large-scale example of the reverse method of keeping a garrison, as it were, at large inside a disturbed city, and the disastrous results which followed from a counter-revolutionary point of view, has already been illustrated in regard to the Russian Revolution of 1917. And it may perhaps be pointed out again that Bésenval's tactics in 1789 and Louis Philippe's in February 1848 were based on a similar misconception of a proper counter-revolutionary strategy.

Fraternization, then, is an important method for tampering with the morale of troops and thereby negativing their resistance to insurrection. It has been shown how the more clear-sighted revolutionaries worked for this technique during the revolution of March 1917 in Russia, considering it far more important to win over blocks of soldiers than to organize and arm rebel bands in order to pit them directly against the troops. But fraternization, as a rule, can only be used where the soldiers are dispersed in relatively small bodies in such a way that there can be personal contact between them and the insurgent population. It requires a general attitude of friend‐

---

[1] Jellinek, *The Paris Commune of 1871*, p. 183; *vide* also p. 182.
[2] *Vide* Lamartine, *The Revolution of 1848*, pp. 552, 553.

liness on the part of the populace towards the troops, and on the part of the troops, it presupposes the existence of a feeling of disgust, however vague, with their position as defenders of a hated regime. It implies any method of winning sympathy, from direct argument and persuasion to the generation by one means or another of that subtle emotional sense of an underlying community of sentiment and interests between troops and people—the atmosphere, in short, which has been so superbly rendered by Trotsky in his description of the streets of Petrograd quoted in a previous chapter.

10

THE POLITICAL CHARACTER OF ARMED FORCES

Various types of armed forces—the influence of composition and character on political vitality and alinement

The particular character of armed forces and their composition not only has an important bearing on the political attitude they are likely to adopt, but also throws a searching light on the system whose interests they are in fact enlisted to uphold. 'The structure of an army', wrote the Bolshevik general and military thinker Tuchachevsky, 'is determined on the one hand by the political aims which it pursues and on the other by the recruiting system which it employs.'[1] This raises the general question of the social material from which officers and men are drawn, and the further question as to whether long-service professional armies or short-service conscript armies are potentially more friable material from a political point of view.

In regard to the second point, thinkers on both sides, e.g. those who regard an army as the guarantee of liberty and fear its arbitrary misuse in the hands of a reactionary government, and those who frankly want it in order to support a conservative system, have reached a similar conclusion. From their different points of view they are agreed that a long-service professional army provides the surest defence for a conservative regime. A century and a half ago Major Cartwright, pioneer of English radicalism, pondered this question in regard to the British regular army of the time as opposed to a national militia. 'The great end of arming a militia', he wrote, 'is to defend the nation against foreign attacks, without exposing it at the same time to that danger to liberty which is justly to be apprehended from all other military establishments; a militiaman is, therefore, the most honourable of all soldiers.'[2] And again: 'A mere soldier, while he fortified

[1] Quoted by Wollenberg, *The Red Army*, p. 172.
[2] Extracts from the standing orders drawn up by Major Cartwright for the use of the Nottinghamshire Militia. (F. D. Cartwright, *The Life and Correspondence of Major Cartwright*, vol. ii, p. 328.)

London might undermine our liberties, and while he preserved the soil might destroy the constitution of our country.'[1]

Cartwright himself had good personal reason to fear the political complexion which a strong and reactionary government can impose upon its armed forces. He had for many years been a zealous and apparently most efficient officer of the Nottinghamshire Militia. In 1789, he was rash enough to attend a meeting to celebrate the fall of the Bastille. That same year he was due for promotion to the command of his regiment, but it was intimated to him that the Duke of Newcastle, in whose hands the preferment lay, could not, consistently with his political opinions, give him the vacant lieutenant-colonelcy. Cartwright was urged to resign his commission, but refused. It took the Government three years to discover a means to turn him out. They finally succeeded by bringing to bear an Act of Parliament which laid down that a field-officer may be discharged at the end of five years.[2]

Cartwright objected to a long-service regular army for the same reasons that Thiers, a military-political thinker from another camp, favoured it. Thiers, for instance, was strongly against the introduction of conscription in France when this was under discussion during the early days of the Third Republic. In his view it was liable 'to put combustible stuff in everyone's head and a gun to the shoulder of every socialist'. He wanted a professional army, 'firm, disciplined, capable of making us respected abroad and at home—very limited in number, but superior in quality'.[3] This was exactly the type of army built up in Germany some fifty years later during the first years of the Weimar Republic.

By the terms of the Peace Treaty, the Germans were forbidden to raise an army based on universal service; instead, they were permitted to maintain a small standing army recruited on a voluntary basis, with a twelve-year term of service for the rank and file and a twenty-five-year term for the officers.[4] In the hands of able commanders, the Reichswehr rapidly became a highly trained and efficient professional force, taught to regard itself as a caste apart, contemptuous of the governments which officially it served, out of touch with the civil population, and unsympathetic to the ideals of liberal and social democracy which were struggling for permanent expression in the nation's new life. In short, it had an exclusively and arrogantly profes-

---

[1] Extracts from Major Cartwright's *Aegis of the Military Energies of the Constitution*. (F. D. Cartwright, *The Life and Correspondence of Major Cartwright*, vol. i, p. 335.)

[2] F. D. Cartwright, *The Life and Correspondence of Major Cartwright*, vol. i, pp. 187–9.

[3] Rousset, *La France sous la Troisième République*, vol. i, p. 375.

[4] *Encyclopaedia Britannica*, 14th edit. s.v. Germany. The proportion of officers and N.C.O.'s to privates is interesting. In 1927 there were 4,291 officers, 20,671 N.C.O.'s, and 74,229 privates.

sional military character; and it has been cogently argued that this complete failure to fashion it into an expression of the Republic is one of the major factors in accounting for the ease with which Hitler later fastened the Nazi regime upon Germany.[1] It is one of the greater ironies of history that the main lineaments of the Reichswehr were originally traced by Mr. Lloyd George who, unfortunately, remembered too well the lessons he had read from the Napoleonic wars. After the defeat of Germany in 1807, the French had fixed a maximum strength for the various German armies which might not be exceeded. But they had omitted to make any rule about the length of service or the form of recruitment. The Germans, therefore, were able to short-circuit the limitation by passing men through the army for short periods only. Thus, within a few years the entire manhood of the nation had been trained to arms, but still within the limited military framework prescribed by Napoleon. Mr. Lloyd George, recalling what had happened after 1807, determined to make such a military revival technically impossible after 1918. Instead, he fell into another and a more disastrous snare.

Bénoist Méchin quotes a significant remark made by a colonel of the German General Staff to a member of the Inter-Allied Commission of Control:

'In designing the Reichswehr, in disembarrassing us of all the elements which go to democratize an army, compulsory service, reserve of officers, you have brought us back to the time of Frederick II. You thought you were making a professional army. You have made the army a vocation.'[2]

In his preference for the long-service professional army, from the point of view of a *status quo* government, Thiers overlooked one important argument in favour of conscript armies which modern anti-revolutionary practice has discovered. This is the device of calling up classes of men to the colours in order to hamstring whole sections of workers, who are thus obviously prevented from acting against the government in power unless they commit a definite act of mutiny. This was done during the great French strike of 1910 when the Government issued a mobilization decree, thereby bringing the strikers under the Minister for War as military servants. Transport workers were then assigned to their own jobs.[3] The same technique had been successfully tried in Italy in 1902 to combat a railway strike on the Mediterranean line. All the men who were reservists were mobilized and ordered to operate the road. Since they were under the articles of war, there was no alternative to obedience short of open mutiny.[4] A further example, already referred to, is the action of Ludendorff in calling up reservists from among the workers during the great Berlin strike of 1917.

[1] Cf. *infra*, pp. 227 sq.
[2] *Histoire de l'armée allemande*, vol. i, p. 18.
[3] Hiller, *The Strike*, p. 261.
[4] McClellan, *Modern Italy* (Princeton Univ. Press), p. 180.

THE POLITICAL CHARACTER OF ARMED FORCES

From a revolutionary position, this is a very important point to take into account when balancing out the pros and cons of various types of armed forces. It is, however, offset to a certain extent by the contention that workers drafted into the army under such conditions would make very doubtful material in the hands of a repressive government faced by a serious political clash.

The power to call up reservists to break strike or revolutionary action raises the question of the relation of the reservist to his trade union. The problem discovers in a particularly acute form the dual personality of the soldier as a unit in the military machine and as a citizen with civilian sympathies and obligations. Either he must break his military allegiance and risk the penalty attaching to mutiny, or he must betray his corporate loyalty as a member of his trade union. Owing partly to the danger and difficulty of this problem, the Left, at least in this country, set its face against a conscript army. In view, however, of the many possibilities of advantage, both political and psychological, to a progressive democracy in power, or to a Left party which seeks to attain power either by constitutional or revolutionary means, of a conscript army as opposed to a long-service professional army, this point of view seems hasty and perhaps ill-considered. From the standpoint of the Left, the ideal solution may well be a short-service democratic army, based on compulsory service, with special safeguards to regulate the calling up of reservists to deal with internal disputes. It is, however, admitted that such a solution would hardly appeal to governments pledged to maintain an existing system of society.

It is, unfortunately, not possible to apply the test of history in any sort of scientific manner to this question whether a conscript army might crack under revolutionary pressure where a professional army would hold firm, since contributing circumstances can never be excluded and have always influenced the result. A rough judgement, however, can be made by inference.

It has already been shown that contact with the civil population during the course of his military life is an important influence in undermining that conception of the impersonal instrument which has been set up for the soldier as his ideal mentality. Detailed examples of the effect of such contacts have been given in regard to the French Army of the *ancien régime*; and in modern times there can be no doubt at all that the disintegration of the Tsarist Army in 1917 and the German Imperial Army in 1918 was accelerated by the flood of recruits coming direct from their civil occupations to repair the wastage of war, a flood which almost completely obliterated the mental barriers between soldiers and people. The importance attached by politicians of the type of Pitt or Thiers to building up these barriers is strong evidence of their necessity in order to keep armies fit for the task of defending political systems which are under attack from the

163

masses. Now, it is obviously much harder to build a palisade between soldiers and people when the soldiers are under arms for a short period only,
and regard their military duty merely as an incident in their lives rather than
the exclusive purpose of their working years. The difference in mentality
between a professional soldier and a citizen under arms in a force of militia
type is fundamental. Modern conscript armies where the term of service is
anything from one to three years probably provide a compromise between
the two. It will be more interesting, however, to discuss the difference at its
greatest points of contrast, and for this purpose there can be no more significant illustration than to trace the fortunes of two characteristically citizen
armies, the traditional English militia and the French National Guard.

The English militia[1] grew out of the Assize of Arms of 1181 and the
Statute of Winchester of 1285. It was laid down that every freeman should
provide himself, or be provided at the county's expense, with certain
weapons and that he should be liable to serve in a military or police capacity on the summons of the sheriff of the county, at the King's command.
From the outset, therefore, the militia was subject to a sort of dual control
which served to emphasize its citizen character. On the one hand, it was
raised, paid, and where necessary equipped by the county organization under
its high officer the sheriff; on the other hand, once embodied, it was at the
orders of the King. Under the Plantagenet and Lancastrian kings, this gave
rise to considerable friction. The militiamen considered that their job was
to defend the realm in case of emergency and when necessary maintain
order within its borders. They served with a good grace in the Scottish
wars, but refused to go abroad as organized county units to fight in France.
When the King wanted soldiers for his foreign wars, he had to pick them
through Commissions of Array and pay them and arm them out of his own
pocket. During the Wars of the Roses, neither side seems to have troubled
much about the militia as an organized force, but during the Parliamentary wars it was again in the limelight, this time as the centre of a struggle
between King and Parliament as to which should have the right to call it to
arms. At the Restoration it was reorganized in such a way that it was given
a definitely upper-class bias.[2]

Deliberate attempts, some of which will be described later, have frequently been made to check unwelcome Leftward tendencies in citizen
armies by manipulating their organization; and the remodelled Restoration militia, even though its makers may well have been unconscious of this
result from their work, is specially interesting from this point of view. It
was laid down that everyone throughout the county with an income of £500

---

[1] *Vide* Maitland, *Constitutional History of England*, pp. 276–9.

[2] For the composition of the Restoration militia and also for its organization
during the eighteenth and nineteenth centuries *vide* Maitland, *Constitutional
History of England*, pp. 455–9.

or a capital of £6,000 in goods must find one horse, horseman, and armour for the militia, and so on in proportion to his wealth. No-one should be forced to serve in person, but anyone refusing to serve was obliged to find a substitute and pay him. The county force was put under the command of the Lord Lieutenant and its officers were appointed by him with certain reservations on the King's behalf. From this scheme, it is clear that the officers of the entire force would be under the influence of the Lords Lieutenant, who would themselves always be prominent members of the ruling class. Cartwright's treatment as a militia officer under the same system, when his opinions were found to clash with those of his superiors, has already been pointed out.

As for the men, since they were provided personally by the well-to-do inhabitants of the county, and had the right to produce substitutes if they were prosperous enough to pay them, it is evident that most of them could be hand-picked from a political point of view and that in any case they would tend to reflect the interests of property. Indeed, theoretically, it would have been hard to devise a subtler scheme for ensuring that a citizen army should be safe and innocuous from the point of view of the ruling class. But in spite of all this, the militiaman still seems, surprisingly enough, to have followed his own emotions in times of crisis. Regiments of the militia, for instance, embodied during Monmouth's rebellion were found to be quite unreliable. The officers would have been prepared to take their share in suppressing the rebellion, but the men sympathized so openly with the Protestant Duke that Churchill, who was in charge of the Government troops, dared not use them. Many men, indeed, deserted to Monmouth's army; and Churchill, so far from being able to use the militia battalions as he had intended as supplementary troops, was obliged to sterilize them by sending them far back to the rear.[1] He was thus forced to rely exclusively on the less politically impressionable soldiers of King James's professional army. Monmouth's rebellion had an eager popular backing in the western counties. It is significant that in the two rebellions which found no popular support in England—the '15 and the '45—the militia throughout remained completely loyal to the Government.

During the eighteenth century the method of recruitment was again altered. Every county was required to provide a certain quota of men and these were to be chosen by ballot, the whole adult population being liable to serve. This method was merely designed to get more men, and certainly not with a view to shading off the class organization of the force, but there can be little doubt that, in spite of the high property qualification retained for the officers, it would tend to have this latter effect. Indeed, all through the chronic troubles of the last years of the eighteenth century and the first decades of the nineteenth, troubles resulting from the spread of Jacobin

[1] Winston Churchill, *Marlborough; His Life and Times*, vol. i, pp. 210, 212.

propaganda and the economic misery due partly to the French wars and partly to the rise of the new industrialism, the militia proved itself an untrustworthy instrument in the hands of the ruling class. One difficulty seems to have been that the men were expected to serve in their own counties. The shrewder supporters of the Government realized the disadvantages of this and pressed to get the system altered. As Lord Anglesey wrote to the Home Office in 1817: 'Indeed, it is very revolting to the feelings of any man to be called upon to attack his neighbours and possibly his kinsfolk.'[1] In this connection it is worth recalling the steps taken by the Tsarist Government in 1905 to ensure that local troops were never employed to suppress disturbances in their own areas.

An even more stringent policy of this kind was adopted for the Spanish Guardia Civil, a force formed partly in order to root out brigandage, but whose main function has always been the suppression of political disorder. The Guardia Civil has been described as perhaps the most important administrative achievement of Spain in the nineteenth century. It was recruited on a strictly selective basis, kept carefully apart from the civil population, housed in barracks, and individual guards were not allowed to serve in their own home districts or even to marry into families coming from localities where they were stationed. As a result, 'the State, which could not count upon its army, secured at least one reliable force which was invariably and integrally at the service of its superiors'.[2] But from the standpoint of the people, the Guard was feared and hated throughout the length and breadth of Spain more deeply perhaps than any other institution of the ruling classes. British governments too understood this psychology in their dealings with Ireland. Men of the Royal Irish Constabulary were housed in barracks and customarily drafted to localities distant from their own home districts.

In most cases, governments are probably safe to rely on this parochial tendency to restrict one's sympathy to one's own locality. Even the English militiamen, whose unreliability was so evident that it was sometimes thought wiser not to call them out at all, could frequently be trusted outside their own areas. Lancashire Fencibles put down a food riot at Seaford in Sussex where the local militia had gone over to the people, and a Cumberland regiment suppressed a riot in Lancashire, to the surprise and chagrin of the insurgents who had believed, no doubt on their knowledge of local battalions, that the men would not fire.[3]

Pitt was gravely concerned over the politically uncertain character of the militia and sought to steady it by creating a new force of volunteers and yeomanry. Since the volunteers were drawn from exactly the same sources

---

[1] Hammond, *The Town Labourer*, p. 87.
[2] Borkenau, *The Spanish Cockpit*, p. 16.
[3] Hammond, *The Town Labourer*, pp. 86, 87.

of the population as the militia, it is a little difficult to understand why Pitt should have expected them to serve the Government more faithfully; in fact, they did no better than the old militia.[1] The yeomanry, however, were an unqualified success. The men had to find their own horses and equipment, which meant that in the shires most of them would be drawn from the farmer class and in the towns from the sons of the relatively well-to-do. The yeomanry therefore was firmly fixed on property, and there was, moreover, a certain public opinion in favour of young men defending their interests in this way. In 1816, for example, a Captain Littlewood is found pressing for the creation of a force of yeomanry in Huddersfield, because 'the better classes ought to get together in this way'.[2] In fine, the social grounding of the yeomanry was emphatically shown up by their action at Peterloo.

Like other citizen armies, they were, however, not much interested in serving the government of the day as such. They were always tempted to back their own political ideas; and the history of this small force is rather specially interesting since it provides a particularly clear example of the political veerings of troops of this type and their loose allegiance to any government they do not like. On the whole, the yeomanry reflected the political feelings of the middle classes; and in 1832, when the Reform agitation was at its height, it is almost certain that the Duke of Wellington, had he formed his Anti-Reform Ministry, would have been unable to rely on them to help him hold down the country. In many districts they had already refused to serve under Tory officers and had resigned without handing in their weapons, a meaningful omission.[3] But the Government, significantly enough, had experienced no difficulty in using them some eighteen months earlier, when they were in action helping to liquidate the Labourers' Revolt.[4]

The history of the various branches of the English citizen army throughout the nineteenth century and its reorganization into the modern Territorial Army provides less striking evidence of its differing political alinements. But a proposal put forward in the autumn of 1938, had it been carried through on any scale, might have had interesting repercussions for the future. This proposal was to form air defence units for individual factories among the hands themselves. It is obvious that in a widespread strike, no government would be able to rely for certain on the assistance of the rank and file of such units against their fellow workers. And where a strike

[1] Hammond, *The Town Labourer*, p. 88.   [2] Ibid., p. 89.

[3] Butler, *The Great Reform Bill*, p. 422. Cf. also Graham Wallas, *Life of Place*, p. 304.

[4] For the Labourers' Revolt, *vide* Hammond, *The Village Labourer*, ch. x. It is surprising to find that in Kent apparently there was a definite feeling amongst the farmers against joining the Yeomanry. The *Kent Herald* asserted that only the dependants of the great landowners would join 'this most unpopular corps', p. 231.

took a political and revolutionary slant, the leaders might well find that they had been presented gratis with the priceless gift of already trained and armed bodies of insurgents.

The passage of soldiers, who have completed their term of service in technical and mechanized units, into trade unions on their re-entry into civilian life provides another such interesting possibility. If these men were induced to put their trade union allegiance before their army allegiance—a dilemma which has already been referred to—it is obvious that their power to menace any government which they disliked would be very great. Nor is it correct to assume that such a menace must necessarily come from the militant Left against a conservative system. We have to consider a possible alinement in which trade unionism might be given a fascist twist as a result of post-war exhaustion, bewilderment, and disillusion.

The story of the French National Guard provides an equally clear example, and on a far larger scale, of the easy and predominant influence of politics in citizen armies. This Guard was first formed in Paris, a day or two before the Bastille rising, by delegates of the sections of the Paris municipality who met at the Hôtel de Ville and decided on the spot to organize a militia of 48,000 men, 800 from each section.[1] The force was entirely distinct from the traditional French militia; its function was to support the revolution and it won its spurs at the storming of the Bastille. The Paris example was imitated throughout France, and the position was regularized by a decree of the Assembly in 1790 which made the Guard responsible for the maintenance of internal order and placed it under the control of local administrations.[2] By June 1791 at least two million National Guards had been enrolled.[3] Recruitment was at first limited to the class of active citizens,[4] e.g. those who paid direct taxes to the value of three days' work and were therefore entitled to vote. This, of course, ensured a certain safeguarding property basis for the Guard, a basis which was further strengthened by the rule that National Guardsmen must find their own equipment. The advanced wing of the revolution found itself continually up against these two regulations, but in February 1792, the Guard was thrown open to all Frenchmen indiscriminately.[5] Passive citizens who were National Guardsmen were given electoral rights after August. In taking this action, the Assembly was no doubt influenced to a considerable extent by the necessity for raising soldiers. The country was alarmingly at war on her frontiers, and in certain provinces internal discontent was ready to flame up into open revolt. During the Thermidorian reaction, an effort— rather half-hearted owing to fear—was made to fix the Guard more firmly on property. Certain special companies which had been dissolved during the Jacobin régime were once more reconstituted and a mounted

---

[1] Mathiez, *La Victoire en l'an II*, p. 18.   [2] Ibid., p. 20.
[3] Ibid., p. 24.   [4] Ibid., p. 21.   [5] Ibid., p. 74.

Guard was formed of men who had to find their own horses and equipment.[1]

These changes in recruitment naturally reflected themselves in shiftings in the political sympathies of the Guard. Moreover, in Paris in particular, the position was further complicated throughout the Great Revolution by the method of enlistment through regional sections. The political position of the Guard as a whole could never be definitely settled, because some sections represented exclusively bourgeois and others exclusively working-class districts, and the companies recruited from the various sections were, of course, composed of local inhabitants. This did not in any way sap its political vitality. It played an important part in every insurrection between the fall of the Bastille and the revolt of Vendémiaire; and an analysis of its actions shows conclusively that, whether it fought as a whole, or whether it split into its component parts of bourgeois and working-class sections, its companies were always swayed by considerations of their own particular political interests. The working-class sections, of course, constituted the great majority of the Guard and their sympathies always followed closely the central drive of the revolution; indeed, it can almost be said that their passion and their correct if instinctive reaction to political developments made this central drive. Thus, it was the workers' sections who stormed the Tuileries on the 10th of August 1792 and finally brought down the monarchy, while the bourgeois sections stood aside and assumed an attitude of neutrality.[2] Again, the working-class sections provided the force to overawe the Assembly on the 2nd of June 1793 and displace the hated Girondins.[3] Here, clearly, they were supporting their own imperative interests. The economic pressure upon the poorer part of the Paris population was exceedingly severe and could only be eased by some form of central commodity control. This necessity the Girondins refused to recognize. With their bourgeois-democratic outlook, they feared above everything else the risk of the rise of some sort of dictatorship based on sans-culotte Paris, and they showed this fear by a bitter antagonism to the growing power of the capital which exasperated the feelings of the Parisians beyond endurance. On the other hand, the National Guard as a whole refused to be drawn into the abortive Hébertist insurrection of March 1794. This was hatched at the Cordeliers' Club, always a focus of extremist opinion, and represented political aims too far to the Left to command anything like wide acceptance at that period. Only one out of the forty-eight sections of the Guard associated itself with the Cordeliers; the rest remained loyal to the Central Committee of the Commune at the Hôtel de Ville and to the National Committee of Public Safety.[4]

[1] Mathiez, *La Réaction thermidorienne*, p. 241.
[2] Kropotkine, *La Grande Révolution*, pp. 354 sq.
[3] Kerr, *The Reign of Terror*, p. 105.   [4] Ibid., p. 345.

THE POLITICAL CHARACTER OF ARMED FORCES

Reference has already been made to the position of the Guard during Thermidor. Here, the sections were curiously divided. Thirteen of them sent their troops to support the Robespierrists at the Hôtel de Ville. Twenty-seven sent commissioners to fraternize with the Central Committee. The rest remained in doubt or supported the Convention.[1] Yet there can be little doubt that the Hôtel de Ville represented the real interests of sans-culotte Paris, that Robespierre still had a large personal following and popularity, and that a victory for the Thermidorians would play direct into the hands of men whose avowed intent was to wreck all the radical side of the revolution. Nevertheless, by hesitations and half-heartedness, the Guard allowed the Thermidorians to win. It behaved, in fact, in a manner which seems to belie its actions at the previous crises of Paris politics, at any rate so far as its working-class sections are concerned. This apparent contradiction is to a large extent explainable. The issue at Thermidor was not an obvious and clearly cut revolutionary issue as it had been on August the 10th or on June the 2nd. It was a power issue between the ruling group and their opponents. In August and June the explosion had boiled up from the passion of the people themselves; at Thermidor they were scarcely aware of the inner contending political currents, or of the reactionary forces which were now hopefully massing behind the groups in the Convention who were intriguing against Robespierre. Moreover, the vivid and spontaneous political fire of the sections had been largely banked down by the Robespierrist dictatorship itself. Thanks to the extreme centralization of the regime, the sections had lost their old capacity for quick action and initiative. Finally, once the affair had come to a head, the Thermidorians could make a certain play with the authority of the Convention, and they did in fact make every effort to rally and influence possible supporters, whereas the Robespierrists, as described in Chapter 9, made little or no attempt to hold and increase the number of their sympathizers.

The National Guard again took action according to class sympathy during the revolt of Vendémiaire 1795.[2] This insurrection was a protest against the decision of the Convention to abrogate the terms of the constitution in its own favour by refusing to hold an unfettered general election and voting itself a further two years of office. The deputies had good grounds to fear that the clean sweep of a general election would drive out the remaining personnel of the Jacobin revolution and leave the road clear for monarchist reaction. In saving themselves, they were saving the last vestiges

---

[1] Kerr, *The Reign of Terror*, p. 479. *Vide* also Louis Blanc, *La Révolution française* (Paris, 1861), vol. xi, p. 244) for a detailed analysis of the positions taken by the various Sections. It is interesting that the Gravilliers section in which 'Hébertism' had particularly flourished was one of the most ardent in favour of the Convention.

[2] *Supra*, p. 21.

of the Great Revolution against the rising tide of bourgeois disillusionment and resentment which was allying itself more and more closely with royalism. This resentment determined the action of the bourgeois sections of the National Guard. Thirty thousand of them marched against the Convention, which was bloodily and successfully defended by Bonaparte using regular troops and a couple of thousand Guards from the working-class sections. The failure of the working-class sections to rally as a whole to the active support of the Convention can be largely explained in terms of general 'revolution-weariness' and uncertainty. The deputies had exhausted the vigorous and enthusiastic spirit which had given them their mandate in 1792 and their leadership was no longer trusted. Moreover, economic discontent was again rife in Paris, but there was no guarantee to the working-classes that support of the Convention would ease their own immediate troubles.

The conflicting class division between the bourgeois and the working-class elements in the Guard was again prominent after the revolution of July 1830, when the regime of Charles X gave place to the bourgeois monarchy of Louis Philippe. This revolution had been made by the middle and lower middle classes, supported for the moment by the working classes.[1] But as Louis Philippe's Government settled down, it became rapidly clear to the working class that a predominantly bourgeois citizen army could act as a bar to their aspirations quite as effectively as any professional armed force. 'The obligation on the National Guards', wrote a later critic, 'to pay a contribution based on property and to furnish their own equipment, in effect restricted recruiting to the propertied classes, and the Government of Louis Philippe, on its side, had never hesitated to promise the support of the army to the citizen militia during times of internal trouble.'[2]

The lesson was not lost upon the politically shrewd members of the English working class who probably realized quickly enough how little their opposite numbers in Paris had gained by their support of the July Revolution. When the agitation for the Reform Bill of 1832 was in full blast

---

[1] *Vide Cambridge Modern History*, vol. xi, p. 25. 'To the lower middle classes, however, who appeared to be deprived of political importance by the smallness of their pecuniary resources, the Government had conceded both a favour and a right. After the revolution of 1830, which they had themselves brought about, they were held worthy to fulfil the functions of police, in the interests of Liberalism and for the maintenance of order, as well as to assist the army in the work of national defence. The National Guard had thus become a fundamental institution of the monarchy—an institution whose practical importance was all the greater from the fact that they could use their muskets against whom they pleased. . . . Its opinions were divided like its functions, half military and half police—or its recruitment—half from the population and half from the middle classes—or its interests—half conservative and half revolutionary.'

[2] Quentin Bauchart, *La Crise sociale de 1848*, p. 216.

and the reformers were urging the arming of the political unions, the more far-sighted working-class leaders hesitated on the grounds that to arm shopkeepers could never be in the long-term interests of their own followers.[1]

The bright bourgeois hopes which had sped the government of Louis Philippe on its way faded as the years dragged on and the bourgeoisie found that its voice in fact carried little weight in the Government's councils. Thus, the position of the National Guard at the outset of the 1848 revolution and during the three months' power of the Provisional Government is particularly significant. It shows at once the disgust of the bourgeoisie with Louis Philippe's regime and also its fear lest a dangerously radical system should supervene. At the onset of the revolution, the Guard was, at any rate tacitly, in sympathy with the party of Reform. 'The National Guard', says Caussidière, who became Prefect of Police under the Provisional Government, 'mustered at the town halls and in the squares, but only to shout "Long live Reform!"'[2] And it is fairly certain that Louis Philippe, who preferred to abdicate rather than precipitate an armed clash between his troops and the people, had good reason for his fear that the National Guard would throw in their lot with the latter. As the event turned out, the Guard took no active and organized part in the revolution, and in the disordered days which followed immediately on the flight of the King, its units seem in fact to have temporarily broken up, and individual guardsmen either abandoned the streets to the victorious insurgents or themselves joined the rebel ranks. 'After a few days no authority could hope to lean upon this citizen militia, official guardian of law and order.'[3] This situation, however, rapidly righted itself, but in the interests of property. Prompted by the instinct for self-preservation, the National Guards, numbering some 50,000, spontaneously re-formed their companies and gradually the Guard was reorganized as a whole and the terms of its employment stretched so that it could occupy military posts left vacant by the withdrawal of the regular troops from Paris.[4]

Thus, within a few weeks of its rise to power, the Provisional Government found itself relying for armed support upon a force which was essentially a bulwark of a middle-class social order. Its conservative character was further ensured by the old property basis of its recruitment.

This position was hardly distasteful to the more moderate members of the Government, but to the Radicals and revolutionaries it presented a very serious problem. It is not too much to say that their failure to solve this problem was one of the major causes responsible for the ultimate failure of the revolution. The Left Clubbists, the followers of Blanqui, and the ad-

[1] Graham Wallas, *Life of Place*, p. 285.
[2] *Memoires*, part I, p. 48.
[3] Quentin Bauchart, *La Crise sociale de 1848*, p. 137.   [4] Ibid., pp. 217, 195.

vanced men generally realized that the old class character of the Guard must be broken up, and a new, more proletarian outlook substituted. They used the decree for universal suffrage as a platform from which to demand 'the right to a gun' for every citizen—a right which the moderates at such a juncture could hardly refuse, and which they had to couple with the undertaking that in future the Government would provide arms and equipment. Ledru Rollin, Radical Minister of the Interior, drove the point home by suppressing the 'special companies', whose members seem to have been specially sieved by the expedient of requiring from them expensive extra equipment.[1] Two days after this move by Ledru Rollin, the doomed companies demonstrated outside the Hôtel de Ville. It is significant of the importance attached by the property-owning classes to the principle which lay behind the immediate point at issue that the demonstrators could muster sufficient support to bring them within appreciable distance of overthrowing the Provisional Government. 'Le jour des bonnets à poil' was undoubtedly critical. The Radicals were unable, however, to take full advantage of the ground thus won.

It was not difficult for the moderates to sabotage the new scheme for arming and equipping the Guard at government expense, and proletarian guards were apt to find that they never got arms. Employers too seem to have put difficulties in the way of doubtful employees who wanted to join the Guard. Moreover, many of the more politically conscious working men preferred, despite the opinion of their more intelligent leaders, to rejoin their own clubs or make groups with old comrades of the barricades when the *rappel* was sounded.[2] Thus it came about that, although the working class had a paper predominance of three to one over the bourgeoisie after the universal right to serve had been granted,[3] yet in practice the Guard retained to a very large extent its old bias; and at periods of crisis, such as the serious riot of April 11th, or the Insurrection of the June Days, after some initial hesitation, it invariably rallied to the support of those parties which stood for moderation.

In 1871 the National Guard brought to birth the Paris Commune—the first working-class government of the world. At this period of its history it was for the first time almost exclusively proletarian in character, and, but for defects in leadership and organization already referred to, could have been shaped to an almost perfect Left revolutionary instrument. Various circumstances account for its proletarian outlook at this time.[4]

In August 1870, almost the whole able-bodied male population of Paris had been enrolled in the ranks of the National Guard, and during the

[1] Quentin Bauchard, *La Crise sociale de 1848*, pp. 217, 218.
[2] Ibid., pp. 226, 228.   [3] Ibid., pp. 217–18.
[4] For the character of the National Guard at the outbreak of the Paris Commune *vide* Jellinek, *The Paris Commune of 1871*, pp. 65 sq.

winter, with the Prussian armies investing the city, the need to serve actively had become imperative, not only from a military point of view, but also because the workers could profit their economic interests in this way. Unemployment was terribly severe owing to the break-up of all normal life during the siege and the position had been exacerbated by the importation into Paris of 200,000 inhabitants from the suburbs. In September, the Government of National Defence promised thirty sous a day to every man who carried a rifle. This thirty sous, guaranteed by their guns, must have stood between thousands of workers and starvation. Patriotism and economic interest combined, therefore, to attach the Paris worker passionately to the National Guard. When the Prussian siege was lifted, the balance of the Guard was further weighted against the middle classes because large numbers of the bourgeois guards, sick of the discomforts of the capital, flocked out of the city to the provinces. It has been estimated that some 150,000 left Paris.[1] The Guard was thus left almost exclusively in the hands of the workers; workers, moreover, who had been ripened for revolution by the tactless, exasperating actions of the Government and the Bordeaux Assembly.

In contrasting the more advanced revolutionary feeling of the National Guard in 1871 with that of the Guard during the Great Revolution, it must also be borne in mind that three generations of growing capitalist industry had gone far towards transforming Paris from a city of small-scale individual producers and traders, whose natural political outlook was that of a petty bourgeoisie, to a great centre of production carried on by large-scale factory methods. The National Guard of 1871 must have been manned to a considerable extent by workers whose outlook was proletarian almost in the Leninist sense. The National Guard of 1789–94 was mainly composed of artisans and shopkeepers working in small establishments or on their own account. Lists are extant of drafts of 'Volunteers' from most of the Paris sections of the Guard which give the civil occupations of the recruits. An analysis of such sample lists gives an overwhelming majority of artisans, craftsmen, and small shopkeepers. The most frequently recurring occupations seem to be those of cobbler, barber, compositor or printer, locksmith, mason, etc. Occasionally a man puts himself down as 'bourgeois' and there is a sprinkling of professional men such as doctors and teachers. The labourers are relatively few.[2]

Thus, in 1871, the Guard remained true to its long tradition of political vitality and, given its proletarian character, launched the fiercest revolt against a conservative social system which has taken place in any European country with the exception of Russia.

The history of these two citizen armies, the English militia and the French

---

[1] Hanotaux, *Contemporary France* (English trans.), vol. i, p. 170.

[2] Chassin et Henet, *Les Volontaires nationaux pendant la révolution*, vol. i.

National Guard, has been sketched in some detail in order to show the political instability of this type of armed force by comparison with a long-service professional army. Citizen armies will go exactly that distance to Right or Left which they think their class interests warrant and governments can only place sure reliance upon them when they can identify the citizen soldiers' supposed class interests with their own policy. Thus intelligent governments of the Right have always tried to ensure their loyalty by placing their recruitment upon some sort of property basis. Herein lies a danger which the Left may have to face from a citizen army, whether the Left be represented by a government constitutionally returned to power, or by an opposition party bent on the capture of power. If a citizen army has been successfully built up so that it reflects to a considerable extent the interests of a ruling class, it may prove politically as difficult to handle as a professional army.

It is essential that a citizen army, true to its name, should reflect the political will of the nation at large. Thanks, then, to its political liveliness, it will be the finest instrument of power that any government based on popular support can hope to control, and the surest guarantee against aggression on the part of any party bent on the destruction of liberty.

By contrast with the soldiers of a citizen army, the rank and file of long-service armed forces are invariably politically inert and devitalized. Governments which are pledged to maintain an existing social order have, in fact, always made the political sterilization of the rank and file a part of their deliberate policy. This has been achieved by methods with which the preceding discussion has already made us familiar. It is therefore only necessary at this point to sum them up.

Segregation from the civilian population is the basis of all such methods. The soldiers are housed in barracks, so that they cannot in any real sense understand or share the lives and difficulties of their civilian comrades, they are discouraged from pursuing any outside interests, they are educated in a narrow *esprit de corps*, based first on the regiment and then on the army. In addition, they are further emasculated by the policy of damping down individual initiative once they have enlisted and treating them as children who require constant supervision rather than as responsible adults. Every circumstance of their service contributes to engender a lack of independence in judgement and action. In comparison with their politically virile brothers of the workshops and factories of civilian life they become robots, who can be brought to life only by the violent impact of circumstances which strike at their own interests inside the ring-fence of the army. It is obvious that the longer the term of service, the more successful the policy of sterilization will be. And it is perhaps significant of its success that, where long-service armies are concerned, the authorities have not found it necessary to base recruitment on selective methods as they have tried to do in order to counteract unwelcome political vitality in citizen armies. Throughout the course of its two hundred years' life, the British Army, until the Great War, for instance, was notoriously recruited anyhow, mostly indeed from the misfits, failures, and dregs of the civilian population. Selective recruitment was confined to the corps of officers, which was in practice based on a high property qualification, thereby making it the almost exclusive preserve of the ruling classes.

It is possible that the lack of independence in the rank and file will be counteracted in the future, to some extent automatically, by the necessities of modern mechanized armies. A mechanized army claims much greater intelligence and initiative from the common soldier than was needed to make an adequate private in a regiment of the line. And it may well be that the man who looks after the engine of a tank or an aeroplane will inevitably acquire a professional and therefore by extension a general outlook more in accord with that of his counterpart in a civilian engineering shop. The soldier mechanic who is responsible for the well-being of a delicate engine requires a different mentality from the footslogging private who spends the best years of his youth doing futile fatigues, drilling on a barrack square, and learning how to fire a rifle. In this connection it is interesting to find that before the war the British Air Force authorities had already altered the system whereby a soldier must always be accompanied and supervised by an N.C.O. in any job he is doing and must cease work on the appearance of an officer. In the Air Force shops, men work apparently much as they do in civilian engineering shops, and they are not necessarily expected to down tools in the middle of some important operation because an officer appears on the scene. Moreover, an N.C.O. may command a plane in which a commissioned officer is serving. It appears, too, that before the war signs of greater elasticity were to be found in the army. By an experiment made in 1937 when Mr. Hore-Belisha was Secretary of State for War, soldiers were in certain circumstances to be allowed to spend the night out of barracks. [1]

The attitude of a modern mechanized army has not yet been tested out in any large-scale political upheaval. It is not therefore possible to say how far this new mentality would go in shaping the soldier's political aims and releasing him from the inhibitions of army life. Definite instances can, however, be given where the application of science to warfare has tended to broaden the political attitude of officers. Even so far back as the Great French Revolution, when engineering knowledge was obviously confined to the sappers and gunners, a shrewd observer of the political sympathies of the officers noted that, compared with the line, the officers of these two branches were free from prejudice and imbued with what he called a

[1] *Vide* B. H. Liddell Hart, *The British Way in Warfare* (Penguin Special), p. 213.

'civic' spirit. The same seems to have been true of the Neapolitan Army of 1860 about the time of Garibaldi's Sicilian campaign. 'At the beginning of 1860, lists of officers supposed to be well inclined to Italy were circulated among the patriotic committees; the artillery and engineeers were the most disaffected branches of the Service.'[1]

A recent and more important instance is the attitude of the officers of the Spanish Air Force. At the outset of the Franco Civil War, as we have seen, they held by their allegiance to the legal Government of the republic, progressive as against fascist, whereas almost the entire officer personnel of both the army and the navy followed the revolting generals.

As against this, we must set the fact that both in Italy and Germany the Air Force was strongly Fascist and Nazi in sympathy during Mussolini's and Hitler's rise to power. In the case of Germany, this may have been due to reaction from the Versailles Treaty which had forbidden the maintenance of an air force. Recruitment for civil flying seems to have been in the hands of extreme Nationalists; and recruits realized clearly that their civil training was a basis for a fighting training when the time was ripe. Since Hitler was identified with the fight against Versailles, young airmen would naturally tend to follow him. But this is probably only a partial explanation. The Nazi revolution was a true revolution in the sense that it was the offspring of deep-seated social discontent. It looks as if the technical branches of armed forces were swayed by political currents outside their tradition to some extent. The danger lies in the fascination of fascism for untrained political minds.[2]

It is important at this point to emphasize the fundamental political distinction which in fact exists as between officer and man in armies where the officers' corps is based on social homogeneity. Officers, as we have seen, have never been indifferent to politics in practice. On a superficial view they may have appeared to be indifferent because, where revolutionary politics came seriously into question, they have almost always been called upon to support a government which represented their own fundamental political assumptions, and have therefore naturally responded without fuss and indeed with enthusiastic loyalty. But, in fact, the notion of the 'impersonal instrument' as regards the corps of officers is a mere convenient fiction. During the two crises of English history, for instance, when the political attachment of the officers clashed gravely with the policy of the government in power, their allegiance was shaken to the extent of open mutiny and widespread resignations. We have already seen how the defection of the officers paralysed both the Government of James II in 1688 and the Asquith Government during the Ulster crisis of 1914. The

[1] *Infra*, p. 191. *Vide* also G. M. Trevelyan, *Garibaldi and the Thousand*, p. 141.
[2] Cf. E. W. Dobert, *Convert to Freedom*. The author was for a time a cadet training for civil flying during the Weimar Republic.

latter case is particularly cogent for this argument, since it can be shown that during the preceding generation the Army had come to be identified with the Conservative party as against the Liberal party, and was, indeed, generally regarded as being the special care of Tory politicians and their followers. When the Liberal Government and the Conservative Opposition clashed on an issue which, for the first time since 1832, carried all the seeds of civil war, a large proportion of officers showed no hesitation in refusing their duty to the Government of the day and adopted a partisan and coercive attitude in support of the Conservative Opposition. In assessing the importance of this defection from a political point of view, it is also worth remembering that, since the Lloyd George budget of 1906 and the Parliament Act of 1911, Conservatives had come increasingly to be regarded as the defenders of property and traditional privilege against the inroads of a new kind of liberalism which had thrown off the safe and gentlemanly mantle of the Whigs and now appeared naked and unashamed as the champion of a radical democracy.

Other countries provide analogous instances of the underlying partisan attitude of an officers' corps and its failure to serve a government whose basic policy it fears and dislikes. In Spain,[1] for instance, it has been well said that the army was simply the permanent officers' corps imposed upon a conscript soldiery unwilling to serve. And Spanish history throughout the nineteenth century may be largely read, as we have seen, in terms of the pronunciamentos of groups of generals, who desired to check unwelcome political tendencies or to push the interests of the classes which buttressed their privileges. In our own day, Primo de Rivera's overthrow of the constitution in 1921 was based on the defensive juntas among the officers, temporarily supported by Catalan big business—Primo himself was the Commander at Barcelona—and was due entirely to disgust with the policy of the Government. 'We have not got to justify our attitude,' he declared in his manifesto, 'the facts justify it. Priests murdered, ex-governors, agents of the authorities assassinated; currency depreciated, a tariff policy suspect by its tendency, and the more so because the man who is directing it openly demonstrates his barefaced immorality.'[2] In its genesis, General Franco's rebellion was simply another such attempt to force out a feared and hated government. It was centred on the army and supported in flank by the political parties of the Right, and the fact that it had been carefully prepared for months beforehand, even to the extent of taking soundings for possible support in Germany and Italy, only serves to emphasize the partisan attitude of the generals. Indeed, so soon as the elections of February 1936 had made it clear that Spanish politics were again swinging definitely

[1] For an account of the Spanish Army *vide* Jellinek, *The Civil War in Spain*, pp. 54 sq.
[2] Jellinek, *The Civil War in Spain*, p. 57.

to the Left, after the three welcome years of Right rule which had followed the fall of the political parties who had made the revolution of 1931, plans for a military rising were set on foot, and only held back for the time being until the Right should have breathing-space to reorganize. Neither the generals nor the politicians of the Right ever had the slightest intention of abiding loyally and constitutionally by a disagreeable result of the polls.[1]

The German Reichswehr[2] provides another case of political partisanship on the part of the officers' corps, but indirect and much more subtle in its methods. The design of the Reichswehr, as a small professional army for the maintenance of internal law and order, was dictated as we have seen by the victorious Allies. The disastrous result in isolating the army from the people was no doubt partly due to the design itself, but it was also in large measure due to the influence of the officers' corps in moulding the Reichswehr to their own desired pattern by making clever use of the framework set up by the Treaty. The Government of the Republic had made the initial mistake of encouraging the available generals and officers of the old Imperial Army to take over the task of enforcing law and order by means of the Free Corps and later of the Provisional Reichswehr. When the professional Reichswehr was formed their influence was firmly entrenched. It is, on the face of it, a little difficult to understand why such men should have volunteered to forge an army for the struggling republic, which stood for an order of political life which was alien to all their traditions and which they hated and despised. But the Reichswehr was formed consciously and deliberately on the principle of the 'impersonal instrument'. Its commander and its chief maker, General Seeckt, openly took the line that his job was to create an efficient professional force which should stand completely apart from current politics, and yet should carry on and revitalize the old tradition of the German Army.

For this purpose he chose his officers from the more restrained elements in the Free Corps and the Provisional Reichswehr, not because they were less alive to the old traditions and more attached to the Republic, but because he was shrewd enough to realize that, if he were to have a clear field to get on with his own conception of his task, he must keep on terms with the civilian leaders of the Republic and prevent the army from falling foul of their regime. So far as the rank and file was concerned he strove to reawaken in the nation its old pride in its army by allowing the soldiers to be 'seen' wherever possible, while at the same time he prevented them from taking any active part in political life. They were not permitted to vote or to belong to a political party or to take part in political manifestations; and

[1] Borkenau, *The Spanish Cockpit*, pp. 59, 60. For a detailed account of Spanish history between the 1931 Revolution and the outbreak of the Franco Rebellion, *vide* Jellinek, *The Civil War in Spain*.

[2] Cf. *infra*, pp. 227 sq.

179

the newspapers which they were allowed in their messrooms were subject to the permission of the Reichswehr Ministry.[1]

Herein may be found the apparently paradoxical key, not only to the situation of the Reichswehr, but also to that of all armies based on the same principle. The fiction of the 'impersonal instrument' paid the officers because it enabled them to build up a rank and file whose allegiance was in reality centred not on a civil government chosen by the nation they were enlisted to serve, but on their own professional *esprit de corps*. By this means the officers could hold the rank and file politically in the hollow of their hands. And their own ostensible allegiance to the Government of the Republic was conditional on this freedom to put a ring fence round the army. It was, in fact, a mere titular allegiance. Thus, this conception of the Reichswehr successfully prevented the civil government from ever obtaining adequate control over its own armed forces; and in the last series of crises before Hitler's seizure of power it had become clear that the army could only be used on those conditions which were acceptable to its generals.

The examples quoted above show clearly enough that in a long-service army the theory of the 'impersonal instrument' works only in so far as the rank and file is concerned. The officers are never apart from politics in any genuine sense, and the rank and file can be so conditioned that they will only be roused from their apathy in rare circumstances. From the standpoint of progressives, the danger of this long-service professional system is therefore as a double-edged blade. On the one hand, it means that a progressive government in office can never rely for certain upon its own armed forces to defend its policy, nor can a progressive party intent on winning power expect support from the army, either moral or physical, unless the corps of officers is to some extent disillusioned and disaffected with the old regime, as in France at the outset of 1789 or during the preliminary moves of 1848. On the other hand, it implies that a reactionary Right party, making a drive for power, would probably be able to command the assistance of the army, even against the expressed will of the people. It is significant, for instance, that some 75 per cent of the rank and file of the Spanish Army followed their officers at the outset of the Franco Revolt. The remaining 25 per cent showed more political independence and by one means or another brought their arms over to the side of the Government. In Barcelona, for instance, after a day or two of fighting, many of the soldiers seem suddenly to have recognized the real face of events. They mutinied against their officers, thereby contributing in considerable measure to the success of the Govern-

[1] Rosenberg, *A History of the German Republic*, p. 146. *Vide* also Mowrer, *Germany Puts the Clock Back*, pp. 73 and 80 sq.
Bénoist Méchin, *Histoire de l'armée allemande*, vol. ii, pp. 123 sq., 144 sq.; *vide* also pp. 110, 112.

ment in holding the city against the rebels. It is to be noted that the rank and file of the navy acted at once with decision and independence. In several cases they successfully seized their own ships, killing or chasing out the rebel officers, and brought them over into the service of the Government. In most navies the rank and file, for some reason, seem to have more independence of mind and action than their opposite numbers in land forces. [1]

It will be seen from the Spanish experience that conscription is not in itself an adequate foundation for a democratic army. The Spanish soldier served only for two years with the colours. Again, the Russian Army which met the 1905 revolution was a conscript army, but here the term of service was so much longer—five years—that the Russian soldier was to all intents a professional.

The salient fact seems to emerge conclusively that in revolutionary situations, with the exception of those placed against a background of unsuccessful war, the attitude of the army will be determined mainly by the attitude of the corps of officers.

The political vitality of such citizen armies as the English militia or the French National Guard can be adduced only to prove the general contention that it is segregation from civilian life which emasculates the soldier as a citizen. The more he is segregated and subjected to the military machine the more he is likely to forget his citizenship. A modern conscript army, if it is to be efficient, cannot be constructed on the model of such militias, and their political attitude cannot therefore be used as proof of what the rank and file of a conscript army will do in time of political unrest. We have no historical evidence to show that in fact the rank and file of a modern conscript army may be expected to go against their officers. Such evidence as there is seems to point the other way. Moreover, a conscript army like any other can be officered from the propertied classes.

From the standpoint of a progressive democracy a conscript army is not, therefore, in itself a sufficient safeguard even against counter-revolution. The basic problem is fundamentally to alter the character of the officers' corps by breaking up its social homogeneity. It is probable that of all European armies combining military efficiency with democratic feeling the Swiss approximates most closely to the ideal model. [2] It is important therefore to investigate how the Swiss have solved this problem, not only of retaining a sense of citizenship in the rank and file, but also even more noteworthily of completely democratizing their officers' corps.

The Swiss Army is correctly described as a militia army, in that no forces

[1] Jellinek, *The Civil War in Spain*, pp. 295, 318; and Borkenau, *The Spanish Cockpit*, p. 224.
[2] For the Swiss Army *vide The League of Nations Armaments Year Book 1933*. Also Julian Grande, *A Citizens' Army*. The latter work describes in detail the character of the Swiss Army at the time of the Great War.

are kept permanently with the colours, except the corps of some 300 instructors. Units are brought together only for periods of training or in the event of mobilization. Every Swiss citizen is liable for military service during a period of twenty-nine years. Over that period, he spends normally only 171 days with the colours, 65 to 92 of these being expended on his course as a recruit.[1] In addition he is expected to put in a certain amount of rifle practice, etc. during his civilian life and as a boy he frequently undergoes at school some sort of preliminary military training, but this is purely voluntary. When he has done his training as a recruit he takes home with him his arms and equipment and keeps them as an honourable symbol of his obligations as a citizen. This last small point throws a spotlight on the contrast between an army which is genuinely the expression of a nation and the army which is the expression of a ruling class. A politician of the type of Pitt or Thiers could never envisage with an easy mind the thousands of rifles slung up in peasant or artisan homes all over the country he is called upon to govern.

No-one can become an officer in the Swiss Army who has not already done his time of training in the ranks. Men who are recommended for commissioned rank are then sent to special schools where they undergo a further period of training for eighty days. They then return to their civilian occupations. The Swiss Army has therefore no professional corps of officers, except its 300 instructors. Consequently there is no chance that an exclusive sense of *esprit de corps* will be built up and possibly set against allegiance to the popular will. The difference in outlook between the Swiss officer and soldier and his counterpart in other countries shows in no uncertain fashion how admirably the system works. It is clearly illustrated by the following extracts from the comments of various Swiss officers who were asked to give a judgement on their military system.

A lawyer, holding the rank of captain, who put in some 420 days of training during his time as a student and his first years of practice at the Bar:

'As officers, we learned to manage to behave towards our subordinates with tact and at the same time with assurance. All my military instructors . . . laid stress on the necessity of the superior considering his subordinate before all things as a human being—a principle which must be strictly observed, especially in a democracy where the humblest individual knows what human dignity means. . . . I, personally, have never known an officer attain high rank if he has failed to abide by this principle, and has treated his soldiers not as men but things. . . .

'After every period of military service I have returned to my own work with renewed pleasure in it and mentally refreshed. Moreover, on the many

[1] N.C.O.s spend about 260–401 days with the colours and officers 342–754 days. Other branches of the service spend rather more.

occasions when I have been doing military service I have become acquainted with two things of inestimable worth: my fellow-countrymen and my own country.... I have come in contact with people of every social class; I have shared their joys and sorrows, and now I know with what manner of soul my own people are endowed.'[1]

An officer of the reserve, at one time Member for Geneva City in the Swiss Parliament writing of the Great War period:

'What we in Geneva felt (on mobilization at the outbreak of the World War) was felt equally by every soldier, non-commissioned officer, and officer in our army from one end of Switzerland to the other, without regard to language, race, or sympathies. With us, devotion to our military institutions is inseparable from devotion to our country and to our democratic institutions. Moreover, the fact that the Swiss Army law of 1907 . . . was accepted by the majority of the people themselves, lent it during the last period of stress a force which no law could ever have possessed which had been merely voted by Parliament or imposed by Government. In taking up arms or obeying their leaders, the people feel that by so doing they are exercising their own will, and even those who voted against the law (in the referendum) feel this, realizing as they do that in a democracy the minority must submit to the majority.'[2]

So far as military capacity is concerned, there seems no reason to doubt that, man for man, the Swiss soldier could hold his own with the soldier of any other country; indeed, in the circumstances of modern war, his self-respect and self-reliance should give him an advantage over the troops of nations which have been bred in the old tradition of 'theirs not to reason why; theirs but to do and die'. As regards his officers, it does not appear that their professional efficiency has ever been called in question.

Such an army is fit for a democracy. Since it is based, both as regards its leadership and its rank and file, on the popular will and is indeed an expression of that will, it can never be used to further sectional interests by force of arms or to thwart the political aspirations of a majority of the people.

[1] Julian Grande, *A Citizens' Army*, pp. 95, 101.   [2] Ibid., p. 116.

11

MAKING AN ARMY TO CONSOLIDATE REVOLUTION

Reorganization of existing armed forces—root-and-branch methods—strength and weakness of a militia organization.

So far, the relation of that triangle of forces, the government, the army, and the people, has been examined during the period which precedes a revolution and during the process of insurrection.

It is now proposed to assume the success of a revolutionary challenge and continue the examination in regard to the fighting forces which every revolution must forge for itself on the morrow of its capture of power. For revolutions which have been won must then be held and consolidated, a task as a rule far more difficult than the winning, which implies much abler powers of organization, clearer thinking, and a cooler and more sustained courage. And the ultimate sanction of a revolutionary, as of any other, political system is armed force.

In normal times, in democratic systems such as the British, this ultimate sanction of armed force is kept discreetly in the background, and not only the government, but also to a considerable extent the day-to-day maintenance of order, rests upon goodwill and the co-operation of the community as a whole. A contemporary British Executive has, of course, at its command adequate machinery for the maintenance of order by force and for the suppression of insurrection, but the current dispositions of police and troops are on the whole designed for a community which rests upon consent and needs only to take into account the haling before justice of individual law-breakers. In practice, the government relies upon a warning alteration in the political barometer, or upon sheer advertisement beforehand on the part of potential insurgents, which will allow time for the massing of police and troops before any serious clash should occur. For example, the events which led up to the great Triple Alliance strike of 1921 gave the Lloyd George Government clear warning of coming trouble, and allowed time to call up reservists and form an armed camp in Hyde Park before circumstances could have ripened a possible revolutionary situation.

In the period succeeding a successful revolutionary seizure of power,

MAKING AN ARMY TO CONSOLIDATE REVOLUTION

however, the political weather has nothing in common with the normal climate of a country. The old tradition of government has been swept away, and with it any tacit pact of consent however based, whether on goodwill, inertia, or a habit of slavery, which may have existed between governors and governed. The community is split up into its component elements and their behaviour is no longer dictated by an ideal of political persuasion and restraint. Since no deep revolution has won to power without leaving in its wake a trail of dispossessed and embittered classes, this implies that a revolutionary government on the morrow of its seizure of power will probably be met with a certain degree of violent opposition, whether spasmodic and spontaneous or organized into open rebellion. Moreover, a deep revolution has serious repercussions on foreign countries and it may well happen, as in the case of Russia in 1919 and of France in 1792, that the revolutionary government finds itself not only faced by internal rebellion, but also by armed foreign support for the rebels, or even by invasion from the troops of frightened foreign governments. It follows, therefore, that a first and basic problem is the creation of revolutionary armed forces, capable not only of liquidating disorder and insurrection at home, but also if necessary of fending off external foes.

The material from which a revolutionary army can be created is in practice very varied both as to its character and its military value. The revolutionary government will almost certainly have behind it a heterogeneous mass of armed or semi-armed adherents. Whether these will have seen any serious active service in street fighting, or otherwise, will depend upon the methods by which the government has seized power. In certain cases, the revolutionary leaders may be able to command the services of highly organized partisan armies which have already formed the main point of pressure in their drive for power, and which, though lacking perhaps in the more technical skills and weapons of modern warfare, are already well skilled and enthusiastic in the unpleasant art of terrorizing opponents. The Fascist Militia and the Nazi S.A. are examples in point. The Irish Republican Army provides another example, and in this case the old rebel force had been tempered by the reality of bitter guerrilla war. In other cases, where a revolution sweeps through developing phases like the French or the Russian, the leaders may find ready to their hand roughly organized bodies of citizen soldiers, formed more or less spontaneously during the opening rush of the revolutionary tide. Such was the French National Guard in its beginnings and the Russian Red Guard as taken over by the Bolsheviks. Finally, there are the armed forces of the old regime. These, in the nature of the case, must almost always be seriously broken in morale, disintegrated to a greater or less extent, and released from their old discipline. What to do with them, and how to rebuild on their shattered foundations, is the core of the problem.

MAKING AN ARMY TO CONSOLIDATE REVOLUTION

Revolutionary governments seem always to have approached this question from one of two widely divergent angles, which in fact represent fundamental differences in ideology. On the one hand, it has been tackled by root-and-branch methods on the lines laid down by Lenin when he said that, in order to consolidate and complete a revolution, the entire administrative machinery of the old regime must be smashed and a new revolutionary machinery built up to take its place. This, of course, was the method chosen by the Bolsheviks, or perhaps it would be more accurate to say, the method dictated by circumstances to the Bolsheviks. It was also used, though to a less far-reaching extent, by the French between 1789 and 1794. In practice, it is a method always modified to some degree by circumstances and by the actual condition of the army which it is proposed to reorganize.

On the other hand, the problem can be approached as it was in France in 1848, or in Germany in 1918. In the former case, the army, which had not been seriously disintegrated, was retained intact by the Provisional Government and subjected only to minor reorganization. In the latter, the old organization was completely broken up by events, but a new army was, as we have seen, formed under officers drawn from the personnel of the old Imperial officers' corps. This method corresponds to the view of those who believe in conciliating as far as possible the servants of the old regime and using their expert services. In theory, this second method is obviously safer from the standpoint of technical efficiency. The strength of a modern army depends to an increasing extent upon expert knowledge and training, and it would seem at first blush wanton to reject the expert services of men who, in spite of their associations with the old regime, are apparently prepared to work for the new. Nevertheless, the experience of the 'K' battalions in first World War suggests that it is possible to train civilians as soldiers and regimental officers in a relatively short space of time, and there seems no reason to suppose that even to-day, given the more complex work of a mechanized army, civilian engineers would be unavailable in sufficient quantity and unable to cope with it successfully. Modern man is almost frighteningly 'engine-minded'. It may well be, too, that the necessity for long professional training has been exaggerated in importance in regard to the higher ranks. In the First World War, these were virtually closed to civilians serving in the British Army, both as regards the administrative and the fighting side of the service. But great administrators and great generals are born, not made; and it seems on the face of it unlikely that a civilian administrator of genius would have found himself unable to turn over his talents to military organization. As for the generals, their records, with few exceptions, in all the armies engaged, suggest that long military experience had atrophied rather than sharpened whatever genius nature might have allotted to them.

Revolutionary or civil wars almost invariably throw up some generals of

186

talent who have either had little previous military experience of handling armies, or who have in a year or two climbed by sheer capacity from the lowest to the top rung of the military ladder. Cromwell was a country squire until, at the age of forty-three, he joined Essex with a troop of sixty horse and fought his first engagement at Edgehill. Washington had never had the opportunity to command more than a handful of troops when he was given supreme command of the American Army at the outset of the War of Independence—and Napoleon's dictum that every private carries a marshal's baton in his knapsack may have been based, not on democratic sentiment, but rather on his observation of the rise of men like Jourdan and Soult. During the American Civil War, no outsider in either army rose to the highest military ranks. The generals whose names have gone down to history, Lee and Stonewall Jackson on the Confederate side, and Grant, Sherman, and Sheridan on the Union side, were professionals whose military education had begun at West Point, but Grant and Sherman had drifted into civil life and come back to the army only in order to fight the war.

Perhaps the strongest case for the retention of men with long military experience can be made in regard to the non-commissioned officers. There can be little doubt that the N.C.O.'s of the pre-war British Army made its backbone, and their use in training the soldiers of the 'K' battalions was invaluable.

These difficulties have always been present in one form or another in the minds of leaders whose job is to consolidate a revolution, and an examination of some post-revolutionary armies reveals the very different lines along which practical attempts have been made to solve them.[1]

The relation of the French Army of the *ancien régime* to the revolution of 1789 has already been analysed in some detail. This analysis, however, was designed to show the astonishingly complete turnover of the army to the revolution and to discover the reasons which made this turnover possible. We must now return to the French Army in order to find out more specifically how the men of 1789–94 succeeded in reconstructing it as a fighting force, capable before it was too late of crushing severe internal rebellion, and strong enough to hold at bay on two frontiers the troops of several European states.

Since the Royal Army was never actually disbanded as happened in the case of the Imperial German and Russian armies, but was rather totally remodelled in character within its old framework, the liquidation of the old military ideas went on to a great extent concurrently with the formation of the new. It will therefore be impossible to avoid a certain amount of

---

[1] There is a good deal of illuminating first-hand discussion on these points in T. Wintringham's book on his experiences in the International Brigade in the Spanish civil war, *English Captain.*

repetition in the succeeding pages, since various points to which reference has already been made in connection with the swing-over of the army to the revolution can be considered with equal correctness as bearing upon its revolutionary reconstruction.

The clearer-headed deputies of the National Assembly seem to have realized from the outset, and certainly long before the flight to Varennes had indicated that a final and irrevocable break with the old regime must sooner or later happen, that, in spite of the apparent adherence of the armed forces to the revolution, there was grave danger latent in a professional army still led by officers whose allegiance had been given to the King. So early as December 1789, Dubois Crancé made a famous speech in the Assembly pleading for compulsory service on militia lines. The theory was developed during the debate by Baron Menou, who sketched a plan for a militia which should renew itself every three years. 'Military conscription', he said, 'favours despotic governments among some peoples, because it is then a law made by a despot; it becomes the safeguard of liberty, when it is ordered by the nation.'[1] As time went on, the more advanced men became more and more concerned about the danger to the Revolution represented by the army. Both Robespierre and Mirabeau seem to have made a suggestion that the army should be disbanded and remodelled on a new basis after it had been drastically purged of its untrustworthy elements. The point at issue was the position of the officers, but the agitation resulted immediately in nothing more severe than the imposition of the rather innocuous first military oath. It was hoped by the moderates that this oath, which stressed loyalty to the nation concurrently with loyalty to the King, would filter out those officers who were definitely opposed to the aims of the revolution. In practice the oath was quite ineffective as a purge, since most Royalist officers at this stage took the line that the monarchy would be more effectively supported if they accepted the oath and remained with their regiments. Robespierre and Antoine both castigated this oath as a weak-kneed compromise. Speaking at the Jacobins' Club, Robespierre said:

'You have destroyed the nobility and the nobility remains at the centre of your army. It is by armies that governments have everywhere reduced men to subjection and you are putting your army under aristocratic chiefs. I say with frankness, perhaps even with bluntness, that whosoever does not advise the discharge of the officers is a traitor.'[2]

The required purge was eventually effected to a very considerable extent by the second and third military oaths to which reference has already been

[1] Buchez et Roux, *Histoire parlementaire de la révolution française*, vol. iii, p. 471.

[2] Quoted by Hartmann, *Les Officiers royales dans la révolution*, p. 216; also by Spenser Wilkinson, *The French Army before Napoleon*, p. 114.

made. These were decreed just before and just after the flight to Varennes in June 1791. About one-fifth of the officers on the establishment, according to Mathiez, refused to take the third oath and presumably emigrated. The drain of emigration, as we have seen, had already begun before the flight to Varennes, and continued through the succeeding months until the fall of the monarchy in August 1792. It might then have been safely reckoned up with some jubilation by the critics of compromise that the French Army had lost more than half the total number of its old corps of officers.

Concurrently with the purge of officers, various other measures were taken with a view to reconstructing the army on a firm revolutionary basis. The militia, which consisted of 75,000 men and acted as a reserve for the regulars, was abolished in March 1791. There seems no particular reason to suppose that the militia had a specially Royalist bias, and it is therefore a little difficult to see why, from a revolutionary point of view, it should have been suppressed. A more obvious move was the disbandment of the Household Troops in June 1791. There were 8,000 of these, and by the terms of their service they were specially attached to the King's person. Finally, the 20,000 Swiss Guards were disbanded in September and October 1792. These were probably considered to be particularly untrustworthy since it was their battalions which had, with disinterested heroism, conducted the defence of the Tuileries against the people in the previous August. This was a bold move, for the Swiss Guards were first-class troops and the army must have lost considerably in efficiency by their elimination.[1]

By the autumn of 1792, therefore, the field was clear for a drastic revolutionary reconstruction. The most pressing problem was the replacement of the officers without a grave sacrifice of efficiency. The French Army of the old regime was one of the finest armies of its time. Its artillery was considered the best in Europe, its drill manuals were the most up-to-date, camps for instruction had been organized, and the non-commissioned officers were picked men, 'always capable of commanding a section, usually fit to command a company'.[2] They seem frequently to have come from good plebeian families and apparently the authorities required that they should be literate. The purge of officers was not, therefore, as disastrous to efficiency as it might have been. For a decree of 1790 had thrown open the officers' corps to promotion from the ranks and N.C.O.s were rapidly promoted. In addition, the soldiers of fortune and the middle-class officers now had their opportunity of rising to the higher ranks denied to them under the old regime. At first the chiefs of the army were drawn from aristocrats

[1] Mathiez, *La Victoire en l'an II*, pp. 47, 48.
[2] Spenser Wilkinson, *The French Army before Napoleon*, p. 97; also Mathiez, *La Victoire en l'an II*, pp. 35, 36; also *Cambridge Modern History*, 'The French Revolution', p. 40.

MAKING AN ARMY TO CONSOLIDATE REVOLUTION

of liberal sympathies such as Lafayette and Custine, or from able adventurers like Dumouriez. Later, these political types were eliminated, and the true generals of the revolution emerged, men like Hoche who was a sergeant in 1792 and a general in 1794 at the age of twenty-four; like Jourdan who was a haberdasher at Limoges in 1789, a sergeant in 1792, and a general in 1793 at the age of thirty-four; like Pichegru who was an N.C.O. in 1789 and a general in 1793 at the age of thirty-three; and like Bonaparte who was a lieutenant in 1789 and a general in 1793 at the age of twenty-four.[1] The youth of all these men when they took high command is a point worth noting. Haig was fifty-four when he took over the command of the British forces in France, and Foch was sixty-six when he became Generalissimo.

With the gradual strengthening and centralization of the Executive under the frightening pressure of war and rebellion, the political sifting of the generals became more intense. In the latter part of 1792 and the first half of 1793, no less than 593 generals[2] were nominated and suspended, and the Executive seems frequently to have acted with an eye to eradicating political undesirables rather than from the point of view of increasing military efficiency. Incompetent amateur soldiers, like Rossignol, who for a disastrous period commanded the revolutionary troops in La Vendée, were sometimes pushed to the fore because their political opinions were specially satisfactory to the men in power in Paris. On the whole, however, the Executive steered with skill between the Scylla of political undesirability and the Charybdis of soldierly incompetence. By 1794, the corps of officers was 'the result of the right kind of selection, the battlefield, the march, and the camp'.[3]

It is worth making a comparison here with the parallel experience of the French Navy. The purge of naval officers had also been drastic. But the Government never succeeded in satisfactorily reorganizing the navy. It has even been asserted that the weakness of the French Navy throughout the nineteenth century, by comparison with the army, was due to the fact that it never recovered its technical and sailorlike efficiency after the revolutionary disintegration. Naval training is obviously a much more serious technical affair than army training; it is therefore harder to replace a naval

[1] Mathiez, *La Victoire en l'an II*, pp. 36, 276.

[2] Spenser Wilkinson, *The French Army before Napoleon*, p. 119.

[3] The spirit of the officers is well shown in the following extract from the memoirs of Marshal Soult:

'The officers gave an example of devotion. Haversack on back, lacking funds . . . they took part in the distributions like the soldiers. They had to produce a voucher to draw a coat or a pair of boots. Yet none thought of complaining of this distress, nor of turning aside from the service which was their sole study and their unique object of emulation. . . . I can say that it was the period of my career during which I worked the hardest and seemed to have the most exigent commanders.' Quoted by Dussieux, *L'armée en France*, vol. ii, p. 387.

MAKING AN ARMY TO CONSOLIDATE REVOLUTION

officer by a seaman promoted from the lower deck or by an amateur with a flair for the sea. The Spanish Government found themselves up against this same difficulty when they lost all their naval officers at the outset of the Franco Rebellion. The officers of the French Navy had been carefully trained and had to pass an examination before they became lieutenants. They were replaced very largely, even in the high ranks, by merchant-seamen, men who were technically not competent to command and manœuvre a ship of the line.[1] Moreover, the special class of seamen-gunners was abolished for *incivisme*, and a new corps of marines commanded by army gunner officers, who knew nothing about this specialized job, was substituted. It is interesting in this connection to compare a sentimental speech made by Jeanbon Saint André, representative on mission at Brest, who held that every gunner ought to have the honourable chance of serving *la patrie* at sea,[2] with the thoughtful and realistic attitude adopted by Antoine in his speech before the Jacobins' Club at the beginning of June 1791. In calling for a complete purge of officers, Antoine was prepared to make an exception in the case of sappers and gunners on account of the difficulty of replacing them with men of the requisite technical knowledge, a difficulty which may have been more acute a hundred and fifty years ago than it would be to-day when mathematical and engineering knowledge is so much more widely used and spread through the community.

'These two arms require long study and rare talents; the sudden replacement of officers would not be easy; besides, since it is true that the better educated a man is, the more remote he becomes from prejudices, so one observes with satisfaction that *civisme* is more the rule in these two corps than in the others.'[3]

As the war against Austria and Prussia, supported by English gold and English ships and joined finally by Spain, increased in extent and intensity, the difficulty of raising sufficient troops became the major preoccupation of the military experts. At the outbreak of war, in May 1792, there were available 135,000 troops of the line and 105,000 relatively untrained citizen volunteers.[4] As time went on, and the necessity for throwing vaster numbers of soldiers into the war grew more imperative, the enlistment of volunteers was increased by every form of persuasion, and the Government came to rely upon the volunteer battalions as the revolutionary backbone of the army. These were recruited, in the early period at any rate, from the ranks of the National Guard. The first great levy was raised in February 1793, about the time of Dumouriez' defeats in Holland and Flanders and subse-

[1] *Cambridge Modern History*, 'The French Revolution,' pp. 447, 449.
[2] Chevalier, *Histoire de la Marine française sous la République*, p. 126.
[3] Hartmann, *Les Officiers royales dans la révolution*, p. 215.
[4] Mathiez, *La Victoire en l'an II*, p. 52.

quent treachery. Three hundred thousand men were called for. This raised the proportion of volunteers to regulars in a dangerous degree from the point of view of efficiency. And the proportion must have been still further increased by the final *levée en masse* in August 1793, when the voluntary system was virtually abandoned and every able-bodied male in certain categories of the population was made liable for service. These French volunteer battalions bear a strange analogy to the British 'K' battalions of the First World War. One recalls the raising of the first hundred thousand, followed by the second, followed by the third, until finally voluntary enlistment, in spite of every method of persuasion, fair and unfair, had to be abandoned in favour of compulsory service. In much the same way too, as the war dragged on, the proportion of citizen soldiers to the old regulars swelled until the regulars were outnumbered many times. Finally, the method of raising both the French volunteers and the 'K' battalions was similar. In both cases, units were raised regionally under the aegis of local and municipal authorities.[1]

Service with the volunteers had certain obvious advantages over service with the line, and was therefore considerably more popular. Recruits came from the same locality and knew each other, they were enlisted for one year only instead of for eight. In addition, the rank and file of the volunteer battalions chose their own officers and promotion was more rapid than in the line, they were under a less strict system of discipline, they had a better rate of pay, and received allowances for their dependants.[2]

The somewhat casual discipline, combined with the limited term of service, was a disturbing factor. Commanders could never be sure that their men, coming to the end of their term of service, might not elect to drift off to their homes regardless of the state of the war in their particular sector or the plans of their generals for the conduct of a campaign. Complaints on this score were frequent. There was, for example, a young volunteer, one Noel from Lorraine, who at the end of October 1792 decided to give in his resignation and was considerably hurt because his captain received it with annoyance. Noel wrote in his journal: 'He told me that he did not expect that from me . . . but I had no hesitation in replying that I had thrown up everything and that I would always throw up everything for my country, that I was ready to start again on twenty campaigns if she were in danger, but he knew very well that nobody made serious war in winter, and that I wanted to spend the winter at home to continue my studies which I had interrupted for the sake of the nation.'[3] We shall find, when the American Revolutionary Army is under discussion a few pages later, that Washington

[1] *Vide* Mathiez, *La Victoire en l'an II*, pp. 52, 53, 65, for proportions of regulars to volunteers.
[2] Mathiez, *La Victoire en l'an II*, pp. 55 sq.   [3] Ibid., p. 102.

experienced exactly the same type of difficulty with his volunteer and militia troops.

There can be little doubt, too, that the volunteers, at any rate until fairly late on in the war, were not always reliable as fighters. It appears, for instance, that the battle of Neerwinden in the spring of 1793 was lost, not only on account of Miranda's bad generalship, but because volunteer troops deserted.[1]

The various governments which administered France between 1792 and 1794–5 were well aware that, although the volunteers excelled the regulars in political enthusiasm, they could not match them as trained soldiers, and methods were frequently under discussion as to how the volunteers could be used to the best advantage, in order to profit from the soldierly discipline and knowledge of the regiments of the line, without losing their own political character. On the eve of the declaration of war, when the necessity for a large and efficient army first became urgent, Narbonne, Louis XVI's Minister for War, proposed to draft the volunteers direct into the line.[2] Narbonne, however, was no revolutionary and was concerned merely with maintaining a professionally efficient army, and his proposal was killed by the more advanced men who feared that the soldiers of the line might infect the volunteers with *incivisme*.

It is not very clear how far the line was, in fact, unreliable from a revolutionary point of view,[3] but the general trend of evidence suggests that the critics exaggerated its unreliability, at least so far as the rank and file were concerned. Lafayette wanted to make a reactionary *coup d'état* in Paris after the rioting in June 1792 on account of the king's unpopular use of his veto, and he doubtless believed that if he could once launch his *coup*, he would have the ultimate support of his Army of the North. But nine months later, this same army showed unmistakably its loyalty to the revolution by a blank refusal to condone or support in any way Dumouriez's open treachery to the Convention. When that general returned from an interview with the enemy Austrians, escorted by a detachment of Austrian dragoons, the troops packed their baggage and marched off to Valenciennes on their own initiative, where they were met and welcomed by the representatives on mission. Moreover, when Lafayette, who was at Sedan at the time of the King's dethronement in August 1792, again conceived the idea of a *coup d'état* in Paris in order to rally the conservative forces in the country, he

[1] Bradby, *The French Revolution*, p. 190. *Vide* also Rousset, *Les Volontaires*, for numerous complaints, on the part particularly of professional generals, about the military unreliability of the volunteers.

[2] Mathiez, *La Victoire en l'an II*, p. 145.

[3] For example, three regiments apparently deserted to the enemy in the opening weeks of the war and Dillon's troops which were due to march on Tournai, murdered their general and fled before the enemy. (Mathiez, *La Victoire en l'an II*, p. 72.)

was foiled in any attempt to put this into execution by the attitude of his troops who refused to act with him in this cause.[1] There were, however, a number of minor incidents in the army which gave ground for the view that its temper was not quite certain and, since many officers of Royalist sympathies still remained with their regiments in spite of the continuous drain to the ranks of the *émigrés*, it is possible that those critics were right who held the opinion that more harm would be done to the revolution if the volunteers were merged in the line, and so lost the individuality and the political stiffening and *esprit de corps* ensured by the system of separate battalions, than could be offset by any extra degree of military efficiency that might be achieved.

Even so late as the period immediately preceding the proscription of the Girondins on the 30th of May 1793, when it is generally agreed that discipline had been successfully restored to the line, two representatives on mission to the Army of the North, Cellez and Varin, wrote from Cambrai to Bouchotte, then Minister for War, complaining of the cowardice and royalism of several regiments and the disaffection among the officers :

'We have already said several times that the line was generally bad ; we think that there might perhaps be a method of turning this to good advantage. It would be to disperse the soldiers who comprise the line into the battalions of the National Guard which are much below strength and would by this means be brought up to their full numbers. It appears to us that this is the best method to follow and perhaps the only one that can be used to take advantage of the soldiers of the line who would all do well when they were dispersed among or incorporated with patriots.'[2]

The representatives, however, took a more rosy view of the situation after they had had an opportunity to distribute revolutionary newspapers such as the *Journal de la Montagne* and the *Père Duchesne*, and to explain to the soldiers the reasons for the move against the Girondins in Paris. 'The soldiers were ignorant of everything that was happening,' they write, 'all the news which arrived in camp was distorted', but after the propagandist attentions of the representatives, 'they are no longer recognizable, they are animated with a totally different enthusiasm. We can guarantee that for the last fifteen days the army without being increased in number has been doubled in strength.'[3]

Reference has already been made to the system of the representatives on mission, and the value of their work in holding the army for the revolution can hardly perhaps be exaggerated. Cellez and Varin, in their proposal to draft regulars into the ranks of the volunteers, had been primarily con-

---

[1] For Lafayette *vide* Mathiez, *La Révolution française*, vol. i, p. 208; also Bradby, *The French Revolution*, p. 155. For Dumouriez *vide* Kerr, *The Reign of Terror*, p. 65.

[2] Rousset, *Les Volontaires*, pp. 203 sq.   [3] Ibid., p. 205.

cerned with the political inadequacy of the regulars. Most of the abler critics, however, seem to have been more troubled by the military inadequacy of the volunteers. And in February 1793, Dubois Crancé had again attacked the problem of how best to organize the relations between the volunteers and the line. He then suggested that they should be incorporated in the line by battalions, with officers to some extent interchangeable between the volunteer and regular units. Concurrently, the line should be given the right to elect freely two-thirds of its own officers. [1] Amalgamation, however, was not finally approved until August of that year, when the Convention decreed that one volunteer battalion should be brigaded with two regular battalions. Later, the amalgamation was made more complete by creating companies of forty volunteers and twenty regulars. [2] The outcome of the revolutionary wars undoubtedly proved this policy successful. The volunteers impregnated the regulars with their own spirit and, fighting with them on successive battlefields, learned the art of soldiering. Moreover, as the wars went on and the number of the volunteers exceeded the regulars in an ever growing proportion, the French Army became a genuinely national force. There is probably little exaggeration in the contention that the final success of French arms was mainly due to this fact. For the first time in history a national army was pitted against the politically indifferent professional soldiers of the European monarchies.

From the outset of the Bolshevik regime, Red Russia was faced with a military problem far more difficult of solution even than that which had confronted the French revolutionary leaders. It has been shown how the French Army was fundamentally altered in character without a break-up of its old framework at any specific point in time. The actual process of disintegration, which is the first step in effecting the swing-over of an army, was stopped in France before the structure of the army had been undermined. But in Russia it was encouraged by the Left until the Bolsheviks were finally in a position to seize power. The result was that during the upheaval of the Bolshevik Insurrection, the old officers' corps disappeared altogether and the rank and file of the army melted away in great masses to their peasant homes. The Russian Army had virtually ceased to exist. Every soldier was sick of the war against Germany, and the well-advertised and self-imposed task of the Bolsheviks was to find an immediate means to peace.

Here, again, the difference between France and Russia must be emphasized. The French had to re-officer, re-form, and enlarge their army in the teeth of war on their frontiers and dangerous rebellion at home. But they had never won their soldiers to the revolution with promises of peace On the contrary, they had from the first exhorted them to defend the newfound liberties of their country by force of arms and had imbued them with

[1] Mathiez, *La Révolution française*, pp. 146, 147.   [2] Ibid., p. 150

a missionary zeal which was entirely lacking to the peasant levies of Russia. The soldiers who fought at Valmy were thus persuaded that they were defending the rights which the revolution had won for them; and the Flanders troops of Dumouriez believed that they were bringing to other lands, on the points of their swords, the freedom which they had themselves learned to prize. But the Russian soldiers who were pouring away from the front in their thousands in the latter part of 1917 were doing so largely to ensure their share in the grab for land, and if they thought of liberating other peoples, it was only in terms of persuading their enemies by fraternization of the benefits of their own new regime and the advantages of a democratic peace. It is true that when the Bolsheviks came to organize an army for themselves to meet White rebellion and Allied intervention, they prescribed a military oath in which the recruit swore to do battle for the cause of socialism and the fraternization of races.[1] And a military thinker like General Tuchachevsky based his ideas for Bolshevik army organization on the theory that the Bolshevik forces should be ready to take their share in any drive in other countries towards a proletarian revolution.[2] But Tuchachevsky was thinking in particular of the position in Germany in the years immediately succeeding the war, and the theory was, as it were, held in cold storage, ready to be translated into action only when international circumstances were ripe. It was never used as a red-hot slogan to kindle enthusiasm.

The Bolsheviks, then, confronted by the virtual disappearance of the army, were compelled at once to sue for peace with Germany. The preliminary armistice was signed in December 1917, and in January 1918 they were forced to accept the cruel terms of the Treaty of Brest-Litovsk. They then had a breathing space in which to begin the creation of a Red Army before the new problem of civil war, complicated by Allied backing, became desperately acute. The first fighting of all, against the disconnected outbreaks which later coalesced into the formidable movements of Kolchak and Denikin, was conducted by detachments of Red Guards and free companies of 'Partisans'. The Partisans, composed of peasants and workers, operated mainly in Siberia and in the Ukraine. In Siberia, particularly, they seem to have developed guerrilla capacity of a high order. But in open warfare, against trained soldiers, they were almost useless. In April 1920, for instance, 30,000 guerrillas left their shelter in the Siberian forest and advanced into contact with Japanese forces who completely routed them, although the Partisans outnumbered their opponents by three to one.[3] The leaders realized from the outset that such troops were quite inadequate and that some sort of disciplined national army must be formed without delay.

The first Red Army was raised by voluntary enlistment (decree of Janu-

[1] Wollenberg, *The Red Army*, p. 179.   [2] Ibid., pp. 171 sq.   [3] Ibid., p. 33.

ary 1918) and a hundred thousand men joined in two and a half months.[1] It proved an almost complete failure. Its discipline and its quality were poor, and its units were apt to be more distinguished for plunder and violence than for military spirit. It seems to have been officered by Bolsheviks who had undertaken illegal military work before the November Revolution, by N.C.O.s of the old Tsarist Army, and by a number of young ex-officers who offered their services immediately after the Bolshevik seizure of power. Typical of the best of these officers was Tuchachevsky, an ex-lieutenant of the Guards, who was given the supreme command of this first Red Army when the Czechs rose in May 1918.[2] The general character of the first Red Army is probably correctly summed up in a telegram sent by one of its leaders in April 1918 to the Supreme War Council. 'The majority of the volunteer units', this telegram reads, 'which arrive in Briansk are distinguished by complete lack of organization and by absence of the most elementary military training. The people absolutely do not recognize their officers or obey their commands.'[3] Its fighting capacity, or perhaps it would be more accurate to say, its absence of fighting capacity, is shown by the fact that the thirty thousand Czech soldiers who had been interned in the south-west and who, mainly through mismanagement and misunderstanding, had thrown in their lot with the counter-revolution, were able in three or four weeks, during May and June 1918, to capture town after town without serious difficulty on their route through Russia from Kiev to eastern Siberia.

The danger of this incompetence was bitterly clear to Trotsky, who had been appointed Commissar for War in February. He began work at once on a plan for the creation of a properly disciplined army which should achieve professional standards of efficiency. A start was made immediately after the clash with the Czechs by conscripting enthusiastic workers from Moscow and Petrograd and from the districts most threatened by rebel invasion, such as the Don Basin and the Kuban and Volga provinces and Siberia. In Moscow and Petrograd, at any rate, there seems to have been a keen response and this principle of recruitment was gradually extended. By the early autumn of 1918, the Red Army had been hammered sufficiently into shape to enable it to recapture Kazan and Simbirsk. The anti-Bolshevik Constituent Assembly, sitting at Samara, was definitely threatened, and the Czechs had faded out of the fighting.[4] Samara, actually, was captured in October.

The basis of Trotsky's plan was compulsory service instead of voluntary enlistment, but the political reliability of the army was guaranteed by excluding from the categories of men liable for service members of the old

---

[1] Chamberlin, *The Russian Revolution*, vol. ii, p. 25.
[2] Wollenberg, *The Red Army*, p. 39; *vide* also pp. 59 sq.
[3] Chamberlin, *The Russian Revolution*, vol. ii, p. 26.   [4] Ibid. pp. 28, 119 sq.

bourgeoisie or the *kulak* class of peasants.[1] The singularly difficult problem of how to officer this new army was tackled by Trotsky with realism, great courage, and far-sighted vision. He was, of course, up against the chronic revolutionary difficulty of combining technical competence with political zeal, a difficulty presented to him by the Russian situation in its most acute form. He himself held firmly to the opinion that an efficient army could not be made without the help of a number of officers from the old regime. And in this connection it is interesting to find that Lenin was even willing that the Red Army should receive technical help from the Allies who, apparently, were ready to co-operate in this regard so long as they still thought there was an opportunity for damaging Germany.[2] This scheme was actually started, but of course petered out completely after the peace with Germany and the subsequent Allied intervention against the Bolsheviks. Trotsky, then, disagreed strongly with those Communist leaders and commanders who believed that the best type of officer would be the worker, or the common soldier, or the old N.C.O. who was politically impeccable and had shown some capacity for initiative and leadership beyond that of his fellows. He also disagreed that the best type of discipline was the loose informal variety of the Partisan band. Under his aegis, the elective method of choosing officers was abolished and discipline was sanctioned by a strict system of punishments. In regard to the election of officers, it is interesting to recall the opposite trend in the French Revolutionary Army, where the elective method of picking regimental officers was increasingly used.

The problem of how to man the officers' corps was thrashed out at the Eighth Communist Party Congress in March 1919. Both Lenin and Trotsky argued for the necessity of putting technical competence first and safeguarding political reliability as best could be done. Their view was carried by fifty-seven votes to thirty-seven in the military section of the Congress.[3] The only possibility was to draw liberally upon the shattered and scattered corps of the Tsarist Army. By August 1920, 48,409 ex-Tsarist officers had been roped by one means or another into the officers' corps of the new Red Army.[4] And this figure excluded thousands more old military officials who were brought in to serve in a non-combatant capacity. As an offset to these ex-Tsarist officers, there were some 40,000 new Bolshevik officers, who had received a training at the Soviet military schools which Trotsky had established.[5] In addition, the Reds drew upon the former N.C.O.s of the old army. Budenny, for example, the brilliant cavalry commander, whose dashing and tenacious tactics at last built up the cavalry superiority of the Red Army, had served in the Russo-Japanese war and was a sergeant-

[1] Chamberlin, *The Russian Revolution*, vol. ii, p. 27.
[2] Louis Fischer, *Soviets in World Affairs*, vol. i, p. 98.
[3] Chamberlin, *The Russian Revolution*, vol. ii, pp. 369, 370.
[4] Ibid., p. 32.   [5] Ibid., p. 32.

major in the Great War. Since the total number of fighting officers at the end of December 1920 was 130,000,[1] it is obvious, however, that the proportion of ex-Tsarist officers was dangerously high from the Bolshevik point of view.

But Trotsky did not leave the question of loyalty to chance. If he felt it necessary to make use of the services of doubtful political elements, he insured against possible treachery by instituting a ruthless system of hostages[2] and by attaching a political commissar to each important officer. Moreover, it is interesting to find that where the war could be given a national character, the old officers seem to have served with genuine enthusiasm. In the war against Poland in 1920, for instance, a number of generals who had hitherto managed to stand aside voluntarily offered their services. Brussilov was one of these. He was then old and a cripple, since he had lost a leg during the earlier days of the civil war. He had long been living in concealment, but he came to the Kremlin and demanded to see Trotsky in order to proffer his help. With characteristic audacity and decision, Trotsky accepted, and a special Advisory Council was formed under Brussilov's chairmanship. This Council was attached to the Bolshevik military headquarters.[3]

It is, on the face of it, difficult to understand how so many ex-Tsarist officers could have been prevailed upon to enter the ranks of the Red Army. The majority probably did so from fear or weakness. Concentration camps had been established for those who refused to serve; and the men who actually went to join Kolchak or Denikin did so at the peril of their own lives and knowing that the families they left behind them would be subject to interference and persecution on their account. Nevertheless, it has been estimated that some 200,000 of the 500,000 officers of the old army did in fact take service under the Whites.[4] Others among the ex-officers, those belonging to the class of men who had been promoted during the war with Germany, served with the Bolsheviks in the same sort of professional spirit that the bourgeois officers of the French Army of the *ancien régime* later served the Revolution. Others again became genuinely loyal and keen supporters of the Soviet regime and some, such as Tuchachevsky, Kamenev, Vatzetis, and Yegorov, rose to the highest commands.

The political quality of the army generally was safeguarded by the system of distributing members of the Communist Party throughout the ranks. These provided a tremendous political stiffening in much the same fashion that the volunteers of 1792–4 made the political backbone of the French Army. They were, however, deliberately not formed into special battalions on the French model, but entered the army as individuals entrusted with

[1] Wollenberg, *The Red Army*, p. 56.

[2] Chamberlin, *The Russian Revolution*, vol. ii, p. 31.

[3] Wollenberg, *The Red Army*, p. 63.   [4] Ibid., p. 72.

the special job of infecting the ordinary soldiers with their own zeal and watching out for discontent and disloyalty. In addition, their organization looked after the cultural education of the troops. By August 1920, there were 278,000 members of the party distributed throughout the army,[1] the total number of men under arms in the previous January being three million, and rising to five and a half million during the year.[2] Finally, the Communist Party worked up amongst the troops its network system of organization by party cells. In addition to the work of the party, loyalty was protected by the appointment of political commissars whose function was closely analagous to that of the French representatives on mission. A quotation from the regulations for the conduct of political commissars shows clearly the duties which they were expected to undertake:

'It is the duty of a War Commissar to prevent the army from showing disrespect to the Soviet authority and to prevent army institutions from becoming nests of conspiracy or employing weapons against workmen and peasants. A War Commissar takes part in all the activities of the commanding officer to whom he is attached; these two persons must receive reports and sign orders jointly. . . . All work must be done under the eyes of the Commissar. The only work which he does not undertake is the special military leadership, which is the task of the military expert with whom he co-operates.

'Commissars are not responsible for the appropriateness of orders given for purely military, operative purposes. . . . If a Commissar cannot approve of a military order, he must not veto it, but must report his opinion of it to the War Soviet immediately superior to his own. A Commissar may prevent the execution of a military order only when he has justifiable grounds for belief that it is inspired by counter-revolutionary motives. . . . Commissars must maintain intact the connection between the institutions of the Red Army and the central and local organizations of the Soviet Government, and assure the support of these organizations to the Red Army.'[3]

As in the case of the French representatives on mission, the importance of the work of these commissars in holding the army for the revolution can perhaps hardly be exaggerated.

The Red Army authorities were troubled with the problem of desertion on a scale which seems to have far exceeded any difficulty experienced on that score by the French. Most of the recruits were peasants who had had enough of war in any cause and ran back to their homes whenever opportunity offered. Again, the kaleidoscopic changes of government and allegiance in some parts of the country, such as the Ukraine, naturally bred political irresponsibility and an utter disregard of any governmental

[1] Chamberlin, *The Russian Revolution*, vol. ii, p. 33.   [2] Ibid., p. 29.
[3] Wollenberg, *The Red Army*, p. 255.

authority and discipline. In 1919 and 1920 it is alleged that there were nearly three million deserters. About a million of these were rounded up in raids and forced back into the army; but over one and a half million seem to have returned to the ranks voluntarily in response to proclamations.[1]

It is hard to assess the capacity of the early Red Army as a fighting force. It was never put seriously to the acid test of large-scale war against the best troops of Europe, who in any case were themselves worn out by more than four years of fighting. It is therefore impossible to compare with any accuracy the methods used to create it with those employed by the French in 1792–4. With the exception of the war with Poland, the Red Army's major operations were against the troops of Kolchak and Denikin and their successors. The White generals too had a large complement of more or less unwilling rank and file, though their officers were, of course, trained men fighting with fanatical zeal; and the ranks must have been considerably stiffened by the numerous ex-officers who served as common soldiers. The Red Army certainly learned at last to hold its own against Kolchak and Denikin, but by the time the decisive battles were being fought against the latter, it had a considerable advantage both in numbers and war material. It was, perhaps, seen in its finest form in such operations as the defence of Petrograd against Judenitch. Braced by the enthusiastic support of the armed workers from the city and exhorted in person by Trotsky, the Red battalions snatched the capital from the closing grip of the Whites when disaster had come so near that by all the rules of war it seemed inevitable.

The personal effort of Trotsky was undoubtedly a valuable weight in the balance of Red success. His whirlwind dashes in an armoured train to crumbling and threatened fronts, where he pulled together breaking units and recharged them with his own confidence, saved more than one imperilled position. One such episode, in the early critical days of the fight against the Czechoslovak Legion, has been described so vividly by Larissa Reissner, the Bolshevik girl who fought in the ranks of the Red Army, that it seems worth reproducing the passage in full. Kazan had just been lost and the routed regiments had retreated on Sviyazhsk:

'Trotsky arrived at Sviyazhsk on the third or fourth day after the fall of Kazan. His armoured train drew up at the little station, with the evident intention of making a long stay. All Trotsky's organizational genius was promptly manifested. He contrived to make effective rationing arrangements and brought further batteries and several regiments to Sviyazhsk, despite the obvious breakdown of the railways—in short, he did everything necessary to cope with the impending attack. . . . In spite of everything, the rations became obviously better; newspapers, overcoats, and boots arrived. And there, in the place where boots were being served out, we found a

[1] Chamberlin, *The Russian Revolution*, vol. ii, p. 30.

genuine, permanent army staff. The army took firm root there and thought no more of flight.'[1]

While the Red Army was preparing to re-take Kazan, a large body of White troops got round to the rear of the Red lines at night and proceeded to attack the railway station:

'Then L. D. Trotsky mobilized the whole personnel of the train—the clerks, telegraphists, ambulance men, and his own bodyguard—in short, every man who could hold a rifle. The staff offices were emptied in the twinkling of an eye; there was no more "base" for anyone. The White Guards thought they were fighting a new, well-organized body of troops; they did not guess that all the opposition they had to encounter was a hastily assembled handful of fighters, behind whom there was nobody but Trotsky himself and Slavin, the commander of the 5th Red Army. That night Trotsky's train remained there without its engine, while not a single unit of the 5th Red Army, which was about to take the offensive and had advanced some considerable distance from Sviyazhsk, had its rest disturbed by a recall from the front to aid in the defence of the almost unprotected town.'[2]

In addition to the inspiration of his gallantry, Trotsky gave the Bolshevik Army invaluable leadership through his cool-headed realism. He certainly believed that a good revolutionary soldier does not fight on bread alone, but he saw clearly that no soldier can give his best without a background of efficient material organization, and he had no use for the current romantic theories of revolutionary war-making. Early in the civil war, he wrote:

'We must now devote our whole attention to improving our material and making it more efficient rather than to fantastic schemes of reorganization. Every army unit must receive its rations regularly, foodstuffs must not be allowed to rot, and meals must be cooked properly. We must teach our soldiers personal cleanliness and see that they exterminate vermin. They must learn their drill properly and perform it in the open air as much as possible. They must be taught to make their political speeches short and sensible, to clean their rifles and grease their boots. They must learn to shoot, and must help their officers to ensure strict observance of the regulations for keeping in touch with other units in the field, reconnaissance work, reports and sentry duty. They must learn and teach the art of adaptation to local conditions, they must learn to wind their puttees properly so as to prevent sores on their legs, and once again they must learn to grease their boots. That is our programme for next year in general and next spring in particular, and if anyone wants to take advantage of any solemn

[1] Wollenberg, *The Red Army*, p. 152. *Vide* also Chamberlin, *The Russian Revolution*, vol. ii, pp. 118 sq.
[2] Wollenberg, *The Red Army*, p. 153.

occasion to describe this practical programme as "military doctrine", he's welcome to do so.'[1]

Trotsky's divergence on matters of policy from the Communists in power at a later phase of the revolution has obscured the value of his early services. It may be that, seen in the perspective of history, his later views will be forgiven and he will some day receive from his country that same title of 'organisateur de la victoire' which was handed to Carnot by his French compatriots for his magnificent work of administration in putting revolutionary France upon a war basis.

The foregoing sketches of French and Russian army organization show the radical method of attack on this problem of how to create competent revolutionary armed forces. In both cases, the problem was solved with success, in that the armies created proved equal to the tasks imposed upon them. The French and Russian solutions, though similar in spirit, show, however, a considerable difference in method. The basic difference is, of course, that in France it was found possible to retain the old military organization as a foundation upon which to build the new and much larger army required for the revolution's defence, whereas, in Russia, the old cadres were quite broken up and reorganization had to start from zero. In neither case was it found possible to do without the services of large numbers of the old corps of officers. In Russia they were persuaded by one means or another to come back and organize the Red Army; in France about half of them remained in their old places throughout the first period of the war. But it is probable that the steady process of elimination which went on continuously resulted in the end in a more complete disappearance of the old personnel of officers than took place for some years in Russia. The point is that in neither case was it found in practice workable to translate completely into action Lenin's law of the clean sweep. And Lenin himself, as has been shown, modified his theory when he had to put it to a large-scale practical test. In both cases, however, the old personnel was used merely as a technical makeshift and every means was employed to render it politically innocuous. The radical approach is seen therefore to be at bottom one of revolutionary psychology. It is not so much a matter of translating the theory of the clean sweep from first to last into action, regardless of circumstances, as of working always in the spirit dictated by that theory.

The experience of the Spanish Government in creating an army to meet the Franco Rebellion is another example of the radical method. Though here, perhaps, radical methods were dictated by external circumstances rather than by any definite revolutionary theory of the necessity for making a new army imbued with fresh ideals to defend a new regime. It has already been shown that from the outset of the rebellion, the Government was faced

---

[1] Wollenberg, *The Red Army*, p. 157.

with the almost total loss of the corps of officers both as regards the army and the navy and the loss of some 75 per cent of the rank and file of the army. Only the air force remained loyal. Of the two semi-police forces, the Civil Guard and the Assault Guard, the first split in its allegiance between the Government and the generals, but the second held by the Government. From the very start, therefore, the Government found itself without trained soldiers in any appreciable numbers and without a military organization. And it was opposed by a regular army, it is true not at first strong in numbers, but which could in addition command the strong support of Moorish legionaries and men and material from Italy and Germany. The situation was therefore more precarious than that of France in 1792 and presented a problem of military organization as difficult and fundamental as that which had confronted the Russians in 1918.

In order to get a clear idea of the complexity of the problem in all its aspects it will perhaps be as well to sketch in the political background on the Government side. The Executive which was met in July 1936 by the generals' pronunciamento was in no sense revolutionary or even socialist. It was republican and bourgeois-democratic in character. When it took office after the February elections, both wings of the Socialist Party had refused ministerial collaboration after some discussion, and there was never any question that the Anarchists—in Catalonia at any rate the strongest grouping among the workers—should enter the government. The relation of this Executive to the socialist and anarchist masses who would have to man the fight against Franco was therefore unsatisfactory at the very start. The Madrid workers, realizing that a victory for the generals would mean the end of all the hopes which had dawned and set and dawned again during the five years since 1931, clamoured for arms. The Executive, fearing armed workers more than it feared reactionary generals, hesitated and temporized with the generals. Then the masses, raking together a scratch collection of weapons, showed themselves in the streets of Madrid and brought down the Government by the mere look they put on the face of the city. Casares Quiroga and his ministers were replaced by a cabinet under Martinez Barrios. Barrios made overtures to the generals for a coalition and fell, again within a few hours, owing to the pressure from outside. It was then clear that the masses would stand for no temporizing with the generals and that unless they were led against them in energetic action, they would undoubtedly rise in revolution on their own account. A third Government was formed under Giral, of which Prieto, the leader of the Right-wing Socialists, rapidly showed himself to be the real energizer, although at that time he held no ministerial post.[1] It was this Government, then, still unrepresentative of the Anarchists, the Communists, or the Left-wing Socialists, which

[1] Borkenau, *The Spanish Cockpit*, pp. 60, 62. *Vide* also Jellinek, *The Civil War in Spain*, p. 305.

MAKING AN ARMY TO CONSOLIDATE REVOLUTION

had to undertake the task of defending Spain against the military revolt. This is an important point to bear in mind in discussing the initial difficulties of military reorganization on the government side. It is well shown up by contrasting it with the Bolshevik Government after November 1918 which was the homogeneous expression of the central and strongest drive of a revolution.

The troops at the immediate disposal of the Giral Government were the workers' militias. Companies of militia totalling 50,000 raised themselves within a week.[1] They were stiffened by the loyal sections of the Civil Guard and the Assault Guard. These militias were not raised by the Government. They were recruited by the various workers' organizations from their own members and controlled by them. In Catalonia, for instance, the anarchist C.N.T. (Confederación Nacional de Trabajo) raised a number of columns commanded by their own leaders.[2] Durruti's at once became famous for its fighting gallantry. The P.S.U.C. (the United Socialist Parties of Catalonia) column held a line at Tardientia.[3] In the Asturias, the miners revived from 1934 their famous companies of dynamiters.[4] The Communists raised more columns, probably the finest from a fighting point of view among the units of this strange spontaneous army. They aimed at an iron discipline and a centralized command, and it was their men who, along with the battalions of the International Brigade, and a contingent of Basques, won the battle of Guadalajara on the Madrid front in March 1937, the first serious victory since the opening engagements of the war and a key success.[5]

The anarchist conception of a military formation, however, with its stress on individualism, 'the organization of indiscipline', dominated the first militias. The smallest unit was a platoon of ten with a leader of its own choosing. Ten such platoons made a century and any available number of centuries a column. Many of the centuries had with them a military technician, a loyal officer from the army or the Assault Guard whose job was to advise and instruct on the technical aspects of warfare. Every century had a political commissioner. The commissioner was responsible for the commissariat in addition to the traditional function of watching out for possible disaffection and instilling enthusiasm. He was a representative of the organization which had raised the unit rather than of the central government.[6]

Wintringham, in his book, referred to above, gives a vivid account of

[1] Duchess of Atholl, *Searchlight on Spain*, p. 93.
[2] Borkenau, *The Spanish Cockpit*, p. 80.
[3] Jellinek, *The Civil War in Spain*, p. 439.   [4] Ibid., p. 312; also pp. 410 sq.
[5] Jellinek, *The Civil War in Spain*; Borkenau, *The Spanish Cockpit*, pp. 268, 535 (*vide* also pp. 206, 207, for the Communist military contribution).
[6] Jellinek, *The Civil War in Spain*, p. 439.

MAKING AN ARMY TO CONSOLIDATE REVOLUTION

the sort of work done by the political commissioners in his battalion of the International Brigade:

'Springhall (the Political Commissar) got together a team of Company Commissars who worked and lived as ordinary riflemen, but had an invaluable influence over their companies. And they did an enormous number of odd jobs. Laundry, and in our last weeks hot baths, and a club with radios and canteen, sing-songs, food, news, mail, were all up to them. For discipline they were more useful than any number of guardrooms, and orderly officers. In their little meetings, through their wall newspapers, and more than all through personal contact and argument and example, they strengthened and organized the morale, the political understanding and determination that was the basis of our discipline. And there were few pieces of work of importance undertaken by Macartney and myself on which Springhall was not consulted.

'. . . It was the most difficult work in Spain and the most valuable . . . somehow they were making rebels disciplined, somehow they were holding up to the job volunteers who got very tired indeed of a wearying and damned unpleasant war—tired sometimes to the point of mutiny and desertion. The usual "sanctions of military discipline" were not there; jailing men was too wasteful of time and goodwill for us to do much of it, and we never shot a volunteer that I know of (except Commandant L.). Discipline had to be maintained mainly by our political work; and I wish I knew how it was done.'[1]

The political basis on which the militias were built up and the consequent lack of any proper hierarchy of discipline and direction to link them to the central government provides a second important clue to the difficulties of the Spanish Government in carrying through the necessary recreation of a competent army. Even in Catalonia, which organized its own defence almost independently of Madrid, the militias hardly took their orders from the Generalidad, the legal governing council of the province. They relied on the anti-Fascist Defence Committees, which had sprung up spontaneously in Barcelona during the revolution which succeeded the defeated attempt of the generals to hold the town in July. These committees seem only gradually to have attained unity among themselves let alone with the Generalidad, and it was many weeks before they were finally subordinated to the Generalidad in anything but name.[2]

This sort of dual control is a frequent phenomenon in revolutions. It will be referred to again in connection with the relation between the Petrograd Soviet and the Provisional Government during the spring and summer of 1917, and between the Commune of Paris and the National Assembly after

[1] *English Captain*, p. 113.
[2] *Vide* Jellinek, *The Civil War in Spain*, pp. 333, 334; also pp. 344, 345; also pp. 472 sq.

206

1789. It is useful from the standpoint of revolutionary drive but hardly a factor in promoting military efficiency.

A third particular difficulty for the central government in reorganizing a national army is to be found perhaps in the federalist features of Spanish politics. Federalism is an old bugbear in Spain; and the centrifugal revolts during the troubled lifetime of the first republic of 1871-4 were one of the weakening factors which caused its downfall. Catalonia had obtained autonomy after 1931 and resented any interference from Madrid. The Basques had long been agitating for self-government. When Prieto shrewdly presented them with their statute, almost immediately after he had taken office with Giral, they determined to organize resistance to Franco almost as a united province. In the Asturias, the miners operated on their own without any real direction or assistance from Madrid. Between these various fronts, therefore, there was no effective liaison and no unification of strategy or command. If one sector were hard pressed, there was no organization to ensure that another sector would attack or send up reinforcements to relieve it. Thus, the Asturians had demanded reinforcements of men and munitions from Bilbao, which at that time could have been lightly held, but the Basques refused to send them, and the Asturians in retaliation held up the products of their province, of which Bilbao stood in need, even though they had been expressly asked to send supplies by the Madrid Government itself.[1]

A fourth special difficulty resulted directly from the dissensions between the various political parties and workers' organizations. Since the militias, as we have seen, were based on these parties and organizations, dissensions and jealousy among them detracted both directly and indirectly from the fighting value of the militias. Consignments of arms and reinforcements, for instance, were not infrequently held up in the rear by some party organization which either wanted to be in a position to secure its own political predominance or which feared the political predominance of a rival.[2] A more serious result of this rivalry was its influence in deferring the achievement of real unity of command. No party dared to forgo its own claims in the interests of a powerful central authority.

The militias themselves exhibited all the strength and all the weakness of this type of troops. As street and guerrilla fighters they were unequalled. By their almost spontaneous action they had saved Barcelona and Madrid at the outset of the rebellion. When General Mola's forces threatened to cross the Sierras and capture the city, they had streamed out to the mountains in their thousands and held the passes of the Guadarrama by sheer heroism against the trained troops thrown against them, an action which can only

[1] Jellinek, *The Civil War in Spain*, p. 424.
[2] Borkenau, *The Spanish Cockpit*, p. 81. *Vide* also Jellinek, *The Civil War in Spain*, p. 344.

be classed with the defence of Petrograd against Judenitch. It has been estimated that only one militiaman in three had a rifle.[1] But as the fighting settled down to the rules of modern warfare, it became clear that the militias, with their loose organization and their obstinate belief that a people's war must be fought by guerrilla methods, could not make headway against the professional operations of the generals with their Italian and German backing and their highly trained Moorish battalions. A few weeks after their heroic defence of the rock-strewn passes of the Guadarrama, they were thrown into the Tagus valley to meet an attack by Moors and Foreign Legionaries. The Tagus valley is treeless, flat, and dry. Here was no satisfying rock-cover to give an illusion of street fighting. Caught in the open by the dead-shot Moorish marksmen, the militias had no knowledge or skill to defend themselves. They broke and deserted in masses.[2]

Thus, after the first weeks, the general trend of the war showed clearly that, if the rebellion was to be held and defeated, two objectives of organization must be achieved on the Government side: unity of command and an army divorced from the political parties and formed on a national and professional basis. Thus Spaniards were discovering about military organization what the Russians had found out before them. And it is interesting that it was the Communist Party which all along pressed for reorganization on these lines and showed by its own battalions how much more could be achieved by troops subject to a serious system of discipline and command.

It is probable that one strong and able man could have drawn in the centrifugal tendencies of the various provinces under a single will and direction, could have imposed singleness of purpose and action upon the various quarrelling parties, and so won a clear field for transforming the militias into a regular army under a real central command. There was an enormous amount of goodwill as well as factional quarrelling and an urgent desire to get things done. Giral, certainly, was not a man of the necessary stature and Prieto had not the quality either. He was an energetic organizer and early established schools to train naval officers intensively, and arranged for some 600 more to be sent abroad to train in countries friendly to the republic. It may well be that he too was responsible for the schools which were founded to train army officers in October 1936.[3]

Giral resigned at the beginning of September in favour of a new and more representative Government led by Caballero. This new war cabinet

[1] Jellinek, *The Civil War in Spain*, p. 313; Duchess of Atholl, *Searchlight on Spain*, p. 93.

[2] Jellinek, *The Civil War in Spain*, p. 394.

[3] Duchess of Atholl, *Searchlight on Spain*, pp. 219, 215.

Prieto became Minister for Air and Marine in September 1936, *vide* Jellinek, *The Civil War in Spain*, p. 403.

included six Socialists and two Communists, a representative from the Catalan Esquerra, and one from the Basque Nationalists. Prieto remained, and was made Minister of Air and Marine. The Anarchist organizations were most unfortunately not represented.[1] Nevertheless, it was hoped that the wider political basis of the cabinet and the position of Caballero as a true representative of the fighting workers would lead to the vigorous and united conduct of the war, which every sane man recognized as imperative. Caballero declared: 'The Minister of War has taken over the supreme command of all military forces, so that the Catalan forces too coincide with all other operations in the General Staff. A new General Staff has been formed, but the problem of the unified command will be solved only when we have appointed in every sector leaders directly responsible to me and to the General Staff.'[2] He also planned a general mobilization and the regularization of the militias. But even Caballero had not the necessary force of will and personality fully to impose his plans in practice. He was no Lenin or Trotsky. And it was the harsh instruction of events rather than individual leadership which finally taught the Spanish parties and regions to sink their outstanding differences and subordinate themselves to a national organization and a centralized direction.

The great offensive against Madrid opened in the early winter and dragged on through perilous months. The city was held, heroically and precariously, thanks partly to mistakes of strategy on Franco's side, and partly to the gallantry of the defenders; certainly not thanks to competent government organization. In February Malaga fell, quite unnecessarily, owing to the slackness and ineptitude of the military staff charged with the defence of the city and the failure to send through essential munitions and supplies.[3]

The fall of Malaga showed up the incompetence of the army organization in a fashion that could not be glossed over. In Valencia and Barcelona, the demand for unity of command and the creation of a regular army became clamorous and universal. It would seem that Caballero might have used this enthusiasm to put through the necessary reforms, but in fact he did little except reiterate that he himself was the supreme commander. One important step was, however, taken. General Miaja, who was popular with the Anarchists, was given sole command of the centre fronts.[4] Unfortunately, the Catalan and northern fronts were left out of this reconstruction. But the unified command in the centre had far-reaching consequences. Almost immediately after it had been put through, the insurgents launched the offensive at Guadalajara. It was met, checked, and turned into a smashing republican victory by Miaja, whose troops put to rout more than thirty

[1] Jellinek, *The Civil War in Spain*, p. 402.   [2] Ibid., p. 405.
[3] Jellinek, *The Civil War in Spain*, p. 533. *Vide* also Koestler, *Spanish Testament*, for an eyewitness account.
[4] Jellinek, *The Civil War in Spain*, p. 535.

MAKING AN ARMY TO CONSOLIDATE REVOLUTION

thousand Italians equipped with all the advantages of modern mechanization. Miaja relied chiefly upon the International Brigade and Communist militia columns. Now the Communists had always pressed for proper discipline and centralization. Their victory at Guadalajara showed beyond a doubt that given those two desiderata, unity of command and a strong system of discipline, the Republican Army could stand up against the best-trained and equipped of the troops that could be thrown against them, unless they became seriously outnumbered owing to the weight of Italian intervention. Guadalajara opened out a new era of confident determination.

Meanwhile, discordant political agitations in Catalonia were gathering to an angry head. In April these burst into armed eruption in the streets of Barcelona.[1] The insurrection was confused politically and petered out almost of its own accord. It was like the bursting of an abscess which, once the poison has been drained out, leaves behind a healthy organism. Almost immediately after its liquidation, General Pozas took over command of the eastern front, thus bringing Catalonia into military line with Madrid; another important step forward.[2] The troubles in Catalonia had, however, prevented any effective help being given to the hard-pressed Basques, and in April Bilbao fell. This serious reverse nevertheless had the negative advantage of contracting and consolidating the area which the Republicans had to defend.

The final step towards military reconstruction was taken when the Caballero Government fell in May, and a cabinet under Negrin took its place. The crisis which resulted in the fall of Caballero had been precipitated by the Communists in the interests of their ideal of centralization, and the new Government which emerged from it was incomparably the strongest which had yet undertaken to conduct the war. Prieto was given control of all forces, land, sea, and air. The anarchist C.N.T. did not participate in the Government but settled down to a position of sincere support.[3] In August, the superiority of the new methods over the old haphazard organization was demonstrated at Brunete, a fight invited by the Republican staff, and the first victory in a chosen battle which the Government could claim.[4]

In October the Executive moved to Barcelona, so eliminating any lingering jealousy of Madrid on the side of the Catalans. Thus all obstacles towards military reconstruction had been gradually but surely swept away. The position in the autumn of 1938 showed the new methods in full action. Military service had become universal and compulsory. The militias had been broken up as separate units and the militiamen absorbed in the

---

[1] Jellinek, *The Civil War in Spain*, pp. 545 sq.   [2] Ibid., pp. 552, 558.

[3] Jellinek, *The Civil War in Spain*, pp. 558 sq. For the C.N.T. general support *vide* pp. 567, 570.

[4] Jellinek, *The Civil War in Spain*, p. 569.

general body of conscripts. Service was for an unlimited period, which no doubt in practice meant for the duration of the war. The officers were trained in special colleges and nominated by the Government. The powers of the political commissars had been cut down. They had now no longer any executive function and concerned themselves solely with educational and cultural affairs in the units to which they were attached. Education in party politics was expressly put outside their purview.[1]

How far these reforms were actually in working order before the fall of Barcelona in January it is difficult to know. The evidence, too, is not yet available as to whether the Spanish Army may not have lost something in enthusiasm and élan through the general merger.

The foregoing attempt to pilot a course through the complicated waters of Spanish politics is necessarily incomplete and perhaps, owing to the difficulty of getting reliable objective information, inaccurate in emphasis at some points. Certain events and tendencies do, however, stand out clearly as 'leading lights' and these I have tried to follow and to relate correctly to the problem of army reconstruction. In so doing, it may be that I have seemed to underestimate the military work of the militias. There can be no doubt that the militias saved the republic. At the outset of the civil war they were the only military force available. But events proved, as they had already proved in Russia, that this type of irregular political army is not adequate to meet trained troops in a long-drawn-out war fought by modern methods.

The armed forces engaged to defend a revolution against serious attack must be organized, trained, and commanded according to normal military methods. The general problem is to effect this reconstruction without losing the impetus of political zeal. It has already been shown how the Bolsheviks and the French revolutionaries of 1792 solved it, each in their own way. The key to the Bolshevik solution was the stiffening of the army by individual members of the Communist Party. The key to the French solution was the brigading of the volunteer units with the units of the regular army. The Bolshevik solution was impossible for Spain, since the revolutionary defence had been manned by a coalition of political parties in which no one party predominated. The French solution might have been used by attaching militia companies to newly formed regular battalions. Instead, the Spanish Government relied on the realization of the people as a whole that the war could only be won by an army formed on a regular model and loyally supported by all parties. How far was the ultimate failure of the republic due to its military methods, and how far was it the result of the increasing pressure of its enemies and their mechanized superiority, thanks to German and Italian intervention? We must wait until our own troubled

[1] This short account of the position (autumn 1938) is taken from information which was courteously supplied to me by the then Spanish Embassy in London.

years are over before we can get satisfactory evidence to assess this point.

The technical side of the problem of army reconstruction is, of course, concerned mainly with the raising of an adequate corps of officers. Here the Spaniards were worse placed than either the Russians or the French, since the services of relatively few old officers were available for their use. They seem, however, to have solved fairly successfully this aspect of their problem. Pre-military training was instituted in the schools, and the rapid establishment of colleges for training officers, though it may not have worked very efficiently at the start, seems finally to have ensured a steady flow of adequate men. Nor was the time-honoured revolutionary method of giving command to men who have shown in action a natural aptitude for soldiering despised. Eighteen months of war brought to the front ranks of officers a number of such natural soldiers. There were Lister, a quarryman, Carlos, a miner, Valentine Gonzalez, a peasant, Cypriano Meru, a mason, Modesto, a carpenter, Gustavo Duran, a composer, and Taguena, a professor of science.[1]

The weaknesses of militia organization and mentality as a basis for an efficient fighting force in serious and sustained warfare also troubled Washington and Lincoln in their respective times; and to overcome them their capacity was taxed to the uttermost. Difficulties which confronted the Spaniards had appeared, some of them in almost identical form, a hundred and fifty years earlier in the War of Independence and again in the Civil War.

The men who fought the redcoats in the first battle of the revolutionary war at Lexington were militiamen[2] who had hurried of their own accord from neighbouring districts to the scene of action. Militiamen also were the defenders of Bunker's Hill, whose marksmanship was so excellent that ninety-two British officers out of a total of 1,040 casualties fell to the muskets of the American 'minute-men'.[3] This was the only type of army that America then possessed. It had been instituted by the first settlers on the English model, and on the whole had proved adequate for frontier warfare and homestead defence against the Indians, and also as an important

[1] Duchess of Atholl, *Searchlight on Spain*, pp. 215, 218.

[2] In these comparisons it is important to bear in mind that, whereas the Spanish workers' militia was at first an unofficial army countenanced rather than run by the Government, the American militia was from the start an official citizen army. It represented the military establishment of the Colonies and had been organized in every colony along with the setting up of government. 'It was as essential a part of the governing machinery as the town meeting in New England or the County Court in Virginia' (Greene, *The Revolutionary War*, p. 288), and was of course historically derived from the traditional English militia. The engagement for service after embodiment was six months.

[3] G. O. Trevelyan, *The American Revolution*, vol. i, p. 315 (rev. ed.).

MAKING AN ARMY TO CONSOLIDATE REVOLUTION

auxiliary to help British regulars in the French-Canadian wars. And without it, during the earlier phases of the War of Independence, it is doubtful whether hostilities could have been maintained long enough to enable a permanent army to be formed for service against the English. Indeed, all through the war, militia units rendered magnificent service from time to time. They hovered on Burgoyne's flanks on his march down from Ticonderoga and their continual harassment was one of the decisive factors which led to his ultimate disaster at Saratoga. In the invasion of the Southern States, the first serious check which Cornwallis suffered after his victory over Gates at Camden was dealt him by militia detachments, and by partisan bands raised by enterprising individuals and which must have had much the same characteristics and indeed the same personnel as the militia. As he advanced into Mecklenburgh county, the famous nest of rebels which had issued its Declaration of Independence immediately on hearing the news of Lexington, he found himself continually nagged at by bands of yeomanry who cut off his foraging parties and killed his couriers. In the autumn Ferguson, who had been sent to recruit the highlands of South Carolina for Tory auxiliaries, was cut off by 3,000 of these 'dirty mongrels', as he called the partisan companies, at King's Mountain; and in an engagement where American marksmanship and mountain skill had full play, the partisans annihilated the British force of 1,125 men, taking 716 prisoners. The total American loss was only 28 killed and 60 wounded.

Irregulars, again, under the leadership of George Rogers Clarke, from a base at Pittsburg, rowed 1,000 miles down the Ohio to its junction with the Mississippi, and then proceeded with astonishing success and daring to clear the small British garrisons and detachments out of that territory north of the Ohio which is now the State of Illinois. In these types of action the militia and the irregulars excelled themselves. Such actions did not expose their inherent defects, but on the contrary emphasized their strong qualities. They were fighting only over short consecutive periods, and in order to carry out some more or less specific adventure or to defend their own districts from English invasion. Their leaders were picked individuals who had undertaken their tasks of their own accord, thanks to native energy and daring. There was no need for central control or a tight system of army organization.[1]

The necessity for a permanent army, based on a properly built-up organization and a real central control, became, however, apparent from the start of the war; and Washington, at any rate, realized at once that it could never be built up from a militia basis. From his point of view, probably the

[1] For general histories of the War of Independence, see G. O. Trevelyan, *The American Revolution*; Fiske, *The American Revolution*; Lecky, *History of England*, vols. iv, v.

worst feature of the militia organization was the short-service engagement, which might and frequently did in practice mean that a man was released from his obligation to serve and free to go home at any critical period of a campaign. That the militiaman frequently took advantage of this freedom was only humanly excusable. More often than not he was a farmer, and the thought of rotting crops or untilled fields at home was more than he could bear:

'In some parishes', wrote Colonel Fitch, of Connecticut, in August 1776, 'but one or two men are left; some have got ten or twelve loads of hay cut, and not a man left to take it up; some five or six under the same circumstances; some have got a great quantity of grass to cut; some have not finished hoeing corn; some if not all have got all their ploughing to do, for sowing their winter grain; some have all their families sick and not a person left to take care of them. . . . It is enough to make a man's heart ache to hear the complaints of some of them.'[1]

With such a picture of his home affairs before him, it is small wonder that the militiaman or the volunteer was not always prepared to give up his whole mind and time to soldiering. After the Battle of Bunker's Hill, militiamen drifted home at will, sometimes taking the trouble to procure a substitute, but more often omitting that duty. In any case their enlistment was due to run out in December and it was feared that if Boston were not taken before that date, there would be no besieging army left. In the face of Washington's personal and earnest entreaty to stop on a month beyond their time, the Connecticut militiamen, for instance, left camp to go home in a body so soon as their enlistment expired. Again, at Christmas 1776, Washington made his audacious plan to cross the Delaware and attack the scattered English garrisons in New Jersey in the knowledge that the majority of his little force of 3,300 men were militia whose service was due to end in a few days' time. Sullivan's failure to take Newport in August 1778 was in part directly attributable to militia defections. To succeed it was essential that he should be able to muster numbers superior to the enemy. At the critical moment 3,000 volunteers, despairing of the quick success of the siege since the French fleet had left them in the lurch by going off to Boston to refit, and panting to get home to gather their harvests, marched away in disgust to attend to their private affairs.[2]

A further weakness of the militia system was in regard to the type of officer which it frequently produced. Theoretically, it is no doubt impressive to fight a revolutionary war on a basis of complete democracy as between officer and man. But in practice, as the organizers of revolutionary armies, including the Russians, have generally found, a certain kind of equality does not make for discipline or efficiency. This kind of false

[1] C. K. Bolton, *The Private Soldier under Washington*, p. 47.
[2] *Vide* Fiske, *The American Revolution*, vol. ii, p. 78.

equality was prevalent among the American militia officers in the earlier periods of the war, with the result that:

'Little conception of the dignity and honour necessary to inculcate discipline was found in them. When captain, lieutenant, and ensign placed their salaries in a common fund with the enlisted men, drawing at the end of the month each the same share, the official intent was doubtless generous and democratic, but such officers commonized themselves and made it easy for Lieutenant Jones to filch Private Smith's blanket.'[1]

In the New England regiments there seems to have been no distinction between officer and man. A lieutenant was tried 'for voluntarily doing the duty of an orderly sergeant'—conduct which his higher commanders regarded as degrading to his rank. A cavalry staff officer was found by visitors to the camp happily shaving one of his men.[2] Other officers distinguished themselves by unwarrantable brutality to their men. Discipline became a sort of seesaw between undesirable familiarity and reprehensible savagery of punishment. Moreover, cowardice was not uncommon. At Bunker's Hill, in particular, the record of many officers was despicable.[3]

The poor type of commissioned officer obtained by the militia was no doubt mainly due to the method of his choice. Any popular member of a community who could enlist the necessary quota for a company became a captain, likewise for a regiment, a colonel. The remainder of the company officers were generally elected by the privates: and the field officers by the company officers. However, in Maryland all the officers were elected by popular vote like municipal officials at a town meeting. The qualifications of an officer were confined to such points as popularity, zeal in raising men, ability to pay the tavern bills. Just how little military knowledge or training influenced selection can be seen from the account of a New Jersey private:

'After this we chose our officers. When on parade, our first lieutenant came and told us he would be glad if we would excuse him from going, which we refused; but on consideration we concluded it was better to consent, after which he said he would go, but we said: "You shall not command us, for he whose mind can change in an hour is not fit to command in the field where liberty is contended for." In the evening we chose a private in his place.'[4]

Washington felt bitterly the inadequacy of the whole military position, and his writings during the war refer frequently to the losses of opportunity which it entailed. On the 20th of December 1776, when he was cogitating his plan for the passage of the Delaware, he wrote:

[1] Canoe, *The History of the United States Army*, p. 12.

[2] C. K. Bolton, *The Private Soldier under Washington*, pp. 128, 129.

[3] C. K. Bolton, *The Private Soldier under Washington*, pp. 131 sq.; also Canoe, *The History of the United States Army*, p. 12.

[4] Canoe, *The History of the United States Army*, pp. 4, 5.

MAKING AN ARMY TO CONSOLIDATE REVOLUTION

'Short enlistments and a mistaken dependence upon militia have been the origin of all our misfortunes.'[1]

And again in August 1780 when American fortunes were perhaps at their lowest ebb:

'Had we formed a permanent army in the beginning . . . we should never have had to retreat with a handful of men across the Delaware in 1776 trembling for the fate of America . . . we should not have been the greatest part of the war inferior to the enemy, indebted for our safety to their inactivity, enduring frequently the mortification of seeing inviting opportunities to ruin them pass unimproved for want of a force which the country was completely able to afford.'[2]

The first serious attempt to create a regular continental army under the orders of Congress was made in June 1775. The earlier armed contingents had been provided by the several states individually and were not responsible to a central authority. Enlistment for the first continental army was fixed at one year, and it was proposed that the strength should be 20,372 officers and men. Washington was appointed Commander-in-Chief. Enlistment was very slow, and after six months less than half the required total were with the colours, and of these many had to be granted furloughs in order to induce them to re-enlist. Recourse therefore had still to be made to the militia. In March 1776, for instance, Washington called out local militia for the attack on Dorchester Heights. Congress then tried out the method of each colony furnishing a quota of men to serve till the end of the war, and various bribes such as bounties and grants of land were put forward to lure in recruits. This method failed also to produce the necessary men, at any rate over a period long enough to train them into competent soldiers, and finally Congress voted for a 'three-year or the duration' term of enlistment. But all through the war the shortage of recruits on the American side was endemic and the difficulties due to inadequate terms of enlistment almost insuperable. So late as November 1779, Washington's army only mustered 26,000 effectives. He himself analysed his roll call as follows:

'Of this number, comprehending 410 invalids, 14,998 are stated as engaged for the war; that the remainder by the expiration of enlistments, will be decreased by December the 31st, 2,051; by the last of March, 6,426; by the last of April, 8,181; by the last of June, 10,158; and shortly after, 12,157.'[3]

These troubles were no doubt partly due to the Americans' almost panic fear of a standing army, inherited from their forebears who, if they were Southern Cavaliers recalled Cromwell and his major-generals, and if they were New Englanders the attempts of the Stuarts to raise regular armies and govern through their sanction.

[1] Quoted by Greene, *The Revolutionary War*, p. 292.   [2] Ibid., p. 292.
[3] Canoe, *The History of the United States Army*, p. 68.

216

MAKING AN ARMY TO CONSOLIDATE REVOLUTION

The continental army was largely held together by Washington's personal magnetism and energy. And even then it was only maintained at perhaps an average strength of 6,000–10,000 men, with the militia in use as a frequent supplement. At no period of the war were there more than 35,000 men in the field at any one time.[1]

By modern standards such small figures can hardly be said to constitute an army at all. Yet the difficulties and faults of organization which made the raising of even this tiny force so grim and disheartening a task are modern enough, and indeed foreshadow difficulties similar to those which have already been discussed in particular in regard to Spain. Most of them can be traced back to the weak position of Congress as a central body of control, coupled with its innate unsuitability for dealing with practical military organization. The lack of effective central authority sprang from the jealousies between the several States, who would have liked to regard themselves almost as small separate sovereignties and were extremely loath to delegate to a central body their State authority. Congress could do little more than register resolutions and hope piously that they would be carried out. There was no central sanction of any sort to enforce its legislation. Applied to army matters this weakness and unsuitability showed itself chiefly in the perpetual struggle to get recruits for the continental army, to equip it, to feed it, and to pay it.

We have already seen how the failure of the continental currency to hold its value reduced the soldiers' effective pay almost to zero, and was responsible to a very large extent for the alarming proportion of desertions in 1780.[2] So far as the commissariat was concerned, Congress merely meddled unnecessarily and incompetently. Until 1777, the commissariat had been managed with reasonable success by Colonel Trumbull. Instead of leaving well alone, and in spite of Washington's opposition, Congress proceeded to appoint two officers, one to buy and the other to issue supplies. Moreover, the subordinate officers were made accountable, not to their own superiors but directly to Congress. Trumbull was put in charge of purchases, but being unable to control his own underlings he resigned, and the department fell into hopeless confusion. As a direct result, the movements of the armies were crippled for the rest of the season. At the end of the year, Washington was actually prevented from carrying out a very promising movement against Lord Howe because two brigades had become mutinous through want of food. For three days they had gone without bread and for two without meat.

The sufferings endured by the troops at Valley Forge resulted much more from gross mismanagement than from any real shortage of supplies.[3] Com-

[1] Greene, *The Revolutionary War*, p. 291.
[2] *Vide supra*, p. 70.
[3] Fiske, *The American Revolution*, vol. ii, p. 28.

MAKING AN ARMY TO CONSOLIDATE REVOLUTION

menting on the failure to clothe the troops properly, dire indeed in the conditions of an American winter, Washington exclaimed disgustedly:

'Perhaps by midsummer the soldier may receive thick stockings, shoes, and blankets, which he will contrive to get rid of in the most expeditious manner. In this way, by an eternal round of most stupid management, the public treasure is expended to no kind of purpose, while the men have been left to perish by inches through cold and nakedness.'[1]

The following winter non-fighting season, which was spent by the main army at Morristown, was just as bad. The whole army would go for days together without bread and a large proportion of soldiers had not enough blankets. Even those who were still in the field fighting were hopelessly equipped for a winter campaign. In November 1779, General Glover wrote bitterly:

'The whole army has gone into winter cantonments excepting General Nixon's and my brigades, who are now in the field (800 of my men without shoe or stocking) enjoying the sweets of a winter campaign.'[2]

If there was very considerable excuse for the British to fail in adequately supplying their armies, there was next to none for the Americans who could amply have supported their small forces had they evolved even an elementary competence of organization.

Congress again showed its unsuitability as an executive instrument in regard to the appointment of general officers. It was continually swayed by personal and inter-state jealousies, and seems to have acquired not the slightest real knowledge of the military capacity of the various men whom it appointed to command or unjustly passed over. Hanging about Philadelphia or writing letters to his supporters in Congress, the soldier-politician was in his element. General Gates, because he was *persona grata* with a large group of Congressmen, was again and again given commands which he was quite unfitted to take up with success; while other men, such as the competent General Philip Schuyler, were persistently passed over purely for reasons of personal or State jealousy. Benedict Arnold's treachery, though it can in no way be condoned on such grounds, can almost certainly be explained on the score of the frequent rebuffs and insults and exasperations which he had received at the hands of Congress, at the very time when he was straining every nerve with brilliant effect in the American cause. Nor was Washington himself immune from attempts to undermine his position.

Concurrently with all these difficulties, Washington had to conduct a war while he made his untrained levies into a fighting force capable of standing up against some of the best troops in Europe. This task might well have proved impossible had it not been for the rigours of the American winter which made winter campaigning on both sides almost impossible. The

[1] Canoe, *The History of the United States Army*, p. 52. [2] Ibid., p. 68.

MAKING AN ARMY TO CONSOLIDATE REVOLUTION

winter provided an off-season from fighting which Washington could use to shape both rank and file and officers into the semblance of a competent army. At Valley Forge in 1778–9 he and his German assistant Baron von Steuben wrought wonders of training, technical instruction, and discipline. They gave the rank and file not only military knowledge but a new soldierly self-respect; and they infused into the slack officers a new responsibility for the health and morale and appearance of their men, a new regard for their fighting efficiency, and a new understanding of how this might be increased.[1]

The value of the winter's work was shown at Barren Hill in May when a force of 2,500 men under Lafayette found itself completely surrounded by British troops. The only means of escape was a ford over the River Schuylkill which could be commanded by the enemy. To extricate the army from such a situation would be a test of the new discipline. The men were formed by their officers without hesitation or confusion, were marched across the stream without crowding, and were well away on the far side before the British discovered their escape.[2] The heterogeneous bunch of tatterdemalions who had built their wooden hutments at Valley Forge in December was now an army in fact as well as name, capable not only of marksmanship—a native accomplishment—but also of cool discipline and the execution of complicated manœuvres. Finally, under Steuben's instruction the continentals added bayonet fighting to their attainments—a form of attack at which the British excelled and which was generally regarded in European circles as the acid test of the courageous and disciplined soldier.

'All the evils of organization', so it has been said, 'that overflowed Washington's cup poured out on Lincoln.' Again, provided it be not pressed too closely, an interesting analogy can be drawn between the position of the Spanish Government in regard to the Franco Rebellion and the position of Lincoln's Government in regard to the secession by the Southern States. The military problem still turned on adequate central control and the transformation of an ill-trained, ill-officered, and ill-organized citizen army into a disciplined and centrally organized and commanded fighting machine.

At the outset of the Civil War, the United States, thanks to its almost pathological fear of militarism, had still an absurdly small army. The total strength of the regular long-service force was only about 13,000 men, and these were strung out in posts over the immense lengths of wild frontier. For the rest, reliance was placed upon the poorly trained citizen militia. The regular officers' corps split gravely, 295 out of about 900 officers joining up with the South. But the rank and file held solidly by the Union. The split in the navy was more favourable to the North; 321 officers went with the South and 1,242 held to their allegiance to the Union.[3] It is, however,

---

[1] Canoe, *The History of the United States Army*, pp. 54 sq.   [2] Ibid., p. 62.
[3] Canoe, *The History of the United States Army*, p. 244, 250; Fish, *The American Civil War*, p. 215.

obvious that the small numbers of regulars would be engulfed owing to the scale on which the war developed and could not seriously influence the result. Nevertheless, at the outset of hostilities, the North was clearly in a much stronger position relative to the South than was the Spanish Government as against Franco. This is a not unimportant matter for reflection having regard to the fact that the North was never hampered by foreign support given to its opponents and that yet it required four years to win the struggle.

The geographical shape which the war took on, with both sides possessing interior lines of communication and more or less homogeneous administrative areas, precluded that type of guerrilla fighting which is perhaps best suited to half-trained soldiers. The nearest approach to guerrilla warfare were the dashing Confederate cavalry raids around and behind Northern camps. 'Three times round and out' was Lincoln's comment when J. E. B. Stuart and his men circled behind McClellan's army for the third time.

Both sides, therefore, had to meet the problem of creating a professional army in the face of serious war; and both had a nucleus round which to build in the professional officers who had divided between the two sides. The Confederates led off with far more intelligence and energy than the North. They at once called out 100,000 men for a year and proceeded to train and handle them, not as a militia, but as a professional army organized on properly centralized lines. They were, perhaps, unusually fortunate in their political leadership. Jefferson Davis seems to have been one of those rare brains who combine political instinct with military acumen and efficiency; and the politicians of the Confederate States had the sense to organize the joint government so that he had the quick and unquestioned central control, and also the man-power that he asked for. Later, the South decreed conscription for every man between eighteen and thirty-five. In the actual administration of the army, Jefferson Davis showed a far shrewder mind than the Union statesmen. He took advantage of every trained soldier of Confederate sympathies. He placed recruits beside old soldiers in the ranks in order to stiffen his battalions. He concentrated his forces into main armies with properly graded commands. And from the start he gave his generals a fair chance to lead,[1] with the result that the North, in spite of its overwhelmingly greater reservoir of man-power and material resources, was held at bay for four years.

Lincoln began the war by calling out a mere 75,000 men of the militia,

[1] Canoe, *The History of the United States Army*, pp. 248, 253. There were exceptions. It has been argued, for instance, that Davis never gave Beauregard a fair chance to show his full capabilities, and that he removed General Johnston from the defence of the Chatanooga section against Sherman for no adequate reason.

and these only for a period of three months.[1] The militia seems to have suffered from the normal weaknesses of poorly trained citizen soldiers. Elected officers who might or might not know their job, short engagements, and no adequate central staff control made up a few of its defects as a serious fighting machine.

It took Lincoln a few weeks only to discover the hopeless inadequacy of this provision for the war, and he at once began the serious struggle to increase the Union armies. In violation of the Constitution, he increased the regular army by 22,714 men and called for 42,834 volunteers for three years. Succeeding months brought further calls for volunteers, much on the lines of the French *levées* or the 'K' armies of the war of 1914–18. But in October 1863 Lincoln decided that the volunteer system would not produce enough men. He therefore issued a proclamation calling for a fixed quota of recruits to be provided by each State, every man of military age being liable for service. This was neither conscription nor freedom, and it gave him the worst of both worlds. It would have been hard to devise an arrangement more calculated to produce graft and sordid shifts. Bounties were offered and in some States rose to 1,000 dollars. Men who would otherwise have been quite willing to serve held back for a rise. Agents combed foreign countries for emigrants who would agree to enlist and hand over a rake-off from the bounty money.

It is arguable that the voluntary system, properly handled, would have given Lincoln sufficient men to win. So long as he could hold Northern enthusiasm for the war, he could afford to go fairly slowly, provided that he kept enough men in the field to prevent a Confederate invasion. He could afford to wait until a process of attrition gradually wore out the Southerners. But the organization of the army was hopelessly muddled. The lack of clear thinking as to consequences produced inefficiency which sometimes became a fantastic nightmare to able commanders who had to fight battles with the material provided for them.

The periods of service were, in practice, almost as confused as those of Washington's army. Enlistments would frequently expire in the middle of a campaign, so that commanders in the field were suddenly shorn of their troops and left without a fighting instrument, or else, they were hurried into actions where lives were merely thrown away. And the general lack of proper preparation or training showed itself in a percentage of disease and desertion which seems beyond all reason. On the Union side 199,105 men deserted.[2] State Governors had the right to appoint all officers below general rank, but local regiments still elected their own officers. The man who had

[1] For the following sketch of Northern Army organization *vide* Canoe, *The History of the United States Army*, chap. viii, and Fish, *The American Civil War*, pp. 244–50.

[2] Canoe, *The History of the United States Army*, p. 297.

raised a unit regarded it as his exclusive concern and allowed no mere State Governor or President to dictate to him who its officers should be or what ranks they should be given. All sorts of negotiations had to be carried on before a general in the field could promote an officer from this or that State.

Thus there was no fixed and certain channel of command running from the general in chief through his subordinates down to the subalterns of a battalion. The position was further confused because, thanks to the jealousies between the different States and even between one locality and another, no central reserve could be formed, since men from one district would not serve in regiments which had been raised in a different part of the Union. Hence it frequently came about that while, through casualties or disease or the expiration of enlistments, one battalion would only be able to muster perhaps 25 per cent of its roll-call, its neighbour might be parading at full strength.

Nor was any attempt made to stiffen the volunteers in their units by contacting them with regulars so far as possible. The French experience of 1792 might have been utilized as an example. It is true that the number of regulars was so small that it would not have been possible to use the system of brigading volunteer and regular battalions together, but at least regular officers could have been used to train the volunteers and provide them with a nucleus of professionally competent leadership.

A final weakness in the layout of the Union armies was the absence of any supreme military command or properly constituted General Staff. The President was legally the supreme commander of the army, and much of the military mismanagement of the first years of the war must lie at his door, even though it can perhaps not fairly be regarded as his fault. Lincoln was essentially a civilian statesman and knew nothing about either strategy or organization of armies. It did not, however, take him long to realize his own limitations in regard to such problems; nor to understand that the first desideratum was to find one competent man and see that he had adequate powers and freedom from interference to organize, administer, and command the army from private to general. But not only had he to find the man, he must also bring into line his civilian political colleagues whose heads were not only as poor at planning military affairs as his own, but were also unendowed with his sound judgement and self-regarding intellectual honesty.

In March 1864, after watching the performances of various generals for many months, Lincoln decided on the appointment of Grant and worked so that he was given supreme command of the armies of the Union. Just over a year later the Confederacy was broken and Lee, a gallant and chivalrous figure to the bitter finish of his soldiering days, handed his sword to the slovenly dressed, rough-mannered, and hard-drinking general whose appointment had caused so much puritanical headshaking throughout the

Union, but who had accomplished to the full in thirteen months the heavy task which the President had entrusted to him. It requires perhaps as much talent successfully to find and delegate to the right man a complex and difficult piece of work as it does to carry through the actual task. And it requires perhaps more strength of character to back the man chosen and support him against calumny and criticism than it does to work personally in the face of opposition and slander. Lincoln searched out the right man and, when he had found him, he backed him loyally and unstintingly. To him, then, in the end as much as to Grant belong the honours of the final Union victory.

Summing up the discussion in this chapter, it may be said fairly conclusively that all the evidence suggests, first, that radical army reconstruction is almost certainly necessary to fight a serious revolutionary war, and secondly, that this reconstruction, if it is to be efficient, must follow professional army lines. A loose type of military organization, without responsibility to a central authority, may be adequate and invaluable for the opening phases of insurrection or for guerrilla warfare; but for a serious war of siege and manœuvre against trained troops it is useless. The informal army mentality is essentially anarchistic; soldiers feel themselves free to go home when they wish; officers are apt to be chosen for reasons other than efficiency; commanders of units dislike interference from above. There can be no centralization of command or administration, no concerted strategy, and therefore no possibility of conducting operations on any large scale.

Apart from the question of how to handle what may remain or what can be regathered of the army of an old regime, the problem posed for revolutionary army organization is to create a regular army out of the raw or half-worked material of the informal band. This is the lesson of the military story of Spain after 1936, of Russia after 1917, of America in 1775 and 1861.

12

MAKING AN ARMY TO CONSOLIDATE
REVOLUTION (*cont.*)

Attempts to incorporate existing armed forces in the new
regime—necessity for a political citizen army pending the
reorganization of regular forces.

W̲e have so far been discussing radical methods of army
reorganization. It is now necessary to look at the methods
used by men who have wished so far as possible to retain
the old personnel and organization and turn it over intact
to the service of the new regime. For this purpose, the experience of France
after 1848 and of Germany after 1918 provides two clear and interesting
examples.

Immediately after the February Revolution of 1848 the shaken army was
withdrawn from Paris, thanks to a last order of the Monarchist ministry,
with the object, apparently, of avoiding possible clashes with the populace,
but with the result of ensuring it every opportunity to reform without disturbing influences.[1] Soon after February there were various minor instances of mutiny, owing, perhaps, more to broken discipline and morale
than to political action, but these were dealt with firmly and at once with
the full support of the Provisional Government in Paris.[2] Moreover, that
Government welcomed back into its service all those generals who were prepared to work for it, in spite of the fact that many of them had been in Paris
on the King's side during the critical days, a few having actually been
wounded in the sporadic fighting against the people. According to Lamartine, almost all the generals were prepared to turn over their services to the
new Government. They came to the Hôtel de Ville to proffer their allegiance
and were given no orders beyond a general instruction to rally their troops
and keep safe communication with Paris outside the barriers.[3] No attempt
was made to check up on their activities after they had returned to their
commands. So far as the rank and file was concerned, Ledru Rollin, playing a lone and difficult radical hand in a government of half-hearted revo-

[1] Quentin Bauchart, *La Crise sociale de 1848*, p. 129.   [2] Ibid., p. 229.
[3] Lamartine, *The Revolution of 1848* (English trans., 1849), p. 145.

lutionaries, seems to have made some effort to work up political zeal among the soldiers through the medium of the Revolutionary Clubs, but the practical result of this was negligible because it was never undertaken on a sufficiently large or enthusiastic scale.[1] After the Left demonstration on April the 16th, sixty-five generals were retired and a number of staff officers and colonels,[2] but it appears that this was done following a spurt of revolutionary pressure from below and not at all as part of the considered and keen policy of the Government.

The willing ease with which the officers drifted over from their allegiance to Louis Philippe into service under the Provisional Government requires perhaps some explanation. This can partly be accounted for by the fact that for some time before the revolution, Louis Philippe had apparently neglected his army and therefore had little personal popularity. 'So long as he is on the throne', a contemporary critic of the period wrote, 'it will be impossible to get the army back on to a good footing. If his reign lasts a long time, the consequences may be grave, and the drift in the army may bring a new revolution.'[3] Moreover, the king had abdicated and fled to England; there was thus no focal point at which the officers' corps could rally for a positive defence of the old regime. Finally, it was from the outset clear that the Provisional Government had no intention of leading a radical revolution which should shake the economic and social foundations of France. It must have appeared therefore to the more politically intelligent officers that the best chance of preserving France from a deep revolutionary upheaval would be to support the moderate men in power at the Hôtel de Ville. The army, then, was for reasons of political opportunism to some extent identified with the Provisional Government, but never in any sense became, as after 1789, an armed expression of the people in revolution. This was in some degree due to the policy of the Left leaders themselves. Blanqui and the Left Clubbists, for instance, seem to have supported the decision to withdraw the army from Paris, a singularly short-sighted policy on their part, since the withdrawal cut off the soldiers from the main source of Left political influence.

In the upshot, the revolution was lost largely on account of the failure to give the troops any understanding of the underlying issues involved or to provide them with the leadership necessary to win permanent success. When General Cavaignac, who had held command under the Duc d'Aumale in Africa and had since returned to Paris, was given plenary powers to liquidate the rebellion of the June Days, he experienced no difficulty in using his troops against the insurgent workers; and when Louis Napoleon made his *coup d'état* some eighteen months later, the army proved

[1] *Vide* note 2 on p. 149.

[2] Caussidière, *Mémoires*, part II, p. 39.

[3] Quoted by Quentin Bauchart, *La Crise sociale de 1848*, p. 229.

his reliable instrument. Yet, there can be little doubt that, given different conditions, the soldiers, in the earlier weeks after February, could have been won to an ardent support of a serious revolutionary government. Caussidière, the shrewdest perhaps of contemporary Left observers, looking back in later years on that period, wrote in his memoirs that there was an enthusiastic feeling for the Republic among the rank and file and the lower officers, and that in his opinion the army could have been bound to the revolution by eliminating undesirable officers and by making changes in promotion. He also suggests that the soldiers would have liked to march to the support of the struggling Liberals in Italy and Poland.[1] Yet there was no trouble with the army when Louis Napoleon ordered his troops to Rome to attack Mazzini's Republic and reinstate the Pope. This was only a year later.

The last remark of Caussidière raises a further point. It is hard to endorse on humanitarian grounds the war-mongering policy of the Girondins, whose crusading zeal forced the declaration of war against Austria in 1792, but a strong case can be made out for them on the score of political strategy. Just as modern dictators may be driven into making war in order to distract their peoples from economic discontents, so the patriotism fanned up by war may be useful to heat a national welding iron in the hands of a revolutionary government. In 1792 such a welding iron proved invaluable. The waverers and the indifferent were aroused by the national danger and, together with the convinced and ardent revolutionaries, merged into their country's service. Thus the revolution itself became identified with the nation and purged of partisanship in the flame of patriotic ardour. The epic struggle of the U.S.S.R. in the present war provides another example, despite the time-lag of twenty-four years between 1917 and 1941.

A foreign war might well have deepened and strengthened the Revolution of 1848 by forcing it to vigorous action and giving it a national certainty of aim. If Lamartine had embarked upon a crusade to help free the oppressed peoples of Poland and Italy, it is possible that the old Jacobin spirit would have swept once more through France and so enabled the political ground won in February and March to be permanently held and consolidated and perhaps even extended.[2] Again, if armed opposition had broken out internally, the Provisional Government might well have been forced to take up a more foursquare revolutionary position, or to make way for keener and more determined men. In either case, the army must then have undergone the healthy sifting and reconstruction which, in fact, never took place. These, however, are surmises of history which it is perhaps idle to make.

---

[1] Caussidière, *Mémoires*, part I, p. 249.
[2] Lamartine discusses his foreign policy in *Trois mois au pouvoir* (ed. 1848), pp. 15–20. *Vide* also his *Manifesto to the Foreign Powers*, pp. 69 sq.; and his *Report to the Assembly on Foreign Relations*, pp. 178 sq.

MAKING AN ARMY TO CONSOLIDATE REVOLUTION

What cannot be questioned is that the soldier of 1848 was never seriously encouraged in any way or by anybody to show his revolutionary mettle. Lamartine's rather self-congratulatory dictum that 'when at the close of an intestine commotion, the soldier remains a soldier, there is no reason to fear that revolution will develop into anarchy'[1] shows clearly that the Provisional Government did not understand or did not agree with the revolutionary maxim that you must first disintegrate the army and then re-create it in a new character.

The military situation in Germany after 1918 provides a particularly interesting example of the methods and psychology of unconfident men who have to remake armies after a revolution. It has already been shown how Ebert's Government, almost from the hour at which it took power, might have had behind it an immense and to all intents and purposes organized body of military support. The armies at the front under Hindenburg's command never broke discipline to the extent of disintegration but showed unmistakably their sympathy with the revolution, and the troops in the rear, who had been the actual makers of the revolution, were naturally eager to support it. So far as the rank and file was concerned, the support pressed exactly at the axis of the revolution. This axis was formed by the moderate Socialist parties, who represented the main body of revolutionary opinion throughout the country, and whose endorsement of the Government held it in place, without at the same time imparting to it any real revolutionary driving force. The soldiers, on the whole, were not theoretical socialists, perhaps because a large proportion were free peasants in civil life. The circumstances of the moment, however, united them closely to the moderate Socialists.

In regard to the officers, circumstances had manœuvred them into a tactical support of the Government as the only guarantee against chaos. Under such conditions, a socialist regime, developing its strength from a moderate start, should have been impregnable.[2] Ebert's Government, by its handling of the military situation, threw away chance after chance. The armistice was signed on November the 11th and the Government was at once confronted by the difficult task of demobilizing the swollen and disaffected army. Every effort was made to complete demobilization by Christmas. This meant that the guarantee of political power was shifted off the army; and the Government was thus left almost entirely without organized military support in the event of insurrection or for police purposes.[3] Such an obvious eventuality might have been foreseen, but no immediate steps were taken to meet it by organizing forthwith a substitute citizen army, composed of the keen workers and elements of the old army who might

[1] Lamartine, *The Revolution of 1848*, p. 328.
[2] *Vide* Rosenberg, *A History of the German Republic*, pp. 4–9.
[3] Rosenberg, *A History of the German Republic*, pp. 47, 48.

have been eager to re-enlist, and officered by progressive men from the old officers' corps. Such an army could have been based on voluntary enlistment and would not therefore have run counter to the subsequent terms of the Treaty of Versailles. This was the first serious mistake and, as will be shown, its disastrous effects were made clear before many weeks.

A second grave error was made by the Government in regard to its relation to the chiefs of the old Imperialist Army. At the outset, the High Command was left in the hands of Hindenburg and Groener; and Ebert and his ministers actually agreed to turn over to them the delicate task of bringing back the defeated troops from the front instead of shouldering this burden themselves.[1] This decision was not perhaps so cowardly as it appears. To get the immense army back in good order was a technical undertaking of tremendous difficulty and had it gone wrong the chaos would have been appalling—Hindenburg and his staff carried it through without serious hitch. But in turning over the task to them, Ebert unquestionably gave the generals a welcome opportunity to begin their work upon the nascent republic. The gibe in the title of Th. Plivier's novel *The Kaiser Goes: The Generals Remain* was not undeserved. Groener not unnaturally disliked the soldiers' and workmen's councils and all that they implied. His desire was to restore order in Germany, and when that was done and the last violent spurts of revolutionary fire extinguished, to fashion a new army, apart from politics, but led by the old Imperialist officers. Such an army would prove a permanent effective damper on any future inflammation of feeling. He understood perfectly the nervousness of Ebert's Executive whenever it was called upon to handle any problem which involved the technical organization of troops and he played upon this nervousness by his offers of professional support and his threats to withdraw support if his views were not complied with. His plan was to seize every opportunity for driving a wedge between the Left and Right wings of the revolutionary movement. Ebert feared the Leftward drive of the revolution and this fear, coupled with his nervousness of military matters, made him virtually a prisoner in the hands of Groener and the General Staff. A symbol of the whole situation was the private telephone line, kept secret from his Left colleagues, which connected his office with that of Groener at Wilhelmshöhe and by which, every evening when the day's work was done, he could communicate with the general and talk over such of his problems as he thought fit.[2]

The first violent crisis for the Government came when the People's Naval Division, a force of a thousand sailors who had come to Berlin in November and considered themselves as a spearhead of the revolution, refused to obey the Government's order to vacate a palace in Berlin where they had

[1] Rosenberg, *A History of the German Republic*, p. 48.
[2] Bénoist Méchin, *Histoire de l'armée allemande*, vol. i, p. 86.

taken up their quarters. A series of fantastic negotiations and considerable disorder followed this refusal, and Ebert made his third mistake by demanding help from the High Command to eject the unruly sailors. There were still a number of undemobilized front-line soldiers about Berlin. These were under the command of General Lequis who was promptly and joyfully ordered by the High Command to restore order. Heavy fighting ensued in the heart of Berlin on December the 24th. Lequis's force, weak though it was, would have succeeded in ousting the sailors had it not suddenly been taken in the rear by a huge and angry crowd of revolutionaries. Lequis was forced to extricate his troops and save his officers from being lynched by the crowd as best he could.[1] The day's honours rested with the sailors and the Left; and superficially it seemed that the Leftward drive of the revolution had received a considerable impetus. The General Staff was in despair, and the old officers' corps, as an organized body, crumbled and broke. Only a few hundred volunteers remained. Nevertheless, the wedge between the two wings of the revolution had been inserted. The Government had thrown itself upon the goodwill of the old generals and, in spite of their weakness, they were in a position to drive home this advantage with shrewd blows.

The crisis increased in gravity. Revolutionary crowds drifted through the streets of Berlin. The demobilized and half-starved soldiers mingled with the civilians. Machine-guns spattered at street corners. The exacerbated feeling flared up into the Spartacus revolt in January under Liebknecht, Ledebour, and Scholze; an ill-starred and unsuccessful affair, though it seemed that the insurrectionaries must have held Berlin in the hollow of their hands. At the end of December, after consultations with General Groener, Ebert had manœuvred his Left colleagues, Barth, Dittmann, and Haase, into sending in their resignations, thus cutting himself adrift once and for all from the advanced line of the revolution. At the same time he sent for Noske, the Majority Socialist leader whose activities at Kiel in November had been largely responsible for the quelling of the mutiny and the restoration of order among the sailors. Noske was entrusted with the task of restoring order in Berlin, and prepared to work hand in glove with Groener and the generals. His attitude was simple. 'One of us', he said, 'must play the part of executioner', and he accepted that part without demur. And for his subordinates, he cast the officers of the old Imperialist Army. 'It is our misfortune,' he wrote later, 'that no leader has arisen from the ranks of the N.C.O.'s or the common soldiers, despite the fact that power was everywhere in their hands. I have thus been obliged to fall back on the officers. Certainly many of them are monarchists, but when one is faced with reconstruction, one must have recourse to professionals. An

[1] Rosenberg, *A History of the German Republic*, pp. 59–62; also Bénoist Méchin, *Histoire de l'armée allemande*, vol. i, p. 120.

army without discipline is a monkey's grimace. Between a bad socialist officer and a good conservative officer, I choose the second.'[1]

The decision to raise such an army was correct in itself. The Government had no alternative but to support itself by force. And Noske's viewpoint was not necessarily counter-revolutionary—it was sound sense. Trotsky had taken much the same line. But he had taken it merely as a means to a revolutionary end and he had safeguarded his revolutionary position by every method that came to hand. Noske arranged no safeguards; and the Free Corps which he helped the generals to raise for the purpose of restoring order rapidly became nests of counter-revolutionary feeling and activity.

The German Government was also too late. It should have seen to the making of an effective revolutionary guard from the very start. Two men only, Barth and Haase, seem to have realized the supreme importance of doing this. Under their influence Ebert had published a decree on December the 12th constituting a Civil Guard. But recruitment was to be purely voluntary and the call for recruits seems to have met with practically no response.[2] The scheme therefore was in practice abortive and without influence on the development of the situation. It is also worth remarking that, at the Congress of Soldiers' Councils which opened in Berlin on December the 16th, Barth demanded the liquidation of the old officers' corps, lock, stock, and barrel. He was outmanœuvred by Ebert and, in spite of the fact that the majority feeling of the meeting seems to have been with him, his proposition fell dead.[3]

The Free Corps, then, which might have been constituted as a true revolutionary guard, became the most serious menace to the revolution's stability. Their leaders hated the movement which had destroyed the Empire they had served, and the men were frequently unemployed adventurers who had no political faith but owned a sort of allegiance to their officers and quickly developed a tough, if politically quite irresponsible, sense of *esprit de corps*. At Noske's orders, the first of them proceeded to a systematic liquidation of the Spartacist positions in Berlin. The fighting lasted for the inside of a week. When it was over the officers of the old army had bought for themselves a licence to enlist Free Corps to their hearts' content. Within a few weeks the Republic found itself saddled with an irresponsible military force without any official central organization or command, whose various units took action more or less haphazard according to the decisions of the individuals who led them. Their temper was shown by the treacherous murder of Liebknecht and Rosa Luxembourg who had been arrested by one of their companies after the January revolt

---

[1] Quoted by Bénoist Méchin, *Histoire de l'armée allemande*, vol. i, p. 131.

[2] Bénoist Méchin, *Histoire de l'armée allemande*, vol. i, p. 99.

[3] Ibid., pp. 105, 106.

and were then killed as prisoners. The murders were allowed to go un-
avenged, since the men who were implicated were tried by their own comrades and either acquitted out of hand or helped to escape after a formal
verdict of guilty.[1] This was only the first and, since Liebknecht and Luxembourg were international figures, perhaps the most dramatic of many such
incidents. Throughout the length and breadth of Germany the Free Corps
were always enthusiastically active in the suppression by fair means or more
frequently by foul of any disorders that might have a revolutionary source.
The murderers they sheltered were seldom brought to justice and, if they
were committed for trial, almost invariably escaped with sentences that
were farcically light. For the Government, too fearful to tackle the military
problem for itself, had also been too nervous to re-staff the judiciary with
men of reliable republican sympathies, and the judges as a rule shared the
feelings of the accused. The result was that the heart was taken out of the
true supporters of the revolution; their confidence in the Government they
had brought to power was being steadily undermined. 'Every suppression
raised up new enemies for the ministry, and especially caused grave suspi-
cions to grow in the minds of the rank-and-file socialists.'[2] Not only were
they disillusioned and devitalized; they were made powerless in practice.
Their position has been bitterly summed up by one of the most clear-
thinking Left critics of the period:

'The political result of the civil war that was waged during the first half
of 1919 in Noske's name was the total destruction of the political power of
the councils. . . . Thus the attempt to found a democracy to succeed to the
revolution was an utter failure. As a result the disarmament of the working
classes was carried out systematically and with the greatest thoroughness by
the officers. . . . By the middle of the year the real power in Germany lay
with the Free Corps and not with the Assembly. Hand in hand with it went
the systematic armament of the propertied middle classes, of estate owners,
students and so forth. . . . The German workmen saw in this development
the victory of the counter-revolution.'[3]

It is worth contrasting here the very different revolutionary psychology
shown by the Socialist leaders, Bauer and Deutsch, after the Austrian revolution in the autumn of 1918. Bauer and Deutsch successfully opposed suggestions that an armed force of demobilized officers should be formed to
maintain order. They also opposed the formation of a Students' Guard and
a Citizen Guard. Instead, they set about organizing a volunteer army of
proletarians taken from the disintegrated ranks of the regular forces.
Companies of Red Guards, which had sprung up before the revolution,
were incorporated in this army. It carried the Red Flag and later

[1] Rosenberg, *A History of the German Republic*, p. 85.
[2] Quigley and Clarke, *Republican Germany*, p. 45.
[3] Rosenberg, *A History of the German Republic*, p. 89.

231

became the Volkswehr.[1] The Free Corps of Germany were transformed into the Reichswehr with all its leanings towards the old imperialism. The composition and psychology of the Reichswehr have already been discussed in regard to its disastrous relation to the new and struggling Republic. It is here only necessary to link up the emergence and particular character of the Reichswehr with the initial failure of Ebert's Government to realize that the consolidation of a revolution depends upon revolutionary measures and revolutionary psychology, and that an army which fails to reflect the new spirit of the people is a menace rather than a guarantee for revolutionary power.

The Spaniards made a similar mistake after the Revolution of 1931, by making half-hearted efforts only to bring the old officers' corps into line with the new spirit of a republican army. Azana, then Minister for War, knew perfectly well that the officer caste was hostile to any genuinely democratic republic, but he could not find the courage to dissolve the corps and reconstruct it with men whose political loyalty was proved, even though their technical ability might be a little suspect. All that Azana did was to retire about half the officers on the establishment, but since the proportion of officers to rank and file had been of fantastic size, this measure in fact only put the army on a more or less normal footing. It was further stultified because the dismissed officers were permitted to form a reserve, retaining their titles, uniforms, arms, and pay.[2] There was thus every opportunity for them to keep up close connections with the active officers. Thus, in effect, thanks to Azana's timidity, the reactionaries were given a blank cheque on the army. Five years later, when General Franco's plane landed in Morocco, this cheque was presented for payment.

History shows that every successful revolution has in fact been protected at the outset by its own soldiery and police. It is not suggested that such *ad hoc* forces can form a permanent military defence. Indeed, much of the foregoing discussion on the formation of revolutionary armies has gone to show that forces of this type are not capable of the sustained and disciplined action, the wide organization, and high degree of centralization which are necessary for modern operations of war on any large scale. But immediately after a seizure of power, their use is invaluable. In all probability, they will be the only troops quickly available, and the fullest possible use must be made of their services until a new regular army can be formed. They will as a rule represent the armed insurgents who have made the revolution, reinforced by companies of revolutionaries who have formed themselves more or less spontaneously in order to defend the new system. Directly after the capture of power there seems to be a natural urge on the

[1] Glaise-Horstenau, *The Collapse of the Austro-Hungarian Empire*, pp. 321–2.
[2] Jellinek, *The Civil War in Spain*, pp. 58, 134. For proportion of officers to men in the pre-Republican Spanish Army, *vide supra*, p. 118.

part of the revolutionary people to express their enthusiasm in an armed guardianship of the new law and order.

Such a desire, for instance, was clearly shown in Paris even after February 1848, though on a small scale and in a manner quite insufficient to guarantee the successful holding of the revolution. Apart from the established National Guard, various *ad hoc* bodies of citizen soldiers and police, directly based on the revolution, were raised immediately after the upheaval. Lamartine, for instance, himself enlisted a corps of Gardes Mobiles to help in the maintenance of order, and there was a Garde Républicaine, whose special work seems to have been the defence of the Provisional Government. Finally, there were the companies of Montagnards raised by Caussidière who had been made Prefect of Police.[1] The sentiment of these companies and of their commander was a good deal more radical than that of the Government, and their rough aspect and vigorous views seem to have disturbed Lamartine and his colleagues who were determined that the revolution should be run on gentlemanly lines. The Montagnards, however, were probably a true expression of the more vital forces behind the movement, and the fact that the moderates succeeded, in May, in ousting Caussidière from the Prefecture of Police is an indication of the way in which the counter-revolutionary tide was beginning to flow.[2]

It is also worth noting in this connection that, even after the mild Spanish revolution of 1931, the revolutionary executive at once raised a new body of soldier-police called the Assault Guard, whose special function seems to have been to check up on possible counter-revolutionary activities of the old and dubious Civil Guard.[3] In 1936 the sagacity of the founders of the Assault Guard was rewarded, for this corps, generally speaking, held loyal to its allegiance to the Republic, whereas many units of the Civil Guard either joined the generals' revolt or allowed it to go unchallenged in the areas under their control.

The great-scale experiments in the formation of political citizen armies to guard a revolution are, of course, the French National Guard after 1789, and the Russian Red Guard. The fortunes of the French Guard have already been traced, and it is only necessary to emphasize here its original character as a spontaneous expression of the people in revolution, and its invaluable work as the guardian of the developing political ideas for which the revolution stood. It is also important to recall that immediately after its spontaneous formation during the Bastille rising, it was wholeheartedly accepted and legalized by the men who had won power and, throughout the years after the fall of the Bastille, always regarded as the protector of the people and the barrier against counter-revolution. Its occasional partial

[1] Quentin Bauchart, *La Crise sociale de 1648*, pp. 195, 220–2.
[2] Lamartine, *The Revolution of 1848*, p. 539.
[3] Jellinek, *The Civil War in Spain*, p. 135.

failure to fulfil this trust has been explained on specific grounds and is no argument against the general validity of its function. It is, however, necessary to distinguish between the early aspect of the Guard as a political army for the defence of a revolution and its later character as a general citizen army charged with the defence of the new regime. Reference will be made to this point again later, when contrasting the organizations of the French Guard and the Russian Red Guard.

The Red Guard[1] sprang up in Petrograd, Moscow, and other industrial centres during the period between the fall of the Tsar and the Bolshevik Revolution of November. It was a proletarian military organization of workers based mainly on individual factories and with elected officers and commanders. It was quite unofficial. But it was not a new phenomenon. The revolutionary workers of 1905–6 had organized similar units in their factories, and the moderate parties of 1917 remembered. Hence they looked upon the Red Guard askance and did everything in their power to suppress it. They tried to sterilize its activities by a decree compelling it to amalgamate with the normal militia or citizen police, the object, of course, being to dilute its separate proletarian character and bring it under bourgeois control. They tried to make it unpopular by suggestion that its secret function was to act as a wedge to divide the people from the army.[2] Thus, driven underground, the Guard could procure arms as a rule only by the secret and uncertain methods available to rebels. But under Bolshevik influence its organization was pushed forward. When the Kornilov push became imminent in August and Kerensky's Government required, whether it liked it or not, the help of the more uncompromising revolutionaries of Petrograd, the Red Guard came into the open and was armed. Within a few days 25,000 workers enrolled, and the Guard became the official armed force of the Petrograd Soviet.[3] The Bolsheviks had become by this date the dominating influence in the Soviet, so that the Guard was in effect under their leadership, a fact of great importance for the future development of the revolution, since it implied that the armed force of the workers in the capital provided a powerful sanction for the most advanced section of political thought.

The defence of Petrograd against Kornilov was almost entirely in the hands of the Red Guard, and after the collapse of Kornilov's push their position was naturally very much strengthened. They were legalized and at any rate to some extent armed in Moscow and other industrial centres.[4] In Petrograd, realizing that the forces of the revolution were driving forward towards an inevitable armed clash between the moderates and the advanced

---

[1] *Vide* Wollenberg, *The Red Army*, pp. 20 sq.; also Chamberlin, *History of the Russian Revolution*, vol. i, p. 307.

[2] Wollenberg, *The Red Army*, pp. 21, 23, 26.

[3] Ibid., p. 24.   [4] Ibid., pp. 24–5.

MAKING AN ARMY TO CONSOLIDATE REVOLUTION

wing, they prepared for the coming Bolshevik insurrection. A further effort was made to disarm them, or at any rate to control their possession of arms, but they were now strong enough to disregard such attempts. Arms seem to have been obtained quite freely, for instance, from sympathizers in the government arsenals. Thus Trotsky reports how a delegation of workers came to him asking for weapons and told him that the Sestoretsk arms factory would be prepared to deliver them on receipt of an order from the Central Executive Committee of the Soviet. Trotsky signed this order and 5,000 rifles were at once handed over.[1]

In this connection it is worth noting how the curious system of dual power—Soviet versus Government—which developed between March and November, and to which Trotsky attached great importance, helped the extreme Left to gain a firm hold over Petrograd and enabled it to control the armed battalions of the workers. In practice, the relation of the Soviet to the Provisional Government was not unlike that between the Paris Commune of the Great Revolution and the National Assembly. Both the Soviet and the Commune gave expression to the revolutionary sentiment of the people of the capital and provided a focus and leadership for their activity. It was thus possible to bring very great revolutionary pressure to bear upon the more timid and slowly moving central Government. Moreover, since the Soviet had won the allegiance of the Red Guard and the Commune had the right to call out the National Guard, both had behind them the sanction of armed revolutionary force. Thus an important machinery was evolved to hustle the hesitant central Governments and to speed up the general tempo of revolution.

It is interesting to recall here the system of dual power which emerged in Catalonia after the revolutionary upheaval which took place in Barcelona following the defeat of the rebel attempt to capture the city in July 1936. This system has already been referred to. Numerous revolutionary committees sprang up, which shared or even wrested control from the Generalidad, the governing council of the province. These committees, in particular, looked after the organization and dispatch to the fighting zones of the militia columns.[2] Such a system will obviously give rise to confusion and a certain dissipation of energy, but there can be no doubt of its general value as a source of revolutionary drive. It is here only necessary to refer to it from the point of view of its effect on military development.

As summer drew into autumn, the Red Guard became the spearhead of the coming attempt to deepen the revolution, a spearhead whose shaft was held in the able hands of the Bolsheviks. Trotsky describes how the worker stood at his bench or lathe with a pack on his back and a rifle by his side

---

[1] *History of the Russian Revolution* (one-vol. ed.), p. 949.

[2] Jellinek, *The Civil War in Spain*, pp. 333 sq.

MAKING AN ARMY TO CONSOLIDATE REVOLUTION

waiting for the final call to action.[1] And when the November explosion came, the Red Guardsmen, with detachments of Kronstadt sailors, made the fighting force on which the Bolsheviks relied.[2] After their seizure and consolidation of power, when the old army dissolved, the Red Guard remained the only assembled military force at the Government's disposal. It played an invaluable part in the first spasmodic fighting of the civil war, staving off disaster while the regular Red Army was in process of formation. Indeed, the first units of that army were largely recruited from its ranks.[3] As time went on, the Guard seems to have been completely merged into the new army and to have lost its identity as a separate force.

The Red Guard provides, perhaps, the most complete example of the proper use and development of a revolutionary fighting force. Its original character of a grouping of armed revolutionaries pledged to defend the first gains of the revolution and to forward its further aims, its subsequent development as the military force on which the revolutionary government relied to combat counter-revolution while a permanent army was being formed, and its final necessary replacement by that army in the interests of increased military efficiency represent the three phases through which a force of this kind must correctly pass.

The French National Guard reflects these phases in a less complete and well-differentiated form. In the middle phase, for instance, the French Guard, in the guise of the volunteer battalions, acted as a stiffening for the regular army, which as we have seen had never dissolved, rather than as the shield behind which a new army could be formed. And the final phase was represented, not by a merger of the Guard in the ranks of the regular army, but by its permanent establishment as an official citizen army, in which capacity it gradually lost its revolutionary character. These differences between the French and Russian Guards are perhaps mainly due to original differences in organization. The Red Guard was drawn to all intents and purposes exclusively from factory workers. This gave it a limited class basis, and further implied that its units were founded on individual factories rather than on territorial districts. The units, composed of men who worked together in their daily life, were homogeneous and closely knit. The French Guard, on the other hand, was recruited on a regional basis. It was open at the peak of the revolution to all citizens, but in the earlier and later periods only to those who were entitled by a certain property qualification

[1] *History of the Russian Revolution* (one-vol. ed.), p. 1036.

[2] Trotsky, *History of the Russian Revolution* (one-vol. ed.), p. 1040.

[3] Wollenberg, *The Red Army*, p. 28. *Vide* also Chamberlin, *History of the Russian Revolution*, vol. ii, pp. 25, 26; and Reed, *Ten Days that Shook the World*, p. 293, for terms of a decree signed by Rykov on November the 10th, ordering all Soviets of Workers' and Soldiers' Deputies to form workers' militias throughout Russia. The military and civil authorities were ordered to give every assistance to the Soviets in this task.

to vote. Thus, taking Paris for example, it was to some extent crippled from a revolutionary point of view since some units were recruited almost exclusively from bourgeois districts. In any case it represented on the whole a radical petty bourgeois rather than a proletarian ideology.

The factory method of recruitment was not, of course, open to the French since the industrial revolution was not sufficiently advanced in 1789. But the fact that there was no real proletariat in the Paris of that day does not invalidate an analysis of the advantages and disadvantages of the two methods; there can be little doubt that, from the viewpoint of an advanced socialist revolution, the Russian method will provide an armed force of a stronger revolutionary temper with a narrower range of political interests and therefore with a sharper concentration. Regional recruitment is bound to entail a certain waste of energy owing to the varying reaction to events of individuals with widely different records and background. In contemporary times, a factory basis for a revolutionary guard would need to be sufficiently flexible to include an armed organization of distributive and transport workers, whose increasing place in the structure of a modern state obviously makes their position in any revolution of the first importance. The factory basis of recruitment would therefore require to be coupled, as it was in Spain for the raising of the militias, with a plan to recruit workers through their own trade organizations. It is also worth noting that, apart from any question of the consolidation of revolutionary power, the factory and trade-union basis would seem to be particularly advantageous from the standpoint of making an insurrection. The difficulty with this type of recruitment is that it provides groups with strongly localized attachments and interests, so that it is almost impossible to impose an adequate general system of discipline or to organize the central control necessary to conduct any large-scale or sustained operations of war.

There remains for discussion the part played by party armies such as the Fascist Militia or the Nazi S.A. in a revolutionary consolidation of power. Forces of this kind are in a quite different relation to the revolution they support; and in assessing their general value, the type of revolution which they were designed to bring about must also be borne in mind. Broadly speaking, the Fascist Revolution was, on one hand, the answer to Communist attempts to break up through strike action the weak and crumbling liberal-democratic regime of Italy, and on the other hand was a disgusted reaction against the failure to govern of that regime. The Nazi Revolution, as has been pointed out again and again, was based on the dispossession through economic circumstances of the middle and lower-middle classes of Germany. It is probable that both the Fascist Militia and the Nazi S.A. represented much the same class composition as the French National Guard; and one may speculate with irony on the savage lash of history which, in one application, drives discontented middle- and lower-middle-class elements into the van of a radical revolution and in another whips them up as supporters of a regime of authoritarian rigidity. The explanation may be that, in the French case, the middle classes had to some extent built up economic power but could make no full use of it owing to their exclusion from political power, and in the other two cases, they had already won political power but could get no value for it owing to their loss of economic security. However this may be, it is clear that both the Fascist and Nazi Revolutions have represented the attempt of an already arrived class to win back a position which it had lost rather than the effort of a young historical class to wrest new power from an old governing society. The organization of force based on such a condition will probably have requirements rather different from those we have been discussing, and it will be interesting to contrast it from the angle of technical efficiency.

Both the Fascist and Nazi private armies had been organized more or less openly for a considerable period before the actual overthrow of the democratic regimes which their leaders were working to supplant. They had already been used to attack individuals and organizations opposed to the Fascist and Nazi movements.[1] This meant that when the leaders took power they had behind them a guarantee of force ready made, nothing less in fact than a disciplined, highly organized, if partly unarmed, army which they had already learned to handle under difficult circumstances and which itself was already versed, if not in warfare, at any rate in the art of putting down internal opposition. The advantage of this was enormous, but it was obviously an advantage that could only have been built up where the government of the old regime was too weak or too blind to prevent a frank and open preparation for rebellion within the borders of its jurisdiction. As a possible means of building a revolutionary force, it must therefore be limited to a particular set of political conditions. The only other example that comes readily to mind of such open organization for rebellion is the methods of Sinn Fein in Ireland.

The function of these private armies before the seizure of power was to undermine possible future resistance by a subtle system of terrorism and by an imposing show of party solidarity and force. They were kept alert and closely knit in their units by continual calls to action of one sort and another, frequently petty and childish, but always effective as a means of creating *esprit de corps* and pumping vitality into the ranks. This was particularly important since the ranks of the Fascist Militia and the Nazi S.A. were not composed of convinced revolutionaries with a positive political aim and a solidarity based on a homogeneous political outlook, but rather of disgruntled individualists, students, adventurers, and petty bourgeois

[1] For the Nazi organization, *vide* Konrad Heiden, *A History of National Socialism*. For the Fascist militia, H. Finer, *Mussolini's Italy*, and Rossi, *The Rise of Fascism*.

elements, all men who for one reason or another found themselves slipping downwards on the greased slide of economic insecurity. This composition created a difficulty for the leaders which other revolutionaries have not had to face in the same measure. It is, however, worth making reference to it, since all revolutions carry a certain proportion of merely disgruntled partisans, and the Fascists and Nazis have ably shown how these can be welded into an effective semi-military force.

A further difference between the Fascist and Nazi armies and the forces of other revolutions appears in regard to the actual methods of organization. In both these cases, the framework of organization was extraordinarily rigid, and constructed so as to give a closely descending stair of central direction from the leader of the party himself down through every grade of officer to the commander of the smallest unit. In the S.A., for instance, the smallest unit was the squad, consisting of four to twelve men, and anyone could form and assume leadership of a squad. But once the squad had been raised, the leader was bound to report its formation to an officer in the grade above him, preferably the leader of a storm detachment (70 to 120 men). He then came under the orders of this leader, and if he had to give up his post it was filled, not by election among the members of his squad, but by an appointment made by the leader of the storm detachment. It is also worth noting, as an example of psychological insight in organization, that Hitler's own regulations for the S.A. laid it down that the squad should 'consist of friends who join themselves together because they are of the same mind and are united by common interests founded on early friendship, on being old schoolfellows, or being engaged in the same kind of work'.[1] The spirit expected of the Fascist Militia is perhaps sufficiently summed up in the eighth and ninth of the ten commandments which were handed out to recruits: (8) Mussolini is always right; and (9) for a volunteer, there are no extenuating circumstances when he is disobedient.[2]

This method of organization bears considerable analogy to that of the Irish Republican Army. And in this connection it is significant to recall that the I.R.A. was the armed expression of a nationalist and not of a social upheaval. For the method appears in fundamental contrast to the organization of any of the classic revolutionary forces. It has been shown how such forces almost always make their first appearance as a spontaneous banding together of revolutionary enthusiasts, and the problem of the leaders, on taking power, has always been that of working scattered and casual units into an official framework and imposing an effective central command. From the outset of their revolutions, the Fascist and Nazi leaders were spared the expenditure of energy necessary to do this, and the immediate striking force at their command was thus relatively very much stronger.

[1] Konrad Heiden, *A History of National Socialism*, pp. 124, 125.
[2] H. Finer, *Mussolini's Italy*, p. 443.

239

MAKING AN ARMY TO CONSOLIDATE REVOLUTION

On psychological grounds it is probable, however, that a rigid and highly centralized system of organization has serious disadvantages in the initial stages of a new revolutionary regime. It seems to run counter to the way in which a revolutionary populace naturally desires to express itself in arms. Even where an established force of long standing, such as the French National Guard, plunges into revolution as it did during the Paris Commune, this tendency to cling to local controls and autonomy is clear. It has already been shown how the battalions of the Guard clung to their loose federal and regional organization and rendered almost useless the various attempts which were made to bring them under a properly unified central control. The loss of fighting efficiency was no doubt incalculable, but there was no lack of gallantry and enthusiasm. A criticism on similar lines might be made of the Spanish militias in the months following July 1936.

It is possible then that any attempt to work up too quickly a military organization on Fascist or Nazi lines, where a deep social upheaval has taken place, would end in the loss of so much spontaneous goodwill and energy and initiative that increased efficiency of administration would be more than cancelled out. Every revolution releases a flood of libertarian feeling among its followers. This in no way conflicts with fighting courage or enthusiasm. The wise revolutionary leader will respect it. But as the revolution deepens and opposition increases, it becomes obvious to the clear-sighted that libertarianism must be subordinated to a highly centralized control in order to win through. This is perhaps more true of the armed forces than of any other revolutionary institution. At this stage it should be possible to transform the incoherent irregular troops, who made the revolution and have defended its opening phase, into the backbone of a new regular and national army, disciplined and united under a single central command. Such an army founded the United States of America, won Fleurus for the French in 1793 thereby turning the tide of the war, and drove back Kolchak and Denikin in 1919 to the borders of Russia.

CONCLUSION

The chemist can isolate the ingredients of his experiments and the ingredients themselves possess the Jehovan attribute of being the same yesterday, to-day, and for ever. He can insert a new factor at will to modify his result and he knows that the altered result has been effected by whatever new factor he has introduced. But in the affairs of humanity, the ingredients which make the processes of history never exactly repeat themselves, and a new factor is always apt to be x, the unknown variable which may vitiate the truth of any forecast. So it seems perhaps a useless undertaking to assemble a group of historical facts and then try to deduce from them generalized conclusions of cause and effect, working hypotheses on which men of action can to some extent rely. Yet, as the evidence collected in the preceding chapters has come under discussion, it does appear that certain quite definite trends of cause and effect have established themselves so obviously that they cannot be brushed aside as having no value for general application. Similar conditions in a revolutionary situation have produced similar results irrespective of time or place, and new factors have sometimes been so clearly recognizable that it has been possible to say that through their agency a result has been modified in such and such a way. It is not, therefore, merely futile to suggest that conclusions can be drawn from the experience of the past which will also on the whole prove valid for the future.

The position of the armed forces in a modern state runs parallel to that of the civil service. The armed forces are responsible for the maintenance of law and order and for the defence of the realm. The civil service is responsible for the administration of communal life. Both are at the orders of the duly chosen government of the day and are constitutionally bound to carry out the policy of that government. This position is, however, rather a constitutional conception than a constitutional fact. So far as the armed forces are concerned the theory has been evolved with the evolution of standing armies in order to guard against the perils of irresponsible military force. But in practical political life it is found that the theory is apt to break down in application at times of crisis; it puts too great a strain on political human nature. Armies are not in fact set apart from politics. In smooth political periods, where there are no particular clashes of interest between governors and governed, or between various sections of a community, the army is to all appearance merely a part of the machinery of government and politically innocuous. But in communities where deep fissures of angry

241

opinion develop to separate classes and political parties the soldiers appear in their true colours and take their political stand on whatever side their sentiments may lie.

Broadly speaking, an army reproduces in its own character the structure of society in which it has grown up. Where this is a class structure it means in practice that the main features of army character will square with those of the traditionally strongest classes in the community. The corps of officers will be chosen from those classes and the rank and file will be subjected to a system of discipline and influence designed to make them so much docile material in the hands of their officers. Experience proves that the process of politically sterilizing the rank and file can be carried through, given favourable conditions of service, to an astonishing degree of success. The importance attached by a politician like Pitt to keeping the army from civil contacts is significant. As a result, an enormous reservoir of power is in effect placed at the disposal of the officers and can be used by them without let or hindrance to further their own political aims. Experience also proves that the officers have seldom hesitated to use this power when their interests have been seriously threatened. Hence, when they are drawn mainly from one particular class of the community, or from the ranks of one particular political party, their power will effectually be at the beck and call of that class or party.

In a static society this condition of affairs offers no particular danger, but where a society is gradually but steadily changing in character it is a different story. In such a case it may easily happen that the army does not keep pace with the rest of society and that its structure still reflects the social forces of an earlier time. Here the danger from the army is obvious. It may at any time clash with the progressive drive of the community. The social and political structure of this country, for instance, evolved slowly but surely all through the nineteenth century away from the traditional balance between Whigs and Tories and in the direction of modern democracy, reaching perhaps its zenith of development under the great Radical Governments of 1906–14. But the social structure of the armed forces showed no parallel development. It lagged behind and was no longer a reflection of the structure of society at large. Thus, when the democratic Liberal Government required the sanction of armed force, not perhaps in a very just but certainly in a legal cause, it found that the army, as represented by its officers, was to all intents and purposes a private army of the Conservative party. Disliking the cause it was asked to support, it had no hesitation in jamming the machine of democratic government.

Where a social structure is crumbling and unstable the chances that the army will back partisan politics by force or the threat of force are even greater. The causes of the crumbling are of secondary importance. It may be that an incapable democracy finds itself unable to rule the differences of turbulent political parties or to ride an economic storm as in Italy and Germany before the triumph of Fascism and Nazism. It may be that, as in nineteenth-century Spain, the system of rule has become so effete and out of touch with the spirit of the times that it can no longer effectively control the machinery of government. The result in any event is the same; the army becomes by one means or other the arbiter of policy.

In modern times, these dangers are enormously increased owing to the complexity and power of modern weapons of war which put a regular army in an invincible position as against amateur levies. The exclusive or preponderating weight of guns, tanks, and aeroplanes, besides munitions, on one side of the balance is decisive. Hence the more modern and efficient the technical equipment of an army, the more it is to be feared by a government with whose policy it seriously disagrees. It follows then that the position of the army in almost any society is the pivot on which that society swings; and in practice this usually means the position of the corps of officers.

Owing to the immense technical superiority of trained and fully equipped troops, it can be laid down that no revolution will be won against a modern army when that army is putting out its full strength against the insurrection. Practical experience proves this to be the case. No revolution has in fact been won under those conditions. And apparent exceptions to this rule show on investigation special features which mean that the striking power of the army has been in effect seriously curtailed and weakened. In a revolutionary situation the attitude of the army is therefore of supreme importance. It is the decisive factor on which will depend success or failure. The army's attitude will be determined in part by the corps of officers and in part by the rank and file. The evidence suggests that widespread disaffection among officers is generally sufficient in practice to paralyse the striking power of the army. We have the testimony of 1688 and of 1913–14 in this country, and in Spain the witness of 1936, where the disaffected officer corps not only paralysed the army by depriving it of leadership but dragged it over almost intact to its own side. Since most armies, and this has been particularly true of the British, are officered by men drawn from the propertied classes of the community, it is scarcely reasonable to suppose that the officers will in any circumstances be drawn over to support a proletarian revolution. In modern times, disaffection in an officers' corps is likely to have other aims. It may be used to further a Fascist revolt against a democratic government as it has been in Spain; or it may be used to hamstring some particular policy of an advanced government bent on reform of the social system, and which has not had the foresight or perhaps the power to reform its army before attacking the system on whose character that army has been modelled.

Revolutionary leaders of the Left depend upon disaffection in the rank and file if they are to gain the support of the army or paralyse its opposition during a revolution. In practice, the rank and file whatever may be their apparent class interests and sympathies, are far more politically sluggish than their officers and far less easily moved to mutinous action on their own account. This is due to the care with which a ring fence is built round them in order to cut them off from civilian interests and provide an empty field in which they may be conditioned to accept unquestioningly their officers' influence. Again and again, as the evidence of the preceding pages has shown, the rank and file have accepted their officers' lead to the extent of breaking an insurrection on whose success their own class interests depended.

Practical grievances relating to conditions of service will have some effect in promoting mutinous agitation among the rank and file. But it is very doubtful how far the discontent they feel can be turned to political ends, unless it is very widespread and deep and is identified in the minds of the men with a particular system of government, and not merely with a particular set of governing officials. This is an important distinction. It is a valid difference between the disaffection in the Stuart Navy in 1692 and the disaffection in the Navy during the Spithead and Nore mutinies. In the Stuart case the king represented the system of society; in the other case the Admiralty represented only a particular ministry and a particular House of Commons. In any event, practical grievances have an inherent weakness which counteracts their strength as solvents fit to disintegrate the rank and file of an army. They can always be remedied by the government of the *status quo* and once the cause for discontent is removed the rank and file slip back to their old position. It has been shown how the Russian Government took care to remedy the soldiers' grievances in 1905-6 thereby checking their temptation to support the revolution. Practical grievances have a second inherent weakness. It is extraordinarily difficult to turn them to revolutionary account because the agitation they occasion is unlikely to be under the control of political leaders, and mutinies will break out regardless of any general revolutionary situation. It has been shown for instance how Wolfe Tone tried to gain direction of the discontent in the British fleet and yet how unready he was to make use of it when the actual explosion came. It will be a mere matter of luck whether such outbreaks can be related to a general revolutionary situation. In the pre-revolutionary period leaders will no doubt exploit them to the fullest possible extent but they will not rely upon them when gauging the attitude that the army will take up when the revolution breaks out.

History suggests that the only solvent likely to disintegrate the rank and file against the will of their officers is an unsuccessful large-scale war. The army will be ripe for disintegration either immediately after the war or towards its end when it is disillusioned by suffering and defeat. The way is cleared for disintegration by two fundamental changes in the character of

CONCLUSION

the army brought about by wartime conditions. One change regards the rank and file. The enormous wastage of modern war added to the necessary expansion of the armed forces means that the ranks must be filled on a vast scale from the civilian population. And the civilians must be taught soldiering in the shortest possible space of time. Hence there is no opportunity to wean them from their civilian interests and cut them off from their civilian background. The rank and file approximates to the type of a citizen army and the soldiers of citizen armies, as has been shown in some detail with reference to the French National Guard and the English militia, are not politically emasculated. The terms of their service prevent this; they carry with them into their military life all the political and class affiliations and sympathies of their civilian life.

The second change regards the corps of officers. Here again the wastage and expansion are both enormous. Thus, as the war drags on, it will be found that the officers' corps is manned more and more by men who have little or nothing in common with those sections of the community from which the old officers' corps was drawn and do not share the old professional and social ideals. It will be manned by promotion from the ranks and by a wide recruitment from all classes of the civil population. In practice this means that the old influence of the officers' corps over the rank and file is completely undermined. It is undermined partly because the rank and file are now politically alive on their own account and partly because the officers' corps has lost every characteristic of a military caste. The army, both officers and men, is in fact the nation in arms. It is an army of individuals subject like other individual citizens to every storm of political passion which may sweep over the country.

From the foregoing summing up of the position of a modern army in the state, and its social and political characteristics and the circumstances in which it may be expected to take partisan political action, as regards both officers and men, two general conclusions may be drawn: the one regards revolutionary action, the other regards the defence of democracy.

Revolutionary action, whether social or nationalist, implies a clash with trained troops who have all the advantage of modern equipment, supplies, and administrative machinery behind them. Where these troops are exerting their full effort it is impossible to win a revolution against them. In certain circumstances an unsuccessful revolt may be worth while on the score of long-term revolutionary strategy. It may frighten and intimidate the government of the *status quo* into making concessions, or it may consolidate and inspire a revolutionary party, as for instance happened in Italy in 1848, in Ireland after the Easter Rebellion, or in Spain after the Asturias Insurrection. On the whole, however, an unsuccessful revolt does not justify itself and frequently does irremediable harm to the movement it seeks to further.

245

CONCLUSION

The object of a revolution is to win it. It follows therefore that the first business of revolutionary leaders will be to assess, before launching the revolution, the probable strength and attitude of the armed forces which will be opposed to them. This assessment will be made, not only in regard to the objective strength and the subjective character of those forces, but also in regard to the special conditions in which the revolution will be fought out. It may happen that the theoretical strength of the opposing forces is in practice sufficiently weakened owing to the circumstances, sometimes geographical, sometimes political, and sometimes both, in which they have to operate. This is particularly true of the American Revolution, where the distance from the base in England and the extreme difficulty of the transport of men and supplies, coupled with the fact that the British Army was on the whole fighting to penetrate a hostile area, contributed in no small measure to the ultimate success of the Colonists. It is also to a large extent true of the Sinn Fein Revolution, where the opposition of a large section of public opinion in England and the fear of awkward repercussions abroad added to the advantages which the Irish derived from conducting guerrilla warfare against the background of a friendly population and in a rural territory, crippled the effective striking power of the British Army and police. These favourable conditions will be more likely to occur in nationalist than in social revolts. In social revolts it is unlikely that the revolutionaries will have the benefit of a homogeneous population behind them. Nor is it likely that they will have the benefit of any compact geographical region to use as an undisturbed base for training their levies and assembling their supplies.

The social revolt presents, therefore, on the whole a more difficult problem than the nationalist revolt. Under certain rather rare conditions, as in France in 1830 and 1848, and in Spain in 1931, social revolt has succeeded without active disintegration of the army. The explanation of this is simple. The government of the *status quo* feels weak and uncertain and prefers to abdicate without provoking a serious armed clash. Charles X, Louis Philippe, and Alphonso XIII never tried out the issue between troops and people. Thus the question of army disintegration did not seriously arise. It was never put to the test whether the common soldier would follow his general or swing back to his natural social place among the revolting populace. But under a strong and courageous government, which is prepared and able to fight out the issue to the bitter end, the disintegration of the armed forces is essential for success. Where armies of the old non-democratic type are in question this disintegration will almost certainly only take place towards the end of or after an unsuccessful war, since it is probable that only unsuccessful war produces a set of conditions sufficiently strong to act as solvents of army unity. Hence, where severe opposition is to be expected, the chances for revolutionary action are most favourable at this period.

CONCLUSION

The apparent exception to this rule, presented by the swing-over of the French Army to the Revolution in 1789, can be explained in terms of special conditions. Outstanding among them was the fact that the officers at first encouraged discontent by their attitude and at no period presented a united active front against the revolution except as émigrés.

In planned insurrections the leaders are in a position to work before the outbreak to increase all conditions favouring disintegration of the army. Practical grievances of the soldiers can be exploited, political propaganda can be carried on, the insurrection can be timed for an advantageous date. Finally, at the moment of outbreak, fraternization can be attempted.

In spontaneous mass uprisings, which catch revolutionary leaders unawares, or before their plans are matured, less will be effected beforehand. It will then be their business to gain control as rapidly as possible of the instinctive revolutionary movement and direct it to the best advantage. Fraternization will be the only means open to them of influencing the morale of the troops.

In those armies which have the character described for citizen armies, the influence of the officers' corps over the rank and file is weak. Hence, at the impact of social revolution, the armed forces may be expected to split according to their class and political interests. This conclusion, however, is based on general reasoning from the behaviour of citizen armies. It has never been put to a large-scale practical test, since no serious social revolution has taken place in those countries which maintain exclusively armies of militia type.

The long-service army with a professional officers' corps is not amenable to influence from the Left in any serious degree, but it does appear markedly amenable to fascist influences coming through Right channels. The reasons for this lie in the character of the officers' corps which makes it in effect the custodian of conservatism and the privileges of property, in the tendency of the officers' corps to support party politics with the sanction of force when their political interests are gravely threatened or their political emotions aroused, and in the ascendancy which the officers' corps gains over the rank and file.

A progressive government which is driving its way along the road of social reconstruction by constitutional means may find itself hamstrung if it maintains an army of this type.

A democracy, struggling against some storm of political disillusion and economic depression which finds a fascist focus, may discover too late that its armed forces are no defence.

What type of army is best suited to defend the interests of a democratic community and in what respects would such an army differ from the types which we have been discussing?

Before trying to answer this question, I should like to get quite clear a political consideration which might confuse the issue. It may turn out that the kind of army best fitted to defend a democracy against fascist attack is also to some extent the kind most open to militant suggestion from the revolutionary Left. That is another story which must be kept separate in our minds from the present discussion.

The answer to our question centres on the twin problems of recruitment and length of service. Unfortunately, the evidence provides only a sure negative answer. It can be laid down that armies where the officers come from the propertied sections of the community and the privates are enlisted for years of service are perilous to democracy. But it cannot be laid down with equal conviction that some other type of army will fulfil with certainty the role of defending a democractic state against fascist attack. There are, however, general tendencies which emerge clearly enough from our evidence, tendencies which show that some methods of composing armed forces are more likely to benefit democracy than others.

Citizen armies of the type of the French National Guard or the English militia have always been politically alive. And there can be little doubt that their political vitality has been due to the fact that the rank and file merged into one conception their rights and aspirations as citizens and their duties as soldiers. They were citizens temporarily bearing arms and they took over into their military life the whole range of their civilian interests and opinions. They were in no sense a will-less weapon in the hands of a professional officers' corps. This is the kind of mentality that a democracy requires in its armed forces. The army must reflect and sum up the will of the whole nation. Armies of this specific type, however, are not technically good enough for modern conditions. This country, for example, could not possibly rely upon its Territorial Army alone. How then can the mental characteristics which distinguish a citizen army best be reproduced in an army where at least a certain period of whole-time training for the rank and file and at least a framework of professional officers and non-commissioned officers must be postulated in the interests of efficiency? The structure of the Swiss Army has already been discussed. It provides perhaps a basis for the successful solution of this problem, though it may well be that in a country like England with many foreign commitments it would be necessary to link the Swiss system with a small professional army for exclusive service abroad.

The first requirement for building up a democratic army is almost certainly that service should be compulsory, not only in order that the burden should fall on all citizens alike, but so that the army should be a true microcosm of the nation at large. Then it must be ensured that the soldier, while undergoing his period of service, is in no way isolated from civilian life. Under modern conditions it is probably not possible to achieve this end either by allowing him to live at home or by billeting him on the civilian population. But if his term with the colours is shortened to the least possible time needed to teach him his military job, and if during that period he is encouraged, not only to take responsibility and use his initiative, but also to hold opinions of his own on any and every aspect of national life, he will not suffer from mental asphyxiation. The methods of work of the British Air Force show that responsibility and initiative can be fostered in the private soldier without destroying discipline, and there is surely no inherent military reason why barrack life should be conducted on the lines of monastic seclusion.

The experience of the Russian Army in the years after the civil war between the Bolsheviks and the White generals and the Polish war of 1920 suggests that the formation and maintenance of a keen and strong army is not incompatible with a burning interest in politics on the part of the troops, and that army life, far from being necessarily a stagnant pond of cultural apathy, can be shaped to carry the living stream of a people's aspirations and enthusiasm, so that the soldier becomes even a fertilizer of popular thought.[1] Observers in Spain noted somewhat similar characteristics among the militiamen of the Government Army, for whom military service became linked with a spontaneous drive to acquire some sort of knowledge and culture other than their old practical experience of the farm or the factory bench. The militiamen exchanged their ploughs and their lathes not only for rifles, but also for books. And the Government saw to it that this desire to learn should find every possible outlet and encouragement by sending round travelling libraries even to the fighting lines.[2] It is probable that enthusiasm of this kind becomes epidemic only during periods of struggle when some great and releasing idea is being tried out in action. It is not suggested that the soldier of any British Army, in normal times, except perhaps as an individual here and there, would be likely to want to emulate his Russian counterpart's programme for non-military hours. Even the Spanish militiaman's less organized political activity and search for knowledge might be too earnest for him. But he should at least have the same liberty and opportunity and stimulus to form his opinions that his civilian fellows enjoy. He should be free to get his views where and when and how he likes, and to express them without fear or favour.

Much is being done to-day to educate our war-time army in the complexities of current problems. But it is not so clear that the methods in use are those best calculated to produce a 'free forum' of opinion—or indeed that all opinions, even if produced, get equal treatment. The start made is, however, the great thing.

Reform of the officers' corps presents a more complicated and more

[1] Webb, *Soviet Communism*, pp. 124 sq.
[2] Duchess of Atholl, *Searchlight on Spain*, p. 225.

pressing problem. It is more pressing owing to the strong influence which a professional corps of officers has over the rank and file and more complicated owing to technical difficulties.

The rank and file can be trained efficiently in a relatively short space of time, but this presupposes that they are trained by men, both non-commissioned officers and commissioned officers, who know their job inside out. It has already been shown, for instance, how the difficulty of making amateur officers efficient in time has always proved the worst part of the problem of raising an army to guard a revolution, or even when, during war, an existing army needs to be expanded. The structure of a permanent army, at any rate in a country with wide foreign commitments, demands a strong framework of whole-time officers and N.C.O.s. Efficient training and instruction obviously cannot be given by men who are themselves a part of the civilian contingent called up at specified times for service with the colours. This means that, even in a modified form, a professional corps of officers must be maintained. How then shall this corps be manned in order that the democratic character of the army may be safeguarded? It is, of course, evident that the social theory that made the armed forces a safe and easy preserve for the sons of the upper classes who for one reason or another were not attracted to the life of a civilian profession must be swept away. Neither the interests of military efficiency nor the interests of democracy are well served by such a theory. Though insistence on harder work and a higher intellectual quality can safeguard the former, they will not necessarily do much to protect the latter. Cadets to the military schools of the British Army required before the war a standard of intelligence on the whole as high as that needed to enter a university, and once started on their military career they had to work and think at least moderately hard on military affairs to keep the pace demanded of them if they were to retain their jobs for more than a few years. The standard required in the German Reichswehr was probably considerably higher. But it does not appear that there was much change of political heart in the officers of the British Army, and the political attitude of the Reichswehr during the life of the Republic and at the time of Hitler's seizure of power needs no further comment. Professional efficiency then does not cancel out class composition.

In the French Army, the officers were partly recruited by direct graduation from the military schools and partly from the ranks of the N.C.O.s after a period of special training, or in a few cases after nomination by the Minister for War.[1] We do not, however, yet know enough about the causes of the collapse of France, or about the relation of the French Army to the Vichy Government, to say that this form of recruitment was inherently unsuited to a democracy. We can only say that promotion from the ranks is

[1] Lewis Clive, *The People's Army*, p. 133. *Vide* also *League of Nations Armaments Book for 1933*, for methods of recruiting French officers' corps.

not in itself an adequate safeguard, and that long-service N.C.O.'s are likely to have the same mentality as professional officers.

The commissioned ranks of the Reichswehr were expressly opened to any common soldier without distinction of class who could pass the necessary tests.[1] The significance of this, however, should not be insisted upon too strongly without the information as to how many soldiers could in fact take advantage of the opening. It is perhaps more convincing evidence that the Civil Guard in Spain, a body of troops raised during the nineteenth century in order to suppress internal disorders and notorious until the Civil War for its harsh methods and its subservience to reactionary governments, was exclusively officered by men who had been promoted from the ranks.[2] At the outbreak of the Franco rebellion its loyalty to the legal government of the Republic was uncertain and at best sectional.

A system of promotion from the ranks with subsequent specialized training is no doubt a foundation for the reform of the officers' corps, but it would seem that it can only be made certainly effective when it is linked with a radical change in the conception of the officer's function, not only in regard to the community, but also in regard to the army itself. In times of revolution the necessity for this has always been instinctively recognized and efforts have always been made to force the change. The election of officers, the formation of regimental committees to control the relations between officers and men, the appointment of political officials to check up on the officers' activities, are all methods, some of them clumsy and disastrous from a military point of view, some of them brilliantly successful, which have been used in an instinctive endeavour to alter the traditional function of the officer in the military machine. This function can perhaps best be defined in terms of personal leadership and control as opposed to professional co-operation for the sake of putting through a job of work. The point can be illustrated by contrasting the position of a regimental officer in relation to his men with the position say of an upper-grade civil servant in regard to the clerks who work under him. Personal leadership can be of two kinds. It can provide an inspiration to action and a sense of reliance on the judgement of the leader in regard to the best means of achieving a given action. But it can also mean an abdication of all initiative and responsibility on the part of the led, and an assumption on the leader's part that he has a right to take responsibility not only for a given objective, but also for the general tenor of the lives of the men under his control. Leadership of the first kind is an essential in army organization, and it must obviously be coupled, as again the experience of revolutionary armies has proved, with the assurance that operative orders will be inevitably obeyed. Leadership of the second kind has always been a part of professional army organization,

[1] *Encyclopaedia Britannica* (14th ed.), s.v. "*Germany*".

[2] Jellinek, *The Civil War in Spain*, p. 64.

at any rate in armies like the British, but there can be no reason whatsoever to suppose that the success of the first and essential kind depends in any way upon it. It has been grafted on to true leadership in order to keep the rank and file conveniently subservient, and because the tradition of the officer class derives in a direct if long line from feudal interference in the concerns of dependants. So far as the British Army is concerned, it might be worth investigating not only how far the old system, whereby individual officers raised and equipped their own battalions, made them feel independent of the State, but also how far it was responsible for handing down the tradition of feudal interference.

It is not suggested that there can be any close analogy between the relations of civil servants and those of army officers to the men under them. The ultimate function of a civil servant will never be to lead a forlorn hope and the gift for direct personal leadership is not one that the community need take pains to foster in its administrators, at any rate not to the same extent that it must seek for it in its army officers. But it can at least be suggested that the general freedom from interference on the part of his superiors which a postman or a tax collector enjoys could be extended to a soldier, and that the spirit in which a civil servant regards his professional function as limited to his work is also proper for an army officer. Nor is it suggested that the methods which revolutionary armies have tried are necessarily the best or the only ones whereby this reform can be brought about. In normal times, other methods would doubtless succeed better. Nor are the methods suitable for one country necessarily suitable for another, since the problem centres on an alteration of psychology.

In England, for instance, there has flourished a theory that leadership is a gift which has been exclusively bestowed upon the upper classes; and the whole system of education for the scions of the governing class has been built up with a view to bringing out and increasing that quality of character, whereas in the education of the working class it has been passed over altogether. Leadership is a quality of individuals and there is not the slightest real evidence to show that the secondary-school boy is naturally more deficient in it that his public-school opposite number. He should at least be given every opportunity to show whether he possesses the gift, and if he does he should be encouraged to use it in a profession where it is important. If, when peace comes again, the military colleges for the training of officers could be made exclusively a charge upon the government and not to a large extent a charge upon the individual cadet, it would be possible for secondary-school boys to enter them on equal terms with public-school boys. And they would bring with them, not only the personal gift for soldiering which had made them choose that profession, but also a new tradition of live and let live drawn from those sections of society who have, fortunately, never been taught that their duty to the community is to mind their subordinates' business more closely than their own. Moreover, an officers' corps which was thus no longer the close preserve of the less intellectually ambitious members of the upper classes would prove far more attractive than at present to boys of spirit and intelligence. Further, the mechanization of the army demands that very interest in practical engineering which is so prevalent to-day.

It is here, perhaps, that the reform of psychology for the officers of the armed forces might begin. Indeed, thanks to the exigencies of the war, it has already begun. It is the civilians' duty to see to it that, when the war is over, there is no swing back to the old system.

If a reform of this kind were really carried out thoroughly and enthusiastically, it would not perhaps matter a great deal whether it were also coupled with an exclusive system of promotion from the ranks. This may have a considerable value in democratic theory, and a certain practical value in enabling men to know at first hand the point of view of the common soldier. But in any case, in a short-service army, promotion from the ranks merely means that men are passed through the ranks before they receive the specialized instruction which is the real heart of their training as officers. Here, again, the experience of the Swiss Army, where the aspirant to commissioned rank receives his special training after he has undergone his normal period in the ranks, is important.

A further essential reform is obviously that the rank and file should be permitted some form of free collective organization for the expression of grievances relating to the organization of their lives.

In sum, then, that implicit governing-class spirit which is the presiding genius of most armies must be eliminated. The promotion of officers from the ranks will not in itself necessarily do this effectively, since experience shows that by one means or another, this spirit can be successfully injected into the rank and file. The reform needed is twofold. In the first place, the rank and file must be given a new sense of independence and self-respect. In the second place, the officers must be drawn from far wider social classes in order to diffuse and break up their political interests; and they must learn a new consideration for the personality of their subordinates and realize that they are commanding not children or serfs, but free citizens.

Reform of the officers' corps on these lines is not, however, in itself a sufficient guarantee against fascism. Fascism is the child of frustration and disillusion and in favourable circumstances it is quite as likely to be adopted by lower-middle-class and by middle-class as by upper-class elements. The political independence of the rank and file is the strongest guarantee against the use of the army for fascist purposes. But this can never be achieved without first a radical reform of the officers' corps. In the hands of an army so reconstructed, the torch of democracy might be held aloft to burn steadily and safely.

A mass popular uprising raises the final question with which this book has attempted to deal. In the last resort a revolution must always be held by armed force during that period when the new power is being consolidated. The strength of the force necessary will naturally depend upon the amount and the violence of the opposition which the revolution has to face after the initial seizure of power. If the dispossessed classes are strong and vital and, in particular, if they feel that they may expect sympathy and perhaps support from their more fortunate fellows who are still in the saddle in other countries, this opposition may take the form of a serious civil war. And the civil war may develop into an international war if governments of other countries take fright and decide to sponsor the anti-revolutionary cause by armed intervention. This has occurred after almost every profound revolution. The French of 1792 found half Europe ranged against them; the Russians of 1919 had to contend with an Allied backing of the White generals; the Spaniards were far more seriously engaged against the military support given to the rebels by Italy and Germany than they were against the native battalions of General Franco. It is then, clear, that a revolutionary government will nearly always require a strong army. How can such an army be organized, rapidly and efficiently, and from what elements should it be recruited? For it can be laid down almost as an axiom that after any deep and violent social upheaval the armed forces of the old regime, whatever their composition, will have disintegrated. The revolution must forge for itself a new military weapon.

The depth and extent of the disintegration will depend in a considerable measure upon the character of the revolution. Where this does not stand for a direct attack on property, disintegration will probably mean little more than bewilderment and a general loosening of the ties of discipline. In such cases it may be expected that the officers, or at any rate a considerable proportion of them, will have adopted an attitude of neutrality to the revolution, and the men will not therefore have been called upon to make a clear-cut choice between firing upon the people or mutinying against their officers. It may then be possible for the revolutionary government to save the old cadres and reorganize, using much of the old personnel. It has already been shown how it was possible to do this in regard to the French Revolutionary Army after 1792, thanks largely to the sympathetic attitude which many officers of the old Royal Army adopted towards the revolution during its opening phases. This prevented a break-up of the whole army organization and gave time to weed out undesirable elements and fill the gaps with loyal men, without the necessity for making a fresh start with a completely new and untried corps of officers. The danger of this method

CONCLUSION

lies, of course, in the uncertain allegiance of the officers to the revolutionary regime. An attitude of benevolent neutrality, which has permitted the first objectives of the revolution to be attained without serious opposition, may be succeeded, as it was to a large extent in France, by definite hostility when the onward sweep of events makes unmistakably apparent the fundamental nature of the social upheaval. This danger may be overcome, as again it was in France, by keeping a close watch on the officers' activities and ruthlessly eliminating all disloyal elements as they appear, even at the expense of temporary technical efficiency. It becomes fatal only when the initial attitude of the officers lulls the revolutionary government into a sense of false security. It has been shown how the numerous offers of allegiance on the part of important officers to the nascent French Republic of 1848 induced the Provisional Government to believe that the army could be trusted and that there was no necessity to proceed with its reconstruction. The fruits of this too easy policy were gathered by the Republicans when three years later the army made possible the success of Louis Bonaparte's bid for power.

Here, again, the distinction between the officers and the rank and file is fundamental. The initial adherence of the officers to the Second Republic had made it possible for the rank and file to support the revolution peaceably. They had never been shaken up by a clear-cut issue and an ultimate choice. Thus, when Louis Bonaparte based his *coup d'état* in 1851 upon overawing Paris by a powerful show of armed force, he was able without difficulty to carry the army with the exception of a few generals.[1] If the Provisional Government had taken steps, not only to purge the officers' corps, but also to give the rank and file a new sense of responsibility and independence, this might have been avoided. In 1789–94, both steps were taken and taken successfully. Napoleon's *coup d'état* in Brumaire, based though it certainly was on the support of the army, cannot in any but the most superficial way be considered as politically analagous to the *coup d'état* of Louis Bonaparte in 1851.[2]

It is clear that in modern times a similar situation might well arise where a Left government, which has enjoyed the tacit support of the armed forces, found itself, for one reason or another, faced with serious discontent settling to a fascist focus. The forecast of such a situation only serves to reinforce the argument that an army must actively represent the will of the people as a whole and not the will of selected groups. If the first Spanish Republican Government of 1931 had had the vision to see this clearly and the strength to take resolute and far-reaching action, its successors of 1934 would not have been faced with a rebellion on anything like the scale of the Franco Revolt.

[1] *Cambridge Modern History*, vol. xi, pp. 135 sq.
[2] *Cambridge Modern History*, 'French Revolution', pp. 676 sq., a fascinating account of the mechanism of Brumaire by H. A. L. Fisher.

CONCLUSION

Where the army has disintegrated because the rank and file have gone over to the revolution while the officers have remained loyal to the old regime, the problem of reconstruction which the revolutionary leaders have to solve becomes more difficult and far-reaching. Disintegration, in this case, means that the men will have chosen open mutiny in preference to their old allegiance and that the cleavage between them and their officers is final. The officers will be left, as it were, in the air with no troops to lead. They will become private individuals who may or may not coalesce later into armed opposition to the new regime. In any event, the result must be a widespread physical break-up of units and a complete breakdown of military administration. The actual process of disintegration may run along differing lines. The officers may disappear altogether as they did in Russia after the Bolshevik revolution and the men may spontaneously disband themselves; or that part of the old army which has held together as an organization through the initial revolutionary upheaval may be later disbanded deliberately through the action of the revolutionary leaders. This happened in Germany after 1918. But, whatever the process of disintegration, the result is the same. The revolutionary government finds itself without the defence of any properly organized armed force. Whatever the political problems which it has to solve, the creation of such a force will take precedence of all of them. What elements are available for the recruitment of a new army and on what lines will it be organized?

A revolution which is the result of a planned rebellion will have immediately ready to its hand the military organization of the insurrection. An organization whose *raison d'être* has been the destruction of an existing regime must necessarily be unsuitable and inadequate in many respects for permanent embodiment. The structure and methods proper for a rebel force are not those best fitted for a regular military organization which can command the resources of a state. It has been shown, for instance, how the Bolsheviks rapidly discovered that the type of rebel force exemplified by their Red Guard was quite unsuitable and insufficient to take over the defence of the regime against seriously organized and trained armed opposition. The old rebel force can be regarded only as a stopgap, but it is a stopgap on which the life of the revolution may well depend. Properly used, it will be competent for the maintenance of revolutionary order until and unless opposition takes the form of organized civil war. It should be taken over by the revolutionary government openly and wholeheartedly. The Bolshevik regime would probably have foundered within a few weeks but for the help of the Red Guard and their co-fighters, the irregular bands. The Treaty Government of Sinn Fein Ireland would have been swept away by de Valera and his dissidents, and the country driven to a further and more bitter clash with Britain, had Cosgrave and Collins dissolved the old rebel organization of the Irish Republican Army on their assumption of power. And it has been shown how the failure of the German Social Democratic government after 1918 to arm and organize the true supporters of the revolution played into the hands of every reactionary element in Germany and paved the way for the development of a situation in which the republic found itself in effect divorced from its army.

The Sinn Fein Revolution was conducted to a detailed strategical plan and the Irish Republican Army was more closely knit and strictly disciplined than is usual with rebel forces. A revolution such as the German or the Russian which is, broadly speaking, the result of a spontaneous popular uprising, throws up a much looser and more individualistic type of military organization. The process has been shown in the sketch of the history of the Russian Red Guard already given.

It is a hard task for a revolutionary government to take over such a force and relate it to a central authority so that it may be used to full capacity for the maintenance of order and the suppression of revolt. The Russians never made a complete success of the Red Guard from this point of view, invaluable though the services of the Guard immediately after the Bolshevik Revolution undoubtedly were. The shifting of the French National Guard from a rebel force, spontaneously formed during the Bastille rising, to an organized body of citizen soldiers enlisted to maintain revolutionary order, was more successful. It may well be that the reason for this lies partly in the different methods of recruitment between these two revolutionary guards. The Red Guard was recruited on a factory basis and its units had the centrifugal characteristics of free companies. The French Guard was recruited on a territorial basis, in Paris through the sections of the Paris municipality. It may have lost something in revolutionary drive, but this loss was more than compensated by the fact that the guard was at the orders of an administration already functioning adequately from the standpoint of the revolution. There was no need to evolve *ad hoc* a system to curb the nonconformist licence of scattered units and bind them to a unified policy under a central control. The Spanish Government found the same difficulty in imposing adequate central control upon their militia columns, most of which were raised exclusively by the different political parties and manned by their members. The gallantry and enthusiasm of these columns is not in question. It is the type of organization that is open to doubt. This may be correct for an insurrection, but not for troops who are at the disposal of a government whose primary function is to maintain a difficult seat in the saddle. Recruitment must be upon a wider basis and the controls must not be subject to the personal views of individual commanders of self-raised units.

It is at this point that the problem of the revolutionary guard merges into the problem of the regular revolutionary army. Unless the guard can be transformed into an army which is a part of the legalized machinery for the maintenance of order, it is suited only to a temporary period of transition. But even where it has been so transformed, it cannot take the place of whole-time armed forces. The creation of such an army must be undertaken from the outset and the task centres on the solution of two main problems. It must be decided whether the new army shall be based on voluntary or compulsory service. And a means must be found to officer it with men who are not only politically ardent but also technically efficient. So far as the recruitment of the rank and file is concerned, it would seem that voluntary service is better suited to the conditions than conscription, at any rate until the new regime has found its level and become the settled social system of a country. Obviously, only those men who are enthusiastic for the cause or whose natural career is soldiering would freely enlist in a revolutionary army. Voluntary service would therefore ensure an army with the homogeneous outlook of a crusading force, an important advantage during a time of internal unrest. But voluntary service may not provide a large enough army. And where armed opposition on a big scale is involved, it will probably be necessary to resort to some form of conscription. Both the Jacobins and the Bolsheviks found that they must decree compulsory service. It will then be essential to devise methods for checking up on possible disloyal elements and for the manufacture of revolutionary zeal—to some extent perhaps a synthetic substitute for the crusader's ardour. The history of revolutionary armies has been shown to provide a variety of such methods.

The practical if prosaic inducement of good pay will help not a little to promote loyal service, as it did in the case of the English Navy during the Parliamentary wars. Trotsky's outburst on the subject of footgear, drawn by the theory that wars can be fought on idealism alone, was prompted perhaps by a similar point of view. But material inducements are in themselves far from sufficient. A stiffening of men picked for their political quality must be incorporated with the ordinary troops, either by sprinkling them throughout the army as individuals—the method used by the Bolsheviks—or by placing them as special units to serve with the regular regiments as the French did with their volunteer battalions. Such a stiffening acts like the hidden steel girders which give to a building its essential strength. Finally, there are the various applications of the system, first brilliantly invented by the French and since used by both the Russians and the Spaniards, of attaching political officers to the military units, whose function is to educate the men in the ideals for which they are fighting and to ensure that disloyalty and inertia are searched out.

In regard to the creation of a new corps of officers, there seems to be no clear channel between the Scylla of political unreliability and the Charybdis of professional incompetence. Officers who are fit to train the rank and file in the methods of modern war cannot train themselves within a few weeks or months, and a revolutionary army is more likely to fail because its officers are inadequate than for any other reason. There are three main sources from which officers can be drawn and which, if properly balanced, will, as experience shows, give successful results.

In the first place, old soldiers serving in the new rank and file can be promoted, and officers of the old regime who have attained commissioned rank on account of their military aptitude rather than their place in society can be given a fair chance to rise to coveted commands, and so bound to the interests of the new regime. Where the revolution has come, and the old army has disintegrated, owing to the pressure of calamitous war, this source of supply should be fairly large. No officers' corps can survive a modern war as a closed caste; the enormous wastage that must be made good involves bringing in numbers of 'outsiders' who are indifferent or even inimical to the old tradition. Every effort must therefore be made to win the professional support of these outsiders and enlist their active interest in the success of the new army. This type of old officer, coupled with the ex-ranker who has been promoted, will best combine political reliability with military efficiency, and from them the backbone of the new officers' corps will be formed.

The second source of supply is the true soldier of the revolution, the man who has fought for his political ideals and found in the process that he has some natural talent for soldiering. He may well be distinguished for valour and enthusiasm and for a gift for personal leadership. But the successful command of a more or less free company of irregulars is not necessarily good training for an officer who has to take his place in the disciplined military hierarchy of an official army. The experience of Russia, shows that it is not always easy to use satisfactorily the services of such men.[1] Moreover, there is always the difficulty that they will be picked for command on account of their revolutionary zeal rather than their true military capacity. The history of the French Revolutionary Army in its earlier period is black-spotted with examples of this kind. In short, this source of supply may throw up individuals of outstanding merit, but as a class it must be considered suspect from a military point of view.

The third source available is what may be called the normal officer of the old regime. In a relatively small army this class may be omitted altogether. But where a great national army must be created, it will inevitably be found necessary to use its services to some extent. The Russians, for instance, found themselves forced to draw a very considerable proportion of their officers from this class. In regard to its use there are two obvious disadvantages for the new regime. In the first place, officers of this type are not likely to offer their services voluntarily. They must be forced in by some form of coercion; and men who have been coerced into serving a cause

[1] Wollenberg, *The Red Army*, p. 39.

they do not love are not likely to bring energy and active loyalty to their work. Where there is a universal liability for army service, it will probably be found possible actually to get hold of men of this type in sufficient numbers. For only those officers who are so deeply hostile to the new regime that they prefer to risk everything rather than serve it would be likely to refuse to answer their call to the colours. The Bolsheviks certainly found that a judicious mixture of persuasion and coercion was adequate to bring in those officers who were not prepared to go to the length of sacrificing their families and their homes in order to join the ranks of the White generals. But, having got the men, the difficulty of ensuring their loyal service still remains. This solves itself to a certain extent, since almost every officer has a professional standard about which he cares, and when engaged on a professional job may, almost against his will, persuade himself to do it well for the sake of his standard. A shrewd government will reinforce this psychology by the inducement of a satisfactory military career on the one hand, and on the other by a strict system of political supervision coupled with severe penalties for slackness or the betrayal in any shape or form of the interests of the revolutionary army. The employment of officers from this class is obviously a dangerous experiment for the new regime and clear-sighted leaders will be likely to resort to it only where the impossibility of raising a sufficient number of technically competent men by any other means makes it urgent and inevitable. It has been shown, for instance, how the employment of such officers by the Weimar Republic, without any real political supervision and with no sanctions against their activities, resulted in the formation of an army alienated from the ideals of the Republic and useless in its defence.

In sum, then, the armed forces of a successful revolutionary state must be built anew after a complete severance with the traditions of the past. This break need not necessarily be physical. In certain circumstances, it may be possible to retain the old cadres and the old framework. But whether the old structure can be used again, or whether a fresh organization must be built up, the spiritual break with the past will be final and irrevocable. There will be no convenient bridge permitted by which the Rubicon can be recrossed.

In this concluding chapter, an attempt has been made, not only to reckon up the various trends in the relations between armed forces and the community which they serve, but also to show how these relations can be used in situations which may at any time develop and involve the whole social and political scheme of our own lives. The Western democracies are like people inhabiting strongholds built upon the verge of a crumbling cliff. We had built ourselves no sea-wall—because of cowardice and cynicism and an indolent refusal to search the future with steady eyes. We prized our

CONCLUSION

Western conception of political freedom and individual value; but we assumed that time was on our side. The eroding waves seemed little waves. Time enough to build that sea-wall against them. But now the waves bear down with violence and laden with the menace of our unknown destiny, so that however we regard our problems, the questions here discussed have a grim practical significance. They are no longer merely a part of the tale of men's struggle and counterstruggle in the past to realize their own conflicting ideas of society, nor can they be shelved against a future which we and our heirs are not likely to see. When the war is over, these problems will take immediate precedence in Europe. It may well happen that not only our own lives, but also the inheritance which we shall hand on to our children, will be irrevocably shaped by the solution that we find for them.

INDEX

Act of Settlement, the, 130

African Colonies, French, 123

Agincourt, Battle of, 15

Air Force, German, 177

Air Force, Italian, 177

Air Force, the Royal, 176, 249

Air Force, Spanish, in the Civil War, 97, 177, 204

Albany, 67, 68

Alekseev, General, 116

Allied intervention in Russia, 124, 198

Alphonso XII (of Spain), 100, 103, 104, 105, 137

Alphonso XIII (of Spain), 246

Alsace, 149

Amadeo of Savoy, 103

America, 17, 18, 63, 65, 67, 72, 216

American Army in the Civil War, 219 sq.; split between North and South, 219; in the War of Independence, 63, 66, 69, 70, 71, 187, 213 sq.

American Civil War, 14; naval superiority of North, 19; advantages of clear-cut areas of control, 20; army organization, 212, 219 sq.

American War of Independence, 14; conflict between duties of a soldier and a citizen—points of view of contemporary soldiers, 17, 18; successful rebellion against professional armed forces, 20, 63 sq.; army organization, 212 sq.

Amherst, Lord, attitude to American War of Independence, 17

Anarchists, Spanish (F.A.I.), 46, 204, 209, 210

Ancona, 77

Andalusia, 75, 104

Anne, daughter of James II, 35, 90

Anglesey, Lord, 166

Annual Mutiny Act, its design as a check on the army, 16

Antoine (Jacobin), 188, 191

Antrim, 93

Aragon, 75

Armed Forces, handling of the, during Insurrection, 112, 113, 154 sq.

Armed Forces, relation of the State to its, 15, 107, 242

Armed Forces, theory of the 'Impersonal instrument', 17, 99, 109, 179, 180

Armies, long-service, political dangers from, 160, 161, 162, 247, 248

Armies, methods of binding to a revolutionary cause after the initial swing over, 116 sq., 148 sq.

Armies, proportions of officers to other ranks, 118

Armies, revolutionary disintegration of, through fraternization, 153 sq.; through internal discontent and mutiny, 128 sq., 140, 244; through unsuccessful war, 108 sq., 244

Army, the English Royal, in 1688, 89 sq.

Army of the North, the French, 193, 194

Army of the Rhine, the French, 150

Arnold, Benedict, 218

Asquith Government, the, and Ulster crisis of 1914, 17, 91 sq., 97, 177

Asquith, H. H., and Ulster Crisis, 91, 94, 96, 97

Assault Guard, Spanish, 204, 205, 233

Assembly, the French National, 140, 143, 145, 149, 168, 169, 188, 206

Assize of Arms, the, 164

Asturias Insurrection, the, 46, 245

Asturias, in the Civil War, 205

Aumale, duc d', 225

262

INDEX

INDEX

INDEX

INDEX

INDEX

INDEX

INDEX

INDEX

INDEX

273

INDEX